Worlds Unrealized
Volume 1

Worlds Unrealized
Volume I

Short Stories of Adolescence
By Canadian Writers

Edited by
Andrew Garrod and Janet Webster

Breakwater
100 Water Street
P.O. Box 2188
St, John's, Newfoundland
A1C 6E6

The Publisher gratefully acknowledges the financial support of The Canada Council, which has helped make this publication possible.

The Publisher acknowledges the financial support of the Cultural Affairs Division of the Department of Municipal and Provincial Affairs, Government of Newfoundland and Labrador, which has made this publication possible.

Cover art, entitled "Metaphor for Life" water colour
by Herzl Kashetsky

Canadian Cataloguing in Publication Data
Worlds unrealized

ISBN 1-55081-036-7 (bound: v. 1). -- ISBN 1-55081-007-3 (pbk.: v.1). -- ISBN 1-55081-038-3 (bound: v. 2). -- ISBN 1-55081-008-1 (pbk.: v. 2)

1. Adolescence -- Fiction. 2. Short stories, Canadian (English) * 3. Canadian fiction (English) -- 20th century. * I. Garrod, Andrew, 1937- II. Webster, Janet Barbara, 1944 -

PS323.A36E67 1991 C813'.0108354 C91-097550-7
PR9197.35.A36W67 1991

Dedication

Jeff and Allan Bailey, David and Mimi Bartell, Scott Bray,
Felicity and Vanessa Callard, Jill and Tony Carter,
Joel Curry, Nigel Davis, Erica and Sarah DeVos,
Sarah and Andrew Dowd, Casey, Tom and Bryan Dowd,
Lisa Down, Ian and Tina Finley, Lisa and Andrew Fleming,
Katie and Fenella Garrod, Gwen Hughes, Maureen Johnson,
David Carroll Kenny, Cameron and Justin Keyes, Shannon Kirk,
Jacqueline and Alison Little, Megan and Bruce MacMillan,
Andrew Nicol, Michael and Valery Simpson, Portia Taylor,
Benjamin Tilson, Karen Vincent, Andrew and Catharine Webb,
Schaefer White, and David Wingrove.

Those who have explored, are exploring, or have yet
to explore the worlds of adolescence.

A.C.G.

Tristan and Lisa
who helped me understand the dark side of adolescence.

Mr. Sykes, an English teacher who always had his nose in a book
and who always took the time to recommend a good "read"
to an adolescent with an insatiable appetite.

J.B.W.

Acknowledgements

A project that is six years in the making inevitably draws into its ken friends and advisors. Among the many who have lent invaluable insight and skills to *Worlds Unrealized: Short Stories of Adolescence by Canadian Writers* are: Felicity Callard, Vanessa Callard, Angelica Drew, Cheryl Howard, Martin James, Jan James, Patrick Lynch, Burns MacMillan, Allison Rowe, Heather Sawyer, Jim Stascavage, Lisa Anne Wilson and Samantha Zee.

Particular thanks are due to Jay Davis for assistance in researching and writing the author biographies.

Table of Contents

Introduction

For most of us, the experiences of our adolescent years are indelible. Their intensity, their vividness, their sense of extraordinary potential, of things happening for the very first time, continue to haunt and tantalize us. Grappling and coming to terms with our adolescent past enables us to reflect on the continuity of our development and to deal more adequately and perhaps more hopefully with the immediate present and more distant future.

The adolescent years are the years of sexual awakening, when the first stirrings of adult sexuality excite the senses and demand attention. Lustful goals and intimacy needs must be coordinated with societal mores, and sexual identity must be incorporated within a changing personality structure. These are the years when we must renegotiate our relationships with parents to ones of greater parity even as we seek self-understanding from and deepening attachment with peers. These are also the years when many of us lose our innocence as our broadening horizons encounter the realities of inequality, prejudice, cruelty, disappointment and death.

Perhaps our greatest challenge in adolescence is in the construction of identity—a sense of personal wholeness that unites past experience, present views, and future possibilities offered by our society. We may try on roles or experiment with an "as if" period. Ultimately, though, identity must be achieved on a number of levels—racial, professional, sexual, ideological and in terms of a coherent philosophy of life. The new capacity for abstract thought that heralds adolescence and is requisite for identity achievement enables us to question more profoundly the "holy writ" handed down by authorities and to detect the hypocrisies of contemporary society as well as the compromises even our loved ones have made. It enables us, too, to think more deeply about the moral choices we make in our lives and their impact on others.

The adolescent, in this way, is analogous to the fool in Shakespeare's plays—disruptor of the peace, powerless, but naggingly insightful.

At no other time, perhaps, does the individual take such dangerous risks. Buoyed by a belief in personal invulnerability or thrilled by flirtations with danger, adolescents seek heightened sensation; alternatively, but equally dangerously, they can become bored, anti-social and alienated. Our culture offers few agreed-upon markers for the transition to adulthood. No formal rites tell us we have left adolescence for adulthood. Just a few hints forewarn us—a growing sense of what we must leave behind, the compromises we must make, the responsibilities attachment involves, the different realities of others' lives. We must gain, necessarily, a surer understanding of "how fearful a thing it is to be an adult" (to use Alistair MacLeod's memorable phrase).

In *Worlds Unrealized,* contemporary Canadian writers explore with different techniques and from various points of view the challenges, relationships, questionings and growth that characterize modern adolescence. The major criteria for inclusion in the volume were high literary merit and that the story deal insightfully with the experience of adolescents. Selection by editors was made from a perusal of thousands of stories and a systematic search of Canadian literary sources over the last six years.

The selections are organized into categories or themes that reflect the central features and tasks of adolescence. Volume I includes nineteen stories under the headings "Sexual Awakening," "Family Relationships," "Friends and the Peer Group," and "Loss of Innocence." Volume II contains twenty stories which have been organized under the headings "Identity," "Religion and Values," "The Dark Side of Adolescence," and "Transition to Adulthood." While the clustering of stories within any one single category is aimed at elaborating that theme fully through variety of age, sex, and point of view, the divisions are by no means discrete. What we have designated as an "Identity" story, for example, could well mark a "Transition to Adulthood." And, many readers, we recognize, may well wish to tackle these stories on a random basis.

The stories in *Worlds Unrealized* originate from every province in Canada. Nearly all were written within the last twenty years, most within the last ten. Of the thirty-nine stories in this two-volume collection, twenty are by men and nineteen by women; nearly a third were written by immigrants to Canada from abroad. The settings range from the West Coast, the prairies, central Canada, to Newfoundland. Five of them, however, have their settings variously in South Africa, India, Scotland and the United States. No other Canadian anthology of which we are aware has dealt so comprehensively with the adolescent experience in literature.

The writers in *Worlds Unrealized* have, through gifts of memory, insight, imagination and reconstruction, penetrated some of the deepest truths of development and life. As Freud said admiringly of imaginative writers, "In the knowledge of the human heart they are far ahead of us common folk, because they draw on sources that we have not yet made accessible to science." It is the hope of the editors that for lovers of good literature, for those who raise or work with adolescents, and for adolescents themselves—in fact, for all of us "common folk"—these stories will stimulate engagement, imaginative extension, selfdiscovery, reflection, and deeper knowledge of the human heart.

Andrew Garrod
Dartmouth College
New Hampshire

Janet Webster
Special Education Services
Yukon

Sexual Awakening

Gall

Brenda Riches

September 13

Her name is Sara. The new girl, the intruder. Red-haired Sara with the fluttering eyes. Who does she think she is, prancing in and choosing the desk in front of Matthew? Who is she, that she gets A's first time?

If they gave marks for what I'm good at I'd get A's. But what would you know about that, precious Mrs. Kirk? You're married to your damn classroom, your withered old specimens.

Those who can't, teach. And today we did the nuptial flight of bees. It figures. Matthew's all eyes for the sleek head in front of him. They'd have garish children, those two. Swarming creatures with striped red and yellow hair.

She can have him. I don't care.

October 13

Today Mrs. Kirk brought a dead stem of goldenrod and told us the lump on it was a gall. It's an abnormal growth induced by a parasite, she told us, and we had to study it and write down our observations.

I wish I could grow on Matthew.

Gall: 1) Before dissection. (I wrote)

> This swelling has forced veins to pull and widen, and magnified the colour so that you can see clearly the shades of silken sand that harbour the grub, the tracery that shelters it. The veins have pulled the skin inwards and I am aware of stress because the parts between have a bloated shape like a peeled tangerine. The swelling is dry and rigid, and when I tap it against my thumb the stem vibrates.

2) After dissection.
The insect is puffy in its tight cavity. The razor has exposed it and I prod it with the ribby stem of the dead plant. I prod. It's like gelatine. The inner faces of the segments are polished chalk under my fingers.

Mrs. Kirk read it through quickly and told me I was supposed to be recording not romanticising, that I shouldn't use first person in scientific observation and that you can't magnify colour. Sara smiled into her book. She got the best mark of course. She's so *precise*. Matthew commented that gall is also that bitter stuff we carry inside us somewhere. Mrs. Kirk said he should make his comments more accurate and told him to go and look up the word in a recognized dictionary. Sara's invited Matthew to Thanksgiving dinner. She hasn't wasted any time, wasping her way in.

November 13

Mrs. Kirk, dear Mrs. Kirk. Cast your eye on this observation. Will you give it an A?

GALL

At that butterfly brief time of the year when lakes have frozen and before snow covers the ice, I skated. The lake was fringed with cattails, reeds and tall gatherings of pampas. I arrived at noon in the clear expectation that the sun would cover the ice and I would skate on gold glass. It would be an afternoon lifted out of time, precious and unreal.

Not so. Skating in the direction of my shadow I was on ice that was grey and black and pitted with trapped bubbles. Little clusters of shredded snow rested like feathers on the surface, and dead leaves were caught on the tops of some of these, so that when I pulled one off it left its imprint behind as a glass fossil.

As I skated towards the bend of the lake, it pleased me to see Sara's face beneath the ice. I stopped for a better look. It was under a part that was cracked, and the jagged edges cut through her face from just above her left eye, and continued diagonally, severing her nose from which spurted a dark red weed, then took a vertical course splitting her soft mouth. Tributary cracks webbed outwards to break her hair close to the scalp, below her ears and level with her throat.

The geography of disfigurement was entrancing. I glided about twenty feet away, turned, and skimmed back over her.

December 13

It hasn't stopped snowing for three days. Even when I close my eyes all I can see is white. It's as if the ground and my brain, both of them together, were being wrapped for burial.

I can't sleep. If I keep Sara under the lake she will feed on its rank and winter feast. She will turn into something with wings.

January 13

Sara is oppressive like a sky that stretches over me, a smothering grey that reaches all the way down to my horizons. Matthew has offered to teach her how to ski. He leaned forward when Mrs. Kirk wasn't looking (when does she ever really look?), touched the back of Sara's neck lightly with one finger, and she turned to face him. He whispered very quietly, but I heard what he said, and I saw her eyes light up. I wanted to throw icy water at them. That would be really something. Sara of the spitting eyes.

February 13

Sara skis *incredibly* well. She must do. Matthew has said so five times so far. Another A for Sara.

Mrs. Kirk is droning on about the way bees dance. On and on like a buzz saw. My eyes are closed.

Sara skis. Yes, I can see her. Sending her body along tracks Matthew has made for her. Sara the quiet shadow, trailing behind him with a noise like taffeta. Now she falls in the snow. She sits up, laughing. He pulls her to her feet and brushes the snow off her clothes. Now they've come to a dusk of pine trees. Sara and Matthew moth-winging to a dark place where they will kiss.

March 13

Today the sun shining through the window pane woke up a blue- bottle. Its glossy buzzing lulled me. Its wings were thin. So thin. How could they send that full body winging through the air? Mrs. Kirk complained about the noise so Sara squished it dead with her thumb. I wish Matthew had been in the room to see her smile as she did it.

April 13

Matthew looks different. He's wearing a loose yellow shirt. Even Mrs. Kirk commented. Button your shirt, Matthew, she told him. Sara is flighty in a new dress. Her mouth is gaudy with lip gloss.

I've written a poem.

Butterfly

Painted lady
I'm watching you
flapping there
over my yellow flower.
How would you like
to be pinned
under glass?
How would you like
to be spread
permanently.

May 13

Earlier this evening I walked down Matthew's back lane. Your fence has gaps in it, Matthew. You should do something about that. Get your backside off the grass and mend your rotten fence.

What keeps you on the grass, Matthew? Sara the scarlet flounce? Tumble-skirted Sara who wants you to smooth her out with your sunwarmed hands?

June 13

At four o'clock I watched them walk out of school. They were holding hands. Their fingers were so twisted together that they looked like one grotesque knot.

Sara and Matthew. Knotted together.

"It's an abnormal growth, induced by a parasite."

Striptease

Al Pittman

The smell of horse, hay, and leather lingered in Mr. Blake's barn long after the last of his animals had been housed there.

The barn wasn't a barn really. It was a stable with two stalls along one side and a hay-loft, no more than waist high, at the far end. The corridor of space between the stalls and the west wall was vacant and the whole interior, though dim, was surprisingly tidy.

The barn was forbidden to us and we ventured there only those times we knew Mr. Blake to be in the sanatorium dying. Even then we'd approach the place cautiously and always in secret.

The Blake house stood close by, separated from the barn by a thin stand of poplars and a rather wretched row of black currant bushes. The door of the barn faced away from the house and opened onto what used to be a hayfield but which was now nothing more than a useless piece of green ground between the road and the brook below.

Mrs. Blake spent all of her days behind the counter in her husband's shop on the far side of the house and was seldom seen in the vicinity of the barn where Mr. Blake spent so much of his time whenever he was home from the san.

Until that summer the barn had been inviolate to us despite the notorious schemes we conspired there. Crouched in the interior twilight, inhaling the heavy sweet smell of long-forgotten hay, we whispered our impossible designs to each other in the close, religious air.

We made our plans with Mr. Blake's imminent death in mind. But it seemed, as time went on, that Mr. Blake had no intention of dying until we were all too slowly grown up, or until the barn preceded him to his decay. So none of this might ever have happened had it not been for Malcolm's prodigious disregard for restriction.

How he got Doreen and Hilda to consent to their part in his scandalous scheme, I could never figure out. But consent they did. The rest was up to Malcolm. And to me.

I wanted no part of it. I made excuses, pleaded incompetence, threatened rebellion, and promised allegiance in all else. But nothing worked.

Against the desperadoes who rode roughshod over the wild west of my imagination, I could stand undaunted 'til doomsday. But confronted with the reality of Malcolm's might, his big bony fists, all my heroics failed me.

I was to hang a rope from the rafters above the loft and test it by swinging from one end of the loft to the other. I was to pass the word and collect the fees. Malcolm would do the rest.

It was, he declared, to be the event of the summer, a secret surprise show worth every penny of the three coppers it cost to get in. And only boys would be allowed.

By Friday, thirteen boys from the road had paid up and six others had promised to pay as soon as they sold some beer bottles. They were told to come to the barn at ten Saturday morning and to make sure no one saw them enter.

That night, I prayed myself to sleep saying the Act of Contrition over and over, and woke next morning to the slish-thump of the wringer washer in the kitchen and my mother singing "The Cashmere Shawl."

By the time I'd struggled through breakfast, the sun was high in the sky.

"It's goin' to be a scorcher," my father said. "Be careful you don't get burnt."

I went out, my scapular medal weighing 'round my neck like an anvil. At the end of Blake's field, I left the road and took the path down the slippery slope to the falls. It would have been a good day to go swimming. The water tumbled silver-white and steep into the sun-streaked pool and the diving rock was already warm to the touch of my hand.

Perhaps, I thought, by afternoon, it'd be over. Nothing will have happened and we'd be here laughing and splashing in the glad summer sun.

I made my way reluctantly up the hill through a tangle of alders, cut across the bottom of the field, and crept like a crook to the barn.

The tense, secretive twilight inside was interrupted only by the thin blades of light knifing across the loft as the mid-morning sun stabbed through the wounds in the dark weathered wall.

"Where's the rest?" Malcolm demanded, out of the black recess beyond the far stall wall.

"They're comin'," I conceded, wishing almost that they wouldn't.

A girl's voice giggled somewhere in the dark.

"Shut up!" Malcolm commanded. "You wanna ruin the whole thing?"

One by one the rest of them came and slipped stealthily inside as I opened the door for each in his turn.

When finally they had assembled, the smaller boys sitting on the floor, the bigger ones leaning against the walls, Malcolm appeared out of the gloom and announced, "Ladies and gentlemen, let's not have no friggin' noise!"

He hopped down from the loft, waded through the throng of boys, and came to lean against the back wall where I stood guarding the door.

There was a moment of expectant silence broken only by the squeak of a girl's voice exclaiming something unintelligible somewhere in the dark beyond anyone's vision.

Then the rope, which had been hanging in a slack curve across the loft, tightened suddenly. And out of nowhere came Doreen, sailing in a quick graceful arc. The boys up front gasped and those behind giggled as they realized, almost too late, that she was stark naked.

Half an audible inhalation later, back she came curving through thin streaks of sunlight, secret segments of girl revealed fleetingly in split seconds of eternal time.

Before any of us could consider what we had seen, Doreen vanished into the dark. The rope fell slack and hung swaying listless in the dim, defiant light.

The coppers I'd collected burned like embers in my pocket. My mind imagined the inevitable eternity of retribution I would suffer. But some pagan part of me wished myself here alone with Doreen swinging forever within my sinful sight.

Malcolm, observing through a crack in the wall the pedestrian traffic to and from Mr. Blake's shop, said, "That ain't nothin'!"

Without warning, the rope whipped tight, and out across the loft came Hilda, spinning vigorously in the forbidden air.

A shocked silence. Whereas Doreen had not even begun to grow out of childhood, Hilda, no less a child, had hair and breasts, all of which she displayed saucily as she swung back and forth through the shafts of sunlight, not once, but twice.

"What a set!" said Cyril, loudly. He was one of the bigger boys.

"Shut up!" whispered Malcolm, sternly. "You want your old woman to barge in?"

The younger boys sat amazed, each absorbed in the mystery of his own masculinity. Here, before their astonished eyes, were revelations dreamed of night after sleepless hell-bent night.

Malcolm turned to me and winked.

Little Mickey Carew said, "I got to go home."

"Was da matter, Mickey?" said Cyril. "D'ya piss in yer pants?"

"I got to go home, is all," said Mickey. He was almost crying.

"Just a minute, Mickey," said Malcolm. "You don't wanna miss the best part, do ya?"

And out across the loft, together, hanging on for dear life, came Doreen and Hilda, a kaleidoscope of flesh flashing in the intermittent light. Back and forth, 'round and 'round they spun, a bewildering contortion of legs, breasts, bottoms, and bellies.

The boys stared, cross-eyed, their confused desires confused further by the spectacle they beheld.

All caution and hell forgotten, I strained for focus in the flickering light, striving for one indelible image to keep unblurred for my solitude.

Then, CRACK! The rope snapped.

The two unclothed aerial artists fell screaming to the loft floor in a tangle of limbs. Doreen wailed and Hilda cursed.

Malcolm threw me one exquisite look of condemnation and made for the exit.

The rest of the boys were on their heels and out the door in a flash, me among them.

Once outside, I took to the woods. The alder branches whipped at my face as I went stumbling blindly down the hill toward the brook.

A minute of reckless descent later, I tripped and fell flat on my face into a small clearing. When I looked up, there was Malcolm glaring at me.

"Gimme the goddamn money," he said.

I stumbled to my feet, dug deep into my pocket, and passed him my handful of coppers. "Now, get lost!" he said, and disappeared in the underbrush.

From where I stood, alone, shivering with guilt, confusion, and fear, I could hear the commotion of Doreen's wail and adult voices shouting.

"What's going on?" said one who sounded like Mrs. Carew.

"What happened?" asked another who might have been Mrs. Blake.

"Her arm is broke," declared someone I couldn't identify.

"Not a stitch on!" exclaimed my mother.

I ran, crashing down the hill, through the woods.

When I reached the falls, my face and hands stained with blood, I fell against the diving rock and wept.

A long time later, when my sobbing had subsided, I said a silent Act of Contrition, summoned up all the courage that had eluded me for so long, climbed to the top of the rock, sat there, and began waiting for them to come and get me.

Crush

Bonnie Burnard

It's Thursday morning and it's hot, hot, hot. The girl is painting the kitchen cupboards. The paint stinks up the kitchen, stinks up the whole house. Her summer blonde pony tail and her young brown shoulders are hidden in the cupboards and a stranger coming into the kitchen, seeing only the rounded buttocks in the terrycloth shorts and the long well-formed legs, might think he was looking at part of a woman.

She's tired. She babysat last night. It isn't the best job she can get; there are other kids, easier kids. She takes the job because of him, because she loves to ride alone with him on the way home. He is Allen, the breadman; she thinks she loves him. She remembers him at the beach, throwing his kids around in the water, teaching them to swim. His back and thighs she will remember when she is seventy and has forgotten others. She does not try to imagine anything other than what she has seen. It is already more than enough.

Her mother stands over the ironing board just inside the dining room door. Thunk, hiss, thunk, hiss. The kitchen table separates them. It is piled high with dishes and tea towels and bags of sugar and flour and pickling salt. Jars of spices are pitched here and there, rest askew in the crevices of the pile. The cupboards are hot and empty. She has nearly finished painting the inside of them.

Neither the girl nor her mother has spoken for over an hour. It is too hot. She leans back out of the cupboards, unbuttons her blouse and takes it off, tossing it to the table. It floats down over the dishes. She wants to take off her bra, but doesn't.

"You be careful Allen doesn't catch you in that state young lady. He'll be along with the bread soon." Her mother doesn't lift her head from the ironing. Her sleeveless housedress is stained with sweat. It soaks down toward her thick waist.

Maybe I want him to, the girl thinks. She does not share this thought with her mother. Her mother doesn't know about backs and thighs.

"Have you picked out the bathing suit you want?" Her mother glances up at her. The bathing suit is to be the reward for the painting. "It's time you started thinking about modesty. It's beginning to matter."

"No." The girl drags the fresh blue paint over the old pale green. But she has picked out her suit. It's the one on the dummy in the window downtown, the one the boys stare at. She knows she won't be allowed to have it. Mrs. Stewart in the ladies shop wouldn't even let her try it on. Said it wasn't suitable for her. But it does suit her. She wants it.

She hears the scream of the ironing board as her mother folds it up and again her mother's voice.

"I'm going downtown for meat. You put that blouse on before I leave."

"Why?" The girl looks at the limp skin on her mother's arm. "Nobody's here."

"Because Allen's coming with the bread soon, that's why. Now get it on. I'm as hot as you are and you don't see me throwing my clothes off."

Her mother stands checking the money in her purse, waiting till the last button is secure before she heads for the back door. "I'll bring you some cold pop." The screen door slams.

The girl steps down from the paint-splattered chair, goes to the sink, turns on the water and lets it run cold. She opens the freezer door, takes out a tray of ice cubes. She fills a glass with ice, slows the tap, watches the water lap around the ice cubes as it seeks the top of the glass. She drinks slowly. She isn't thirsty, but it's the only way to get something cold inside her. She pulls an ice cube out of the glass, holds it in her hands, feels it begin to melt against the heat of her palm. She raises her hand to her forehead, rubs the ice against her skin, back into her hair, over her neck, down into the sweaty shadow between her breasts. The ice cube is small now, just a round lump. Her hand is wet.

When he danced with her at the Fireman's dance, his hand was wet. Not the same wet though, not the same at all. His buddies hollered things about him liking the young stuff and they all laughed, even the wives. She laughed too, pretended she understood how funny it was, his touching her. But the skin on her back can still feel the pressure of his arm, how it moved her the way he wanted her to move. It should have been hard to move together. But it was easy, like a dream.

She wonders how close he is to their house. She dries her hand on the tea towel hanging from the stove door. She undoes the top button of her blouse then the next and the next and the next. It falls from her hand in a heap on the floor. She unfastens her bra, slips it down over her brown arms, lets it drop on top of the blouse.

She climbs up on the chair, begins to paint again. She can't smell the paint anymore or feel the ache in her arm that the movement brings.

Turning, she sees him standing there in the kitchen with her, the basket of baking slung round his neck. She comes down from the chair, steps over the blouse and bra, stands in front of him, as still as the surface of a hot summer lake. There is no sound but the catch of his breathing, no movement but the startled rhythm of his eyes moving from her face to her warm bare skin and back again.

"Jesus," he says.

"I wanted to show you, that's all."

He goes out the door quickly, doesn't leave Thursday's two loaves of white and one whole wheat.

Her mother's voice at the door hits the girl like an iceberg. She stands frozen, knowing that she will be caught and that she will be punished. Punished in some new way. She bends down, picks up her bra.

He's in the truck and he's wishing he had farther to go than the next block. Jesus. Bread to deliver. After that. What the hell was she trying to do.

He checks the rearview mirror. Maybe her mother thinks he was in on it; she could come roaring out after him any minute. He's a sitting duck in this damned truck. A drive. He'll go for a drive, just to clear his head. Christ.

He drives out past the gas station, past the local In and Out store, out of town, onto a grid road. He goes a few miles, lets the hot breeze blow the sweat away. He pulls over.

His wife. What if it gets back to her? She'll find some way to blame him. He should go right now and tell her the truth. Shit. She wouldn't believe him. He doesn't believe it and he was there. He'll just lie low and hope, pray, that her mother is too embarrassed to tell anyone.

The mother. What if she does think he was in on it? Maybe he should go back there right now, tell her straight out. She could watch his hands shake. No. If it's going to come up it'll come up soon and he'll just say it was a surprise and he won't be lying.

The girl has never given him one small clue that she was thinking in those terms. She's a good kid. He enjoys talking to her and he always makes a point of being nice to her when he picks her up to sit and when he drives her home. She always hides herself behind a huge pile of books held up tight to her sweater. And she helped him teach the kids to swim 'cause his wife wouldn't and he didn't even look at her, can't even picture her in a bathing suit.

So damned hot. He leans back in his seat, unbuttons his shirt, lights a cigarette. The sight of her comes back through the smoke that hangs around him. Not centrefold stuff, not even as nice as his wife before the kids but nice just the same, yeah, nice. It's been a long time since he's seen fresh, smooth, hard ones. He shifts around in his seat. Damn.

It's like she just discovered she had them. Or maybe she just got tired of being the only one who knew. Now he knows. And what's he supposed to do about it? Jesus. What she said made it sound like it was supposed to be some kind of gift. Man, this is too complicated for a Thursday morning.

The picture comes back again and this time he holds it and looks it over a little more carefully. He's sure they've never been touched. He thinks about dancing with her that once and how easy she was in his arms. Not sexy, just easy. Like she trusted him. He can't remember ever feeling that before. They sure didn't trust him when he was seventeen, had no business trusting him. And what he gets from his wife isn't trust, not exactly.

Kids are sometimes just crazy. She's crazy. But he remembers her eyes and whatever it was they were saying, it had nothing to do with being crazy.

Back the picture comes again and Jesus it is like a gift. He closes his eyes and the breasts stay in his eyes and he thinks he sees his own hands going to them and he feels a gentleness come into his hands and he sits up straight and he starts the truck and he tells himself you're crazy, man, that's who's crazy.

The mother stands watching the girl do up the last of the buttons on her blouse. She holds the package of meat in one hand, the bottle of pop in the other. The paper around the meat is dark and soft where blood has seeped out. She walks over to the fridge, puts the meat in the meat keeper and the pop beside the quarts of milk on the top shelf. She closes the fridge door with the same care she would use on the bedroom door of a sleeping child. When she turns, the girl has climbed up on the chair in front of the cupboards and is lifting the brush.

"Get down from that chair," she says.

The girl puts the brush across the top of the paint can and steps down.

"I could slap you," the mother says, calmly. This is not a conversation she has prepared herself for. This is not a conversation she ever expected to have. She cannot stop herself from looking at the girl's body, cannot stop the memory of her own body and the sudden remorse she feels knowing it will never come back to her. She longs for the sting of a slap, longs to feel it on her own hand and to imagine it on the girl's cheek. But she puts the anger someplace, out of the way. She pulls a chair from the table, away from the mess of cupboard things piled there and sits in the middle of the room, unprotected.

"Sit down," she says.

The girl sits where she is, on the floor, her brown legs tucked under her young bum as they were tucked through all those years of stories, fairy tales. But the mother can smell her fear.

"How much did you take off?"

The girl does not answer. She looks directly into her mother's eyes and she does not answer.

The mother begins the only way she knows how.

"I had a crush on your father. That's how it started with us, because I had a crush on him. He was only a little older than me but I think it's the same. I don't know why it should happen with you so young but I think it's the same. The difference is I didn't take my clothes off for him. And he wasn't married. It's wrong to feel that way about someone if he's married and it's wrong to take your clothes off. Do you understand?"

The girl picks at a scab on her ankle.

"The way you feel has got nothing to do with the way things are. You've embarrassed him. I could tell at the gate he was embarrassed. You won't be babysitting for them anymore. He'll tell his wife and they'll laugh about it. You've made a fool of yourself."

The girl lifts the scab away from her skin. The mother wants to gather her in her arms and carry her up to bed.

"You will feel this way from now on. Off and on, from now on. You have to learn to live with it. I wish it hadn't happened so soon. Now you just have to live with it longer. Do you understand?"

The girl shakes her head no.

"Women have this feeling so they will marry, so they will have children. It's like a system. And you've got to live within the system. There will be a young man for you, it won't be long. Maybe five years. That's all. You've got to learn to control this thing, this feeling, until that young man is there for you."

The mother gets up from her chair and goes to the fridge. She takes the pop out and opens it, divides it between two glasses. She hands one to the girl.

"If you don't control it you will waste it, bit by bit, and there will be nothing left. There will be no young man, not to marry. And they'll take it from you, all of them, any of them, because they can't stop themselves from taking it. It's not their responsibility. It's your responsibility not to offer it. You just have to wait, wait for the one young man and you be careful who he is, you think about it for a long time and then you marry him and then you offer it."

The girl gets up from the floor and puts her glass on the counter by the sink.

"Can I go now?" she asks.

The mother feels barren. She is not a mother anymore, not in the same way. It is as if the girl's undressing has wiped them both off the face of the earth.

The girl has run away from the house, out past the gas station and the beer store onto the grid road that divides the corn fields. She is sitting in a ditch, hidden, surrounded by long grass and thistles.

She likely has ruined it, likely will never babysit for them again. Not because he was embarrassed. He wasn't embarrassed, he was afraid. It's the first time she's ever made anyone afraid. She will find a way to tell him that she didn't mean to make him afraid.

She wishes her mother had slapped her. She didn't like hearing about how her mother felt about her father, it was awful, and all that talk about controlling it and getting married someday, she knows all of that. That's what everybody does and it's likely what she'll do because there doesn't seem to be any way to do anything else. Except maybe once in a while. If she learns not to get caught. And not to scare anyone.

She feels really alone and she likes it. She thinks about his back and his thighs and she thinks about standing there in front of him. It's the best feeling she's ever had. She won't give it up. She'll just be more careful. She crosses her arms in front of her, puts one hand over each small breast and she knows she isn't wrong about this feeling. It is something she will trust. She leans back into the grass, throws her arms up over her head and stares, for as long as she can, at the hot July sun.

Hurricane Hazel

Margaret Atwood

The summer I was fourteen, we lived in a one-room cabin, on a hundred acres of back-concession scrub farmland. The cabin was surrounded by a stand of tall old maples, which had been left there when the land was cut over, and the light sifted down in shafts, like those in pictures I had seen in Sunday school, much earlier, of knights looking for the Holy Grail, helmets off, eyes rolled up purely. Probably these trees were the reason my parents had bought the land: if they hadn't, someone else would have bought it and sold off the maples. This was the kind of thing my parents were in the habit of doing.

The cabin was of squared timber. It hadn't been built there originally, but had been moved from some other location by the people who had owned it before us, two high-school teachers who were interested in antiques. The logs had been numbered, then dismantled and put back together in the original order, and the cracks had been re-chinked with white cement, which was already beginning to fall out in places; so was the putty on the small panes of the windows. I knew this because one of my first jobs had been to wash them. I did this grudgingly, as I did most jobs around the house at the time.

We slept on one side of the room. The sleeping areas were divided off by parachutes, which my father had bought at the war-surplus store, where he often bought things: khaki-coloured pants with pockets on the knees, knife, fork and spoon sets which locked together and snapped apart and were impossible to eat with, rain capes with camouflage markings on them, a jungle hammock with mosquito- netting sides that smelled like the inside of a work sock and gave you a kink in the back, despite which my brother and I used to compete for the privilege of sleeping in it. The parachutes had been cut open and were hung like curtains from lengths of thick wire strung from wall to wall. The parachutes inside the house were dark green, but there was a smaller orange one set up outside, like a tent, for my three-year-old sister to play in.

I had the cubicle in the southeast corner. I slept there on a narrow bed with wire coil springs that squeaked whenever I turned over. On the other side of the cabin, the living side, there was a table coated with ruined varnish and a couple of much-painted chairs, the paint now cracked like a dried mud flat so that you could see what colours had been used before. There was a dresser with plates in it, which smelled even mustier than the rest of the things in the cabin, and a couple of rocking chairs, which didn't work too well on the uneven boards of the floor. All this furniture had been in the cabin when we bought it; perhaps it was the schoolteachers' idea of pioneer décor.

There was also a sort of counter where my mother washed the dishes and kept the primus stove she cooked on when it was raining. The rest of the time she cooked outdoors, on a fireplace with a grate of iron rods. When we ate outside we didn't use chairs: instead we sat on rounds of logs, because the ground itself was damp. The cabin was in a river valley; at night there was heavy dew, and the heat of the morning sunlight made an almost visible steam.

My father had moved us into the cabin early in the summer. Then he'd taken off for the forests on the north shore of the St. Lawrence, where he was doing some exploration for a pulp-and-paper company. All the time we were going through our daily routine, which revolved mainly around mealtimes and what we would eat at them, he was flying in bush planes into valleys with sides so steep the pilot had to cut the engine to get down into them, or trudging over portages past great rocky outcrops, or almost upsetting in rapids. For two weeks he was trapped by a forest fire which encircled him on all sides, and was saved only by torrential rains, during which he sat in his tent and toasted his extra socks at the fire, like wieners, to get them dry. These were the kinds of stories we heard after he came back.

My father made sure before he went that we had a supply of split and stacked wood and enough staples and tinned goods to keep us going. When we needed other things, such as milk and butter, I was sent on foot to the nearest store, which was a mile and a half away, at the top of an almost perpendicular hill which, much later, got turned into a ski resort. At that time there was only a dirt road, in the middle of what I thought of as nowhere, which let loose clouds of dust every time a car went past. Sometimes the cars would honk, and I would pretend not to notice.

The woman at the store, who was fat and always damp, was curious about us; she would ask how my mother was getting along. Didn't she mind it, all alone in that tumbledown place with no proper stove and no man around? She put the two things on the same level. I resented that kind of prying, but I was at the age when anybody's opinion mattered to me, and I could see that she thought my mother was strange.

If my mother had any reservations about being left alone on a remote farm with a three-year-old, no telephone, no car, no electricity, and only me for help, she didn't state them. She had been in such situations before, and by that time she must have been used to them. Whatever was going on she treated as normal; in the middle of crises, such as cars stuck up to their axles in mud, she would suggest we sing a song.

That summer she probably missed my father, though she would never say so; conversations in our family were not about feelings. Sometimes, in the evenings, she would write letters, though she claimed she could never think of what to say. During the days, when she wasn't cooking or washing the dishes, she did small tasks which could be interrupted at any time. She would cut the grass, even though the irregular plot in front of the house was overgrown with weeds and nothing would make it look any more like a lawn; or she would pick up the fallen branches under the maple trees.

I looked after my little sister for part of the mornings: that was one of my jobs. At these times my mother would sometimes drag a rocking chair out onto the bumpy grass and read books, novels of historical times or accounts of archaeological expeditions. If I came up behind her and spoke to her while she was reading, she would scream. When it was sunny she would put on shorts, which she would never wear when other people were around. She thought she had bony knees; this was the only thing about her personal appearance that she showed much awareness about. For the most part she was indifferent to clothes. She wanted them to cover what they were supposed to cover and to stay in one piece, and that was all she expected from them.

When I wasn't taking care of my sister, I would go off by myself. I would climb one of the maples, which was out of sight of the house and had a comfortable fork in it, and read *Wuthering Heights;* or I would walk along the old logging road, now grown up in saplings. I knew my way around in the weedy and brambly jungle back there, and I'd been across the river to the open field on the other side, where the next-door farmer was allowed to graze his cows, to keep down the thistles and burdock. This was where I'd found what I thought was the pioneers' house, the real one, though it was nothing now but a square depression surrounded by grass-covered ridges. The first year, this man had planted a bushel of peas, and he'd harvested a bushel. We knew this from the schoolteachers, who looked up records.

If my brother had made this discovery, he would have drawn a map of it. He would have drawn a map of the whole area, with everything neatly labelled. I didn't even attempt this; instead, I merely wandered around, picking raspberries and thimbleberries, or sunning myself in the tall weeds, surrounded by the smell of milkweed and daisies and crushed leaves, made dizzy by the sun and the light reflected from the white pages of my book, with grasshoppers landing on me and leaving traces of their brown spit.

Towards my mother I was surly, though by myself I was lazy and aimless. It was hard even to walk through the grass, and lifting my hand to brush away the grasshoppers was an effort. I seemed always to be half asleep. I told myself that I wanted to be doing something; by that I meant something that would earn money, elsewhere. I wanted a summer job, but I was too young for one.

My brother had a job. He was two years older than I was, and now he was a Junior Ranger, cutting brush by the sides of highways somewhere in northern Ontario, living in tents with a batch of other sixteen-year-old boys. This was his first summer away. I resented his absence and envied him, but I also looked for his letters every day. The mail was delivered by a woman who lived on a nearby farm; she drove it around in her own car. When there was something for us she would toot her horn, and I would walk out to the dusty galvanized mailbox that stood on a post beside our gate.

My brother wrote letters to my mother as well as to me. Those to her were informative, descriptive, factual. He said what he was doing, what they ate, where they did their laundry. He said that the town near their camp had a main street that was held up only by the telephone wires. My mother was pleased by these letters, and read them out loud to me.

I did not read my brother's letters out loud to her. They were private, and filled with the sort of hilarious and vulgar commentary that we often indulged in when we were alone. To other people we seemed grave and attentive, but by ourselves we made fun of things relentlessly, outdoing each other with what we considered to be revolting details. My brother's letters were illustrated with drawings of his tent-mates, showing them with many-legged bugs jumping around on their heads, with spots on their faces, with wavy lines indicating smelliness radiating from their feet, with apple cores in the beards they were all attempting to grow. He included unsavoury details of their personal habits, such as snoring. I took these letters straight from the mailbox to the maple tree, where I read them over several times. Then I smuggled them into the cabin under my T-shirt and hid them under my bed.

I got other letters too, from my boyfriend, whose name was Buddy. My brother used a fountain pen; Buddy's letters were in blue ball-point, the kind that splotched, leaving greasy blobs that came off on my fingers. They contained ponderous compliments, like those made by other people's uncles. Many words were enclosed by quotation marks; others were underlined. There were no pictures.

I liked getting these letters from Buddy, but also they embarrassed me. The trouble was that I knew what my brother would say about Buddy, partly because he had already said some of it. He spoke as if both he and I took it for granted that I would soon be getting rid of Buddy, as if Buddy were a stray dog it would be my duty to send to the Humane Society if the owner could not be found. Even Buddy's name, my brother said, was like a dog's. He said I should call Buddy "Pal" or "Sport" and teach him to fetch.

I found my brother's way of speaking about Buddy both funny and cruel: funny because it was in some ways accurate, cruel for the same reason. It was true that there was something dog-like about Buddy: the affability, the dumb faithfulness about the eyes, the dutiful way he plodded through the rituals of dating. He was the kind of boy (though I never knew this with certainty, because I never saw it) who would help his mother carry in the groceries without being asked, not because he felt like it but simply because it was prescribed. He said things like, "That's the way the cookie crumbles," and when he said this I had the feeling he would still be saying it forty years later.

Buddy was a lot older than I was. He was eighteen, almost nineteen, and he'd quit school long ago to work at a garage. He had his own car, a third-hand Dodge, which he kept spotlessly clean and shining. He smoked and drank beer, though he drank the beer only when he wasn't out with me but was with other boys his own age. He would mention how many bottles he had drunk in an offhand way, as if disclaiming praise.

He made me anxious, because I didn't know how to talk to him. Our phone conversations consisted mostly of pauses and monosyllables, though they went on a long time; which was infuriating to my father, who would walk past me in the hall, snapping his first two fingers together like a pair of scissors, meaning I was to cut it short. But cutting short a conversation with Buddy was like trying to divide water, because Buddy's conversations had no shape, and I couldn't give them a shape myself. I hadn't yet learned any of those stratagems girls were supposed to use on men. I didn't know how to ask leading questions, or how to lie about certain kinds of things, which I was later to call being tactful. So mostly I said nothing, which didn't seem to bother Buddy at all.

I knew enough to realize, however, that it was a bad tactic to appear too smart. But if I had chosen to show off, Buddy might not have minded: he was the kind of boy for whom cleverness was female. Maybe he would have liked a controlled display of it, as if it were a special kind of pie or a piece of well-done embroidery. But I never figured out what Buddy really wanted; I never figured out why Buddy was going out with me in the first place. Possibly it was because I was there. Buddy's world, I gradually discovered, was much less alterable than mine: it contained a long list of things that could never be changed or fixed.

All of this started at the beginning of May, when I was in grade ten. I was two or three years younger than most of the others in my class, because at that time they still believed in skipping you ahead if you could do the work. The year before, when I'd entered high school, I had been twelve, which was a liability when other people were fifteen. I rode my bicycle to school when other girls in my class were walking, slowly, langorously, holding their notebooks up against their bodies to protect and display their breasts. I had no breasts; I could still wear things I'd worn when I was eleven. I took to sewing my own clothes, out of patterns I bought at Eaton's. The clothes never came out looking like the pictures on the pattern envelopes; also they were too big. I must have been making them the size I wanted to be. My mother told me these clothes looked very nice on me, which was untrue and no help at all. I felt like a flat-chested midget, surrounded as I was by girls who were already oily and glandular, who shaved their legs and put pink medicated makeup on their pimples and fainted interestingly during gym, whose flesh was sleek and plumped-out and faintly shining, as if it had been injected under the skin with cream.

The boys were even more alarming. Some of them, the ones who were doing grade nine for the second time, wore leather jackets and were thought to have bicycle chains in their lockers. A few of them were high-voiced and spindly, but these of course I ignored. I knew the difference between someone who was a drip or a pill, on the one hand, and cute or a dream on the other. Buddy wasn't a dream, but he was cute, and that counted for a lot. Once I started going out with Buddy, I found I could pass for normal. I was now included in the kinds of conversations girls had in the washroom while they were putting on their lipstick. I was now teased.

Despite this, I knew that Buddy was a kind of accident: I hadn't come by him honestly. He had been handed over to me by Trish, who had come up to me out of nowhere and asked me to go out with her and her boyfriend Charlie and Charlie's cousin. Trish had a large mouth and prominent teeth and long sandy hair, which she tied back in a pony tail. She wore fuzzy pink sweaters and was a cheerleader, though not the best one. If she hadn't been going steady with Charlie, she would have had a reputation, because of the way she laughed and wiggled; as it was, she was safe enough for the time being. Trish told me I would like Buddy because he was so cute. She also mentioned that he had a car; Charlie didn't have a car. It's likely that I was put into Buddy's life by Trish so that Trish and Charlie could neck in the back seat of Buddy's car at drive-in movies, but I doubt that Buddy knew this. Neither did I, at the time.

We always had to go to the early show—a source of grumbling from Trish and Charlie—because I wasn't allowed to stay out past eleven. My father didn't object to my having boyfriends, as such, but he wanted them to be prompt in their pick-up and delivery. He didn't see why they had to moon around outside the front door when they were dropping me off. Buddy wasn't as bad in this respect as some of the later ones, in my father's opinion. With those, I got into the habit of coming in after the deadline, and my father would sit me down and explain very patiently that if I was on my way to catch a train and I was late for it, the train would go without me, and that was why I should always be in on time. This cut no ice with me at all, since, as I would point out, our house wasn't a train. It must have been then that I began to lose faith in reasonable argument as the sole measure of truth. My mother's rationale for promptness was more understandable: if I wasn't home on time, she would think I had been in a car accident. We knew without admitting it that sex was the hidden agenda at these discussions, more hidden for my father than for my mother: she knew about cars and accidents.

At the drive-in Buddy and Charlie would buy popcorn and Cokes, and we would all munch in unison as the pale shadowy figures materialized on the screen, bluish in the diminishing light. By the time the popcorn was gone it would be dark. There would be rustlings, creakings, suppressed moans from the back seat, which Buddy and I would pretend to ignore. Buddy would smoke a few cigarettes, one arm around my shoulders. After that we would neck, decorously enough compared with what was going on behind us.

Buddy's mouth was soft, his body large and comforting. I didn't know what I was supposed to feel during these sessions. Whatever I did feel was not very erotic, though it wasn't unpleasant either. It was more like being hugged by a friendly Newfoundland dog or an animated quilt than anything else. I kept my knees pressed together and my arms around his back. Sooner or later Buddy would attempt to move his hands around to the front, but I knew I was supposed to stop him, so I did. Judging from his reaction, which was resigned but good-natured, this was the correct thing to do, though he would always try again the next week.

It occurred to me very much later that Trish had selected me, not despite the fact that I was younger and less experienced than she was, but because of it. She needed a chaperone. Charlie was thinner than Buddy, better-looking, more intense; he got drunk sometimes, said Trish, with an already matronly shake of her head. Buddy was seen as solid, dependable, and a little slow, and so perhaps was I.

After I had been going out with Buddy for a month or so, my brother decided it would be in my own best interests to learn Greek. By that he meant he would teach it to me whether I liked it or not. In the past he had taught me many things, some of which I had wanted to know: how to read, how to shoot with a bow, how to skip flat rocks, how to swim, how to play chess, how to aim a rifle, how to paddle a canoe and scale and gut a fish. I hadn't learned many of them very well, except the reading. He had also taught me how to swear, sneak out of bedroom windows at night, make horrible smells with chemicals, and burp at will. His manner, whatever the subject, was always benignly but somewhat distantly pedagogical, as if I were a whole classroom by myself.

The Greek was something he himself was learning; he was two grades ahead of me and was at a different high school, one that was only for boys. He started me with the alphabet. As usual, I didn't learn fast enough for him, so he began leaving notes about the house, with Greek letters substituted for the letters of the English words. I would find one in the bathtub when I was about to take a bath before going out with Buddy, set it aside for later, turn on the tap and find myself drenched by the shower. (*Turn off the shower*, the note would read when translated.) Or there would be a message taped to the closed door of my room, which would turn out to be a warning about what would fall on me—a wet towel, a clump of cooked spaghetti— when I opened it. Or one on my dresser would announce a Frenched bed or inform me that my alarm clock was set to go off at 3 a.m. I didn't ever learn much real Greek, but I did learn to transpose quickly. It was by such ruses, perhaps, that my brother was seeking to head me off, delay my departure from the world he still inhabited, a world in which hydrogen sulphide and chess gambits were still more interesting than sex, and Buddy, and the Buddies to come, were still safely and merely ridiculous.

My brother and Buddy existed on different layers altogether. My brother, for instance, was neither cute nor a pill. Instead he had the preternatural good looks associated with English schoolboys, the kind who turned out to be pyromaniacs in films of the sixties, or with posters of soldiers painted at the time of World War One; he looked as if he ought to have green skin and slightly pointed ears, as if his name should have been Nemo, or something like it; as if he could see through you. All of these things I thought later; at the time he was just my brother, and I didn't have any ideas about how he looked. He had a maroon sweater with holes in the elbows, which my mother kept trying to replace or throw out, but she was never successful. He took her lack of interest in clothes one step further.

Whenever I started to talk like what he thought of as a teenager, whenever I mentioned sock hops or the hit parade, or anything remotely similar, my brother would quote passages out of the blackhead-remover ads in his old comic books, the ones he'd collected when he was ten or eleven: "Mary never knew why she was not POPULAR, until.... Someone should tell her! Mary, NOW there's something you can do about those UGLY BLACKHEADS! *Later*.... Mary, I'd like to ask you to the dance. (*Thinks*: Now that Mary's got rid of those UGLY BLACKHEADS, she's the most POPULAR girl in the class.)" I knew that if I ever became the most popular girl in the class, which was not likely, I would get no points at all from my brother.

When I told Buddy I would be away for the summer, he thought I was "going to the cottage," which was what a lot of people in Toronto did; those who had cottages, that is. What he had in mind was something like Lake Simcoe, where you could ride around in fast motorboats and maybe go water-skiing, and where there would be a drive-in. He thought there would be other boys around; he said I would go out with them and forget all about him, but he said it as a joke.

I was vague about where I was actually going. Buddy and I hadn't talked about our families much; it wouldn't be easy to explain to him my parents' preferences for solitude and outhouses and other odd things. When he said he would come up and visit me, I told him it was too far away, too difficult to find. But I couldn't refuse to give him the address, and his letters arrived faithfully every week, smeared and blobby, the handwriting round and laborious and child-like. Buddy pressed so hard the pen sometimes went through, and if I closed my eyes and ran my fingers over the paper I could feel the letters engraved on the page like braille.

I answered Buddy's first letter sitting at the uneven table with its cracked geological surface. The air was damp and warm; the pad of lined paper I was writing on was sticking to the tacky varnish. My mother was doing the dishes, in the enamel dishpan, by the light of one of the oil lamps. Usually I helped her, but ever since Buddy had appeared on the scene she'd been letting me off more frequently, as if she felt I needed the energy for other things. I had the second oil lamp, turned up as high as it would go without smoking. From behind the green parachute curtain I could hear the light breathing of my sister.

Dear Buddy, I wrote, and stopped. Writing his name embarrassed me. When you saw it on a blank sheet of paper like that, it seemed a strange thing to call someone. Buddy's name bore no relation to what I could really remember of him, which was mostly the smell of his freshly washed T-shirts, mixed with the smell of cigarette smoke and Old Spice aftershave. *Buddy*. As a word, it reminded me of *pudding*. I could feel under my hand the little roll of fat at the back of his neck, hardly noticeable now, but it would get larger, later, when he was not even that much older.

My mother's back was towards me but I felt as if she were watching me anyway; or listening, perhaps, to the absence of sound, because I wasn't writing. I couldn't think of what to say to Buddy. I could describe what I'd been doing, but as soon as I began I saw how hopeless this would be.

In the morning I'd made a village out of sand, down on the one small available sandbar, to amuse my sister. I was good at these villages. Each house had stone windows; the roads were paved with stone also, and trees and flowers grew in the gardens, which were surrounded by hedges of moss. When the villages were finished, my sister would play with them, running her toy cars along the roads and moving the stick people I'd made for her, in effect ruining them, which annoyed me.

When I could get away, I'd waded down the river by myself, to be out of range. There was a seam of clay I already knew about, and I'd gouged a chunk out of it and spent some time making it into beads, leaving them on a stump in the sun to harden. Some of them were in the shape of skulls, and I intended to paint these later and string them into a necklace. I had some notion that they would form part of a costume for Hallowe'en, though at the same time I knew I was already too old for this.

Then I'd walked back along the river bank, climbing over the tangles of fallen trees that blocked the way, scratching my bare legs on the brambles. I'd picked a few flowers, as a peace offering to my mother, who must have known I'd deserted her on purpose. These were now wilting in a jam jar on the dresser: bladder campion, jewelweed, Queen

Anne's Lace. In our family you were supposed to know the names of the things you picked and put in jars.

Nothing I did seemed normal in the light of Buddy; spelled out, my activities looked childish or absurd. What did other girls the age people thought I was do when they weren't with boys? They talked on the telephone, they listened to records; wasn't that it? They went to movies, they washed their hair. But they didn't wash their hair by standing up to their knees in an ice-cold river and pouring water over their heads from an enamel basin. I didn't wish to appear eccentric to Buddy; I wished to disguise myself. This had been easier in the city, where we lived in a more ordinary way: such things as my parents' refusal to buy a television set and sit in front of it eating their dinners off fold-up trays, and their failure to acquire an indoor clothes dryer, were minor digressions that took place behind the scenes.

In the end I wrote to Buddy about the weather, and said I missed him and hoped I would see him soon. After studying the blotchy X's and O's, much underlined, which came after Buddy's signature, I imitated them. I sealed this forgery and addressed it, and the next morning I walked out to the main road and put it in our loaf-shaped mailbox, raising the little flag to show there was a letter.

Buddy arrived unannounced one Sunday morning in August, after we had done the dishes. I don't know how he found out where we lived. He must have asked at the crossroads where there were a few houses, a gas station, and a general store with Coca-Cola ads on the screen door and a post office at the back. The people there would have been able to help Buddy decipher the rural-route number; probably they knew anyway exactly where we were.

My mother was in her shorts, in front of the house, cutting the grass and weeds with a small scythe. I was carrying a pail of water up the slippery and decaying wooden steps from the river. I knew that when I got to the top of the steps my mother would ask me what I wanted for lunch, which would drive me mad with irritation. I never knew what I wanted for lunch, and if I did know there was never any of it. It didn't occur to me then that my mother was even more bored with mealtimes than I was, since she had to do the actual cooking, or that her question might have been a request for help.

Then we heard a noise, a roaring motor noise, exaggerated but muffled too, like a gas lawnmower inside a tin garage. We both stopped dead in our tracks and looked at one another; we had a way of doing that whenever we heard any machine-made sound out on the main road. We believed, I think, that nobody knew we were there. The good part of this was that nobody would come in, but the bad part was that somebody might, thinking our place uninhabited, and the sort of people who would try it would be the sort we would least want to see.

The noise stopped for a few minutes; then it started up again, louder this time. It was coming in, along our road. My mother dropped her scythe and ran into the house. I knew she was going to change out of her shorts. I continued stolidly up the steps, carrying the pail of water. If I'd known it was Buddy I would have brushed my hair and put on lipstick.

When I saw Buddy's car, I was surprised and almost horrified. I felt I had been caught out. What would Buddy think of the decaying cabin, the parachute curtains, the decrepit furniture, the jam jar with its drooping flowers? My first idea was to keep him out of the house, at least. I went to meet the car, which was floundering over the road towards me. I was conscious of the dead leaves and dirt sticking to my wet bare feet.

Buddy got out of the car and looked up at the trees. Charlie and Trish, who were in the back seat, got out too. They gazed around, but after one quick look they gave no indication that they thought this place where I was living was hardly what they had expected; except that they talked too loudly. I knew though that I was on the defensive.

Buddy's car had a big hole in the muffler, which he hadn't had time to fix yet, and Charlie and Trish were full of stories about the annoyed looks people in the backroads villages had given them as they'd roared through. Buddy was more reserved, almost shy. "You got my letter, eh?" he said, but I hadn't, not the one that announced this visit. That letter arrived several days later, filled with a wistful loneliness it would have been handy to have known about in advance.

Charlie and Trish and Buddy wanted to go on a picnic. It was their idea that we would drive over to Pike Lake, about fifteen miles away, where there was a public beach. They thought we could go swimming. My mother had come out by this time. Now that she had her slacks on she was behaving as if everything was under control. She agreed to this plan; she knew there was nothing for them to do around our place. She didn't seem to mind my going off with Buddy for a whole day, because we would be back before dark.

The three of them stood around the car; my mother tried to make conversation with them while I ran to the cabin to get my swimsuit and a towel. Trish already had her swimsuit on; I'd seen the top of it under her shirt. Maybe there would be no place to change. This was the kind of thing you couldn't ask about without feeling like a fool, so I changed in my cubicle of parachute silk. My suit was left over from last year; it was red, and a little too small.

My mother, who didn't usually give instructions, told Buddy to drive carefully; probably because the noise made his car sound a lot more dangerous than it was. When he started up it was like a rocket taking off, and it was even worse inside. I sat in the front seat beside Buddy. All the windows were rolled down, and when we reached the paved highway Buddy stuck his left elbow out the window. He held the steering wheel with one hand, and with the other he reached across the seat and took hold of my hand. He wanted me to move over so I was next to him and he could put his arm around me, but I was nervous about the driving. He gave me a reproachful look and put his hand back on the wheel.

I had seen road signs pointing to Pike Lake before but I had never actually been there. It turned out to be small and round, with flattish countryside around it. The public beach was crowded, because it was a weekend: teenagers in groups and young couples with children mostly. Some people had portable radios. Trish and I changed behind the car, even though we were only taking off our outer clothes to reveal our bathing suits, which everybody was going to see anyway. While we were doing this, Trish told me that she and Charlie were now secretly engaged. They were going to get married as soon as she was old enough. No one was supposed to know, except Buddy of course, and me. She said her parents would have kittens if they found out. I promised not to tell; at the same time, I felt a cold finger travelling down my spine. When we came out from behind the car, Buddy and Charlie were already standing up to their ankles in the water, the sun reflecting from their white backs.

The beach was dusty and hot, with trash from picnickers left here and there about it: paper plates showing half-moons above the sand, dented paper cups, bottles. Part of a hot-dog wiener floated near where we waded in, pallid, greyish-pink, lost-looking. The lake was shallow and weedy, the water the temperature of cooling soup. The bottom was of sand so fine-grained it was almost mud; I expected leeches in it, and clams, which would probably be dead, because of the warmth. I swam out into it anyway. Trish was screaming because she had walked into some water weeds; then she was splashing Charlie. I felt that I ought to be doing these things too, and that Buddy would note the omission. But instead I floated on my back in the lukewarm water, squinting up at the cloudless sky, which was depthless and hot blue and had things like microbes drifting across it, which I knew were the rods and cones in my eyeballs. I had skipped ahead in the health book; I even knew what a zygote was. In a while Buddy swam out to join me and spurted water at me out of his mouth, grinning.

After that we swam back to the beach and lay down on Trish's oversized pink beach towel, which had a picture of a mermaid tossing a bubble on it. I felt sticky, as if the water had left a film on me. Trish and Charlie were nowhere to be seen; at last I spotted them, walking hand in hand near the water at the far end of the beach. Buddy wanted me to rub some suntan lotion onto him. He wasn't tanned at all, except for his face and his hands and forearms, and I remembered that he worked all week and didn't have time to lie around in the sun the way I did. The skin of his back was soft and slightly loose over the muscles, like a sweater or a puppy's neck.

When I lay back down beside him, Buddy took hold of my hand, even though it was greasy with the suntan lotion. "How about Charlie, eh?" he said, shaking his head in mock disapproval, as if Charlie had been naughty or stupid. He didn't say Charlie and Trish. He put his arm over me and started to kiss me, right on the beach, in the full sunlight, in front of everyone. I pulled back.

"There's people watching," I said.

"Want me to put the towel over your head?" he said.

I sat up, brushing sand off me and tugging up the front of my bathing suit. I brushed some sand off Buddy too: his stuck worse because of the lotion. My back felt parched and I was dizzy from the heat and brightness. Later, I knew, I would get a headache.

"Where's the lunch?" I said.

"Who's hungry?" he said. "Not for food, anyways." But he didn't seem annoyed. Maybe this was the way I was supposed to behave.

I walked to the car and got out the lunch, which was in a brown paper bag, and we sat on Trish's towel and ate egg-salad sandwiches and drank warm fizzy Coke, in silence. When we had finished, I said I wanted to go and sit under a tree. Buddy came with me, bringing the towel. He shook it before we sat down.

"You don't want ants in your pants," he said. He lit a cigarette and smoked half of it, leaning against the tree trunk—an elm, I noticed—and looking at me in an odd way, as if he was making up his mind about something. Then he said, "I want you to have something." His voice was offhand, affable, the way it usually was; his eyes weren't. On the whole he looked frightened. He undid the silver bracelet from his wrist. It had always been there, and I knew what was written on it: *Buddy*, engraved in flowing script. It was an imitation army I.D. tag; a lot of the boys wore them.

"My identity bracelet," he said.

"Oh," I said as he slid it over my hand, which now, I could tell, smelled of onions. I ran my fingers over Buddy's silver name as if admiring it. I had no thought of refusing it; that would have been impossible, because I would never have been able to explain what was wrong with taking it. Also I felt that Buddy had something on me: that, now he had accidentally seen something about me that was real, he knew too much about my deviations from the norm. I felt I had to correct that somehow. It occurred to me, years later, that many women probably had become engaged and even married this way.

It was years later too that I realized Buddy had used the wrong word: it wasn't an identity bracelet, it was an identification bracelet. The difference escaped me at the time. But maybe it was the right word after all, and what Buddy was handing over to me was his identity, some key part of himself that I was expected to keep for him and watch over.

Another interpretation has since become possible: that Buddy was putting his name on me, like a *Reserved* sign or an ownership label, or a tattoo on a cow's ear, or a brand. But at the time nobody thought that way. Everyone knew that getting a boy's I.D. bracelet was a privilege, not a degradation, and this is how Trish greeted it when she came back from her walk with Charlie. She spotted the transfer instantly.

"Let's *see*," she said, as if she hadn't seen this ornament of Buddy's many times before, and I had to hold out my wrist for her to admire, while Buddy looked sheepishly on.

When I was back at the log house, I took off Buddy's identification bracelet and hid it under the bed. I was embarrassed by it, though the reason I gave myself was that I didn't want it to get lost. I put it on again in September though, when I went back to the city and back to school. It was the equivalent of a white fur sweater-collar, the kind with pom-poms. Buddy, among other things, was something to wear.

I was in grade eleven now, and studying Ancient Egypt and *The Mill on the Floss*. I was on the volleyball team; I sang in the choir. Buddy was still working at the garage, and shortly after school began he got a hernia, from lifting something too heavy. I didn't know what a hernia was. I thought it might be something sexual, but at the same time it had the sound of something that happened to old men, not to someone as young as Buddy. I looked it up in our medical book. When my brother heard about Buddy's hernia, he sniggered in an irritating way and said it was the kind of thing you could expect from Buddy.

Buddy was in a hospital for a couple of days. After that I went to visit him at home, because he wanted me to. I felt I should take him something; not flowers though. So I took him some peanut-butter cookies, baked by my mother. I knew, if the subject came up, that I would lie and say I had made them myself.

This was the first time I had ever been to Buddy's house. I hadn't even known where he lived; I hadn't thought of him as having a house at all or living anywhere in particular. I had to get there by bus and streetcar, since of course Buddy couldn't drive me.

It was Indian summer; the air was thick and damp, though there was a breeze that helped some. I walked along the street, which was lined with narrow, two-storey row houses, the kind that would much later be renovated and become fashionable, though at that time they were considered merely old-fashioned and inconvenient. It was a Saturday afternoon, and a couple of the men were mowing their cramped lawns, one of them in his undershirt.

The front door of Buddy's house was wide open; only the screen door was closed. I rang the doorbell; when nothing happened, I went in. There was a note, in Buddy's blotchy blue ball-point writing, lying on the floor: COME ON UP, it said. It must have fallen down from where it had been taped to the inside of the door.

The hallway had faded pink rose-trellis paper; the house smelled faintly of humid wood, polish, rugs in summer. I peered into the living room as I went towards the stairs: there was too much furniture in it and the curtains were drawn, but it was immaculately clean. I could tell that Buddy's mother had different ideas about housework than my mother had. Nobody seemed to be home, and I wondered if Buddy had arranged it this way on purpose, so I wouldn't run into his mother.

I climbed the stairs; in the mirror at the top I was coming to meet myself. In the dim light I seemed older, my flesh plumped and flushed by the heat, my eyes in shadow.

"Is that you?" Buddy called to me. He was in the front bedroom, lying propped up in a bed that was much too large for the room. The bed was of chocolate-coloured varnished wood, the head and foot carved; it was this bed, huge, outmoded, ceremonial, that made me more nervous than anything else in the room, including Buddy. The window was open, and the white lace-edged curtains—of a kind my mother never would have considered, because of the way they would have to be bleached, starched, and ironed—shifted a little in the air. The sound of the lawn-mowers came in through the window.

I hesitated in the doorway, smiled, went in. Buddy was wearing a white T-shirt, and had just the sheet over him, pulled up to his waist. He looked softer, shorter, a little shrunken. He smiled back at me and held out his hand.

"I brought you some cookies," I said. We were both shy, because of the silence and emptiness. I took hold of his hand and he pulled me gently towards him. The bed was so high that I had to climb half onto it. I set the bag of cookies down beside him and put my arms around his neck. His skin smelled of cigarette smoke and soap, and his hair was neatly combed and still a little wet. His mouth tasted of toothpaste. I thought of him hobbling around, in pain maybe, getting ready for me. I had never thought a great deal about boys getting themselves ready for girls, cleaning themselves, looking at themselves in bathroom mirrors, waiting, being anxious, wanting to please. I realized now that they did this, that it wasn't only the other way around. I opened my eyes and looked at Buddy as I was kissing him. I had never done this before, either. Buddy with his eyes closed was different, and stranger, than Buddy with his eyes open. He looked asleep, and as if he was having a troublesome dream.

This was the most I had ever kissed him. It was safe enough: he was wounded. When he groaned a little I thought it was because I was hurting him. "Careful," he said, moving me to one side.

I stopped kissing him and put my face down on his shoulder, against his neck. I could see the dresser, which matched the bed; it had a white crocheted runner on it, and some baby pictures in silver stands. Over it was a mirror, in a sombre frame with a carved festoon of roses, and inside the frame there was Buddy, with me lying beside him. I thought this must be the bedroom of Buddy's parents, and their bed. There was something sad about lying there with Buddy in the cramped formal room with its heavy prettiness, its gaiety which was both ornate and dark. This room was almost foreign to me; it was a celebration of something I could not identify with and would never be able to share. It would not take very much to make Buddy happy, ever: only something like this. This was what he was expecting of me, this not very much, and it was a lot more than I had. This was the most afraid I ever got, of Buddy.

"Hey," said Buddy. "Cheer up, eh? Everything still works okay." He thought I was worried about his injury.

After that we found that I had rolled on the bag of cookies and crushed them into bits, and that made everything safer, because we could laugh. But when it was time for me to go, Buddy became wistful. He held onto my hand. "What if I won't let you go?" he said.

When I was walking back towards the streetcar stop, I saw a woman coming towards me, carrying a big brown leather purse and a paper bag. She had a muscular and determined face, the face of a woman who has had to fight, something or other, in some way or another, for a long time. She looked at me as if she thought I was up to no good, and I became conscious of the creases in my cotton dress, from where I had been lying on the bed with Buddy. I thought she might be Buddy's mother.

Buddy got better quite soon. In the weeks after that, he ceased to be an indulgence or even a joke, and became instead an obligation. We continued to go out, on the same nights as we always had, but there was an edginess about Buddy that hadn't been there before. Sometimes Trish and Charlie went with us, but they no longer necked extravagantly in the back seat. Instead they held hands and talked together in low voices about things that sounded serious and even gloomy, such as the prices of apartments. Trish had started to collect china. But Charlie had his own car now, and more and more frequently Buddy and I were alone, no longer protected. Buddy's breathing became heavier and he no longer smiled good-naturedly when I took hold of his hands to stop him. He was tired of me being fourteen.

I began to forget about Buddy when I wasn't with him. The forgetting was deliberate: it was the same as remembering, only in reverse. Instead of talking to Buddy for hours on the phone, I spent a lot of time making dolls' clothes for my little sister's dolls. When I wasn't doing that, I read through my brother's collection of comic books, long since discarded by him, lying on the floor of my room with my feet up on the bed. My brother was no longer teaching me Greek. He had gone right off the deep end, into trigonometry, which we both knew I would never learn no matter what.

Buddy ended on a night in October, suddenly, like a light being switched off. I was supposed to be going out with him, but at the dinner table my father said that I should reconsider: Toronto was about to be hit by a major storm, a hurricane, with torrential rain and gale-force winds, and he didn't think I should be out in it, especially in a car like Buddy's. It was already dark: the rain was pelting against the windows behind our drawn curtains, and the wind was up and roaring like breakers in the ash trees outside. I could feel our house growing smaller. My mother said she would get out some candles, in case the electricity failed. Luckily, she said, we were on high ground. My father said that it was my decision, of course, but anyone who would go out on a night like this would have to be crazy.

Buddy phoned to see when he should pick me up. I said that the weather was getting bad, and maybe we should go out the next night. Buddy said why be afraid of a little rain? He wanted to see me. I said I wanted to see him, too, but maybe it was too dangerous. Buddy said I was just making excuses. I said I wasn't.

My father walked past me along the hall, snapping his fingers together like a pair of scissors. I said anyone who would go out on a night like this would have to be crazy, Buddy could turn on the radio and hear for himself, we were having a hurricane, but Buddy sounded as if he didn't really know what that meant. He said if I wouldn't go out with him during a hurricane I didn't love him enough. I was shocked:

this was the first time he had ever used the word *love*, out loud and not just at the ends of letters, to describe what we were supposed to be doing. When I told him he was being stupid he hung up on me, which made me angry. But he was right, of course. I didn't love him enough.

Instead of going out with Buddy, I stayed home and played a game of chess with my brother, who won, as he always did. I was never a very good chess player: I couldn't stand the silent waiting. There was a feeling of reunion about this game, which would not, however, last long. Buddy was gone, but he had been a symptom.

This was the first of a long series of atmospherically supercharged break-ups with men, though I didn't realize it at the time. Blizzards, thunderstorms, heat waves, hailstones: I later broke up in all of them. I'm not sure what it was. Possibly it had something to do with positive ions, which were not to be discovered for many years; but I came to believe that there was something about me that inspired extreme gestures, though I could never pinpoint what it was. After one such rupture, during a downpour of freezing rain, my ex-boyfriend gave me a valentine consisting of a real cow's heart with an actual arrow stuck through it. He'd been meaning to do it anyway, he said, and he couldn't think of any other girl who would appreciate it. For weeks I wondered whether or not this was a compliment.

Buddy was not this friendly. After the break-up, he never spoke to me again. Through Trish, he asked for his identification bracelet back, and I handed it over to her in the girls' washroom at lunch hour. There was someone else he wanted to give it to, Trish told me, a girl named Mary Jo who took typing instead of French, a sure sign in those days that you would leave school early and get a job or something. Mary Jo had a round, good-natured face, bangs down over her forehead like a sheepdog's, and heavy breasts, and she did in fact leave school early. Meanwhile she wore Buddy's name in silver upon her wrist. Trish switched allegiances, though not all at once. Somewhat later, I heard she had been telling stories about how I'd lived in a cowshed all summer.

It would be wrong to say that I didn't miss Buddy. In this respect too he was the first in a series. Later, I always missed men when they were gone, even when they meant what is usually called absolutely nothing to me. For me, I was to discover, there was no such category as absolutely nothing.

But all that was in the future. The morning after the hurricane, I had only the sensation of having come unscathed through a major calamity. After we had listened to the news, cars overturned with their drivers in them, demolished houses, all that rampaging water and disaster and washed-away money, my brother and I put on our rubber boots and walked down to the old, pot-holed and now pitted and raddled Pottery Road to witness the destruction first-hand.

There wasn't as much as we had hoped. Trees and branches were down, but not that many of them. The Don River was flooded and muddy, but it was hard to tell whether the parts of cars half sunk in it and the the mangled truck tires, heaps of sticks, plants and assorted debris washing along or strewn on land where the water had already begun to recede were new or just more of the junk we were used to seeing in it. The sky was still overcast; our boots squelched in the mud, out of which no hands were poking up. I had wanted something more like tragedy. Two people had actually been drowned there during the night, but we did not learn that until later. This is what I have remembered most clearly about Buddy: the ordinary-looking wreckage, the flatness of the water, the melancholy light.

Family Relationships

Cages

Guy Vanderhaeghe

Here it is, 1967, the Big Birthday. Centennial Year they call it. The whole country is giving itself a pat on the back. Holy shit, boys, we made it.

I made it too for seventeen years, a spotless life, as they say, and for presents I get, in my senior year of high school, my graduating year for chrissakes, a six-month suspended sentence for obstructing a police officer, and my very own personal social worker.

The thing is I don't *need* this social worker woman. She can't tell me anything I haven't already figured out for myself. Take last Wednesday, Miss Krawchuk, who looks like the old widow chicken on the Bugs Bunny Show, the one who's hot to trot for Foghorn Leghorn, says to me: "You know, Billy, your father loves you just as much as he does Gene. He doesn't have a favourite."

Now I can get bullshit at the poolroom any time I want it—and without having to keep an appointment. Maybe Pop *loves* me as much as he does Gene, but Gene is still his favourite kid. Everybody has a favourite kid. I knew that much already when I was only eight and Gene was nine. I figured it out right after Gene almost blinded me.

Picture this. There the two of us were in the basement. It was Christmas holidays and the old man had kicked us downstairs to huck darts at this board he'd give us for a present. Somehow, I must've had horseshoes up my ass, I'd beat Gene six games straight. And was he pissed off! He never loses to me at nothing ever. And me being in such a real unique situation, I was giving him the needle-rooney.

"What's this now?" I said. "Is that six or seven what I won?"

"Luck," Gene said, and he sounded like somebody was slowly strangling him. "Luck. Luck. Luck." He could hardly get it out.

And that's when I put the capper on it. I tossed a bull's-eye. "Read 'er and weep," I told him. That's what the old man says whenever he goes out at rummy. It's his needle-rooney. "Read 'er and weep."

That did it. The straw what broke the frigging camel's back. All I saw was his arm blur when he let fly at me. I didn't even have time to *think* about ducking. Bingo. Dead centre in the forehead, right in the middle of the old noggin he drills me with a dart. And there it stuck. Until it loosened a bit. Then it sagged down real slow between my eyes, hung for a second, slid off of my nose, and dropped at my feet. I hollered bloody blue murder, you better believe it.

For once, Pop didn't show that little bastard any mercy. He took after him from room to room whaling him with this extension cord across the ass, the back of the legs, the shoulders. Really hard. Gene, naturally, was screaming and blubbering and carrying on like it was a goddamn axe murder or something. He'd try to get under a bed, or behind a dresser or something, and get stuck halfway. Then old Gene would really catch it. He didn't know whether to plough forward, back up, shit, or go blind. And all the time the old man was lacing him left and right and saying in this sad, tired voice: "You're the oldest. Don't you know no better? You could of took his eye out, you crazy little bugger."

But that was only justice. He wasn't all that mad at Gene. Me he was mad at. If that makes any sense. Although I have to admit he didn't lay a hand on me. But yell? Christ, can that man yell. Especially at me. Somehow I'm the one that drives him squirrelly.

"Don't you *never, never* tease him again!" he bellowed and his neck started to swell. When the old man gets mad you can see it swell, honest. "You know he can't keep a hold of himself. One day you'll drive him so goddamn goofy with that yap of yours he'll do something terrible! Something he'll regret for the rest of his life. And it'll all be your fault!" The old man had to stop there and slow down or a vein would've exploded in his brain, or his arsehole popped inside out, or something. "So smarten up," he said, a little quieter, finally, "or you'll be the death of me and all my loved ones."

So there you are. I never pretended the world was fair, and I never bitched because it wasn't. But I do resent the hell out of being forced to listen to some dried-up old broad who gets paid by the government to tell me it is. Fuck her. She never lived in the Simpson household with my old man waiting around for Gene to do that *terrible thing*. It spoils the atmosphere. Makes a person edgy, you know?

Of course, Gene has done a fair number of *bad things* while everybody was waiting around for him to do the one great big *terrible thing*; and he's done them in a fair number of places. That's because the old man is a miner, and for a while there he was always telling some foreman to go piss up a rope. So we moved around a lot. That's why the Simpson household has a real history. But Gene's is the best of all. In Elliot Lake he failed grade three; in Bombertown he got picked up for shoplifting; in Flin Flon he broke some snotty kid's nose and got sent home from school. And every grade he goes higher, it gets a little worse. Last year, when we were both in grade eleven, I'm sure the old man was positive Gene was finally going to pull off the *terrible thing* he's been worrying about as long as I can remember.

It's crazy. Lots of times when I think about it, I figure I don't get on with the old man because I treat him nice. That I try too hard to make him like me. I'm not the way Gene is, I respect Pop. He slogs it out, shift after shift, on a shitty job he hates. Really hates. In fact, he told me once he would have liked to been a farmer. Which only goes to show you how crazy going down that hole day after day makes you. Since we moved to Saskatchewan I've seen lots of farmers, and if you ask me, being one doesn't have much to recommend it.

But getting back to that business of being nice to Dad. Last year I started waiting up for him to come home from the afternoon shift. The one that runs from four p.m. in the afternoon until midnight. It wasn't half bad. Most nights I'd fall asleep on the chesterfield with the TV playing after Mom went to bed. Though lots of times I'd do my best to make it past the national news to wait for Earl Cameron and his collection of screwballs. Those guys kill me. They're always yapping off because somebody or something rattled their chain. Most of those characters with all the answers couldn't pour piss out of a rubber boot if they read the instructions printed on the sole. They remind me of Gene; he's got all the answers too. But still, quite a few of them are what you'd call witty. Which Gene is in his own way too.

But most times, as I say, I'd doze off. Let me give you a sample evening. About twelve-thirty the lights of his half-ton would come shooting into the living-room, bouncing off the walls, scooting along the ceiling when he wheeled into the driveway like a madman. It was the lights flashing in my eyes that woke me up most nights, and if that didn't do it there was always his grand entrance. When the old man comes into the house, from the sound of it you'd think he never heard of door knobs. I swear sometimes I'm sure he's taking a battering-ram to the back door. Then he thunks his lunch bucket on the kitchen counter and bowls his hard hat into the landing. This is because he always comes home from work mad. Never once in his life has a shift ever gone right for that man. Never. They could pack his pockets with diamonds and send him home two hours early and he'd still bitch. So every night was pretty much the same. He had a mad on. Like in my sample night.

He flicked on the living-room light and tramped over to his orange recliner with the bottle of Boh. "If you want to ruin your eyes, do it on school-books, not on watching TV in the goddamn dark. It's up to somebody in this outfit to make something of themselves."

"I was sleeping."

"You ought to sleep in bed." *Keerash*! He weighs two hundred and forty-four pounds and he never sits down in a chair. He falls into it. "Who's that? Gary Cooper?" he asked. He figures any movie star on the late show taller than Mickey Rooney is Cooper. He doesn't half believe you when you tell him they aren't.

"Cary Grant."

"What?"

"Cary Grant. Not Gary Cooper. Cary Grant."

"Oh." There he sat in his recliner, big meaty shoulders sagging, belly propped up on his belt buckle like a pregnant pup's. Eyes red and sore, hair all mussed up, the top of his beer bottle peeking out of his fist like a little brown nipple. He has cuts all over those hands of his, barked knuckles and raspberries that never heal because the salt in the potash ore keeps them open, eats right down to the bone sometimes.

"How'd it go tonight?"

"Usual shit. We had a breakdown." He paused. "Where's your brother? In bed?"

"Out."

"Out? Out? *Out?* What kind of goddamn answer is that? Out where?"

I shrugged.

"Has he got his homework done?" That's the kind of question I get asked. *Has your brother got his homework done*?

"How the hell would I know?"

"I don't know why you don't help him with his school-work," the old man said, peeved as usual.

"You mean do it for him."

"Did I say that? Huh? I said help him. Didn't I say that?" he griped, getting his shit in a knot.

He thinks it's that easy. Just screw the top off old Gene and pour it in. No problem. Like an oil change.

"He's got to be around to help," I said.

That reminded him. He jumped out of the chair and gawked up and down the deserted street. "It's almost one o'clock. On a school night. I'll kick his ass." He sat down and watched the screen for a while and sucked on his barley sandwich.

Finally, he made a stab at acting civilized. "So how's baseball going?"

"What?"

"Baseball. For chrissakes clean out your ears. How's it going?"

"I quit last year. Remember?"

"Oh yeah." He didn't say nothing at first. Then he said: "You shouldn't have. You wasn't a bad catcher."

"The worst. No bat and no arm—just a flipper. They stole me blind."

"But you had the head," said the old man. And the way he said it made him sound like he was pissed at me for mean-mouthing myself. That surprised me. I felt kind of good about that. "You had the head," he repeated, shaking his own. "I never told you but Al came up to me at work and said you were smart back there behind the plate. He said he wished Gene had your head."

I can't say that surprised me. Gene is one of those cases of a million-dollar body carrying around a ten-cent head. He's a natural. Flop out his glove and, smack, the ball sticks. He's like Mickey Mantle. You know those stop-action photos where they caught Mickey with his eyes glommed onto the bat, watching the ball jump off the lumber? That's Gene. And he runs like a Negro, steals bases like Maury Wills for chrissake.

But stupid and conceited? You wouldn't believe the half of it. Give him the sign to bunt to move a runner and he acts as if you're asking him to bare his ass in public. Not him. He's a big shot. He swings for the fence. Nothing less. And old Gene is always in the game, if you know what I mean? I don't know what happens when he gets on base, maybe he starts thinking of the hair pie in the stands admiring him or something, but he always dozes off at the wheel. Once he even started to comb his hair at first base. Here it is, a 3 and 2 count with two men out, and my brother forgets to run on the pitch because he's combing his hair. I could have died. Really I could have. The guy is such an embarrassment sometimes.

"He can have my head," I said to Pop. "If I get his girls."

That made the old man wince. He's sure that Gene is going to knock up one of those seat-covers he takes out and make him a premature grandpa.

"You pay attention to school. There's plenty of time later for girls." And up he jumped again and stuck his nose against the window looking for Gene again. Mom has to wash the picture window once a week; he spots it all up with nose grease looking for Gene.

"I don't know why your mother lets him out of the house," he said. "Doesn't she have any control over that boy?"

That's what he does, blames everybody but himself. Oh hell, maybe nobody's to blame. Maybe Gene is just Gene, and there's nothing to be done about it.

"I don't know what she's supposed to do. You couldn't keep him in if you parked a tank in the driveway and strung barbed wire around the lot."

Of course that was the wrong thing to say. I usually say it.

"Go to bed!" he yelled at me. "You're no better than your brother. I don't see you in bed neither. What'd I do, raise alley cats or kids? Why can't you two keep hours like human beings!"

And then the door banged and we knew the happy wanderer was home. Gene makes almost as much noise as the old man does when he comes in. It's beneath his dignity to sneak in like me.

Dad hoisted himself out of the chair and steamed off for the kitchen. He can move pretty quick for a big guy when he wants to. Me, I was in hot pursuit. I don't like to miss much.

Old Gene was hammered, and grinning from ass-hole to ear-lobes. The boy's got a great smile. Even when he grins at old ladies my mother's age you can tell they like it.

"Come here and blow in my face," said my father.

"Go on with you," said Gene. All of a sudden the smile was gone and he was irritated. He pushed past Pop, took the milk out of the fridge and started to drink out of the container.

"Use a glass."

Gene burped. He's a slob.

"You stink of beer," said the old man. "Who buys beer for a kid your age?"

"I ain't drunk," said Gene.

"Not much. Your eyes look like two piss-holes in the snow."

"Sure, sure," said Gene. He lounged, he swivelled over to me and lifted my Players out of my shirt pocket. "I'll pay you back tomorrow," he said, taking out a smoke. I heard that one before.

"I don't want to lose my temper," said Dad, being patient with him as usual, "so don't push your luck, sunshine." The two of them eye-balled it, hard. Finally Gene backed down, looked away and fiddled with his matches. "I don't ride that son of a bitch of a cage up and down for my health. I do it for you two," Dad said. "But I swear to God, Gene, if you blow this year of school there'll be a pair of new work boots for you on the back step, come July 1. Both of you know my rules. Go to school, work, or pack up. I'm not having bums put their feet under my table."

"I ain't scared of work," said Gene. "Anyways, school's a pain in the ass."

"Well, you climb in the cage at midnight with three hours of sleep and see if *that* ain't a pain in the ass. Out there nobody says, please do this, please do that. It ain't school out there, it's life."

"Ah, I wouldn't go to the mine. The mine sucks."

"Just what the hell do you think you'd do?"

"He'd open up shop as a brain surgeon," I said. Of course, Gene took a slap at me and grabbed at my shirt. He's a tough guy. He wasn't really mad, but he likes to prevent uppityness.

"You go to bed!" the old man hollered. "You ain't helping matters!"

So off I went. I could hear them wrangling away even after I closed my door. You'd wonder how my mother does it, but she sleeps through it all. I think she's just so goddamn tired of the three of us she's gone permanently deaf to the sound of our voices. She just don't hear us any more.

The last thing I heard before I dropped off was Pop saying: "I've rode that cage all my life, and take it from me, there wasn't a day I didn't wish I'd gone to school and could sit in an office in a clean white shirt." Sometimes he can't remember what he wants to be, a farmer or a pencil-pusher.

The cage. He's always going on about the cage. It's what the men at the mine call the elevator car they ride down the shaft. They call it that because it's all heavy reinforced-steel mesh. The old man has this cage on the brain. Ever since we were little kids he's been threatening us with it. *Make something of yourself,* he'd warn us, *or you'll end up like your old man, a monkey in the cage*! Or: *What's this, Gene? Failed arithmetic? Just remember, dunces don't end up in the corner. Hell no, they end up in the cage*! *Look at me*! My old man really hates that cage and the mine. He figures it's the worst thing you can threaten anybody with.

I was in the cage, once. A few years ago, when I was fourteen, the company decided they'd open the mine up for tours. It was likely the brainstorm of some public relations tit sitting in head office in Chicago. In my book it was kind of like taking people into the slaughterhouse to prove you're kind to the cows. Anyway, Pop offered to take us on one of his days off. As usual, he was about four years behind schedule. When we were maybe eleven we might have been nuts about the idea, but just then it didn't thrill us too badly. Gene, who is about as subtle as a bag of hammers, said flat out he wasn't interested. I could see right away the old man was hurt by that. It isn't often he plays the buddy to his boys, and he probably had the idea he could whiz us about the machines and stuff. Impress the hell out of us. So it was up to me to slobber and grin like some kind of half-wit over the idea, to perk him up, see? Everybody suffers when the old man gets into one of his moods.

Of course, like always when I get sucked into this good-turn business, I shaft myself. I'd sort of forgotten how much I don't like tight places and being closed in. When we were younger, Gene used to make me go berserk by holding me under the covers, or stuffing a pillow in my face, or locking me in the garage whenever he got the chance. The jerk.

To start with, they packed us in the cage with twelve other people, which didn't help matters any. Right away my chest got tight and I felt like I couldn't breathe. Then the old cables started groaning and grinding and this fine red dust like chili powder sprinkled down through the mesh and dusted our hard hats with the word GUEST stencilled on them. It was rust. Kind of makes you think.

"Here we go," said Pop.

We went. It was like all of a sudden the floor fell away from under my boots. That cage just dropped in the shaft like a stone down a well. It rattled and creaked and banged. The bare light bulb in the roof started to flicker, and all the faces around me started to dance and shake up and down in the dark. A wind twisted up my pant-legs and I could hear the cables squeak and squeal. It made me think of big fat fucking rats.

"She needs new brake shoes," said this guy beside me and he laughed. He couldn't fool me. He was scared shitless too, in his own way.

"It's not the fall that kills you," his neighbour replied. "It's the sudden stop." There's a couple of horses' patoots in every crowd.

We seemed to drop forever. Everybody got quieter and quieter. They even stopped shuffling and coughing. Down. Down. Down. Then the cage started to slow, I felt a pressure build in my knees and my crotch and my ears. The wire box started to shiver and clatter and shake. *Bang*! We stopped. The cage bobbed a little up and down like a yo-yo on the end of a string. Not much though, just enough to make you queasy.

"Last stop, Hooterville!" said the guide, who thought he was funny, and threw back the door. Straight ahead I could see a low-roofed big open space with tunnels running from it into the ore. Every once in a while I could see the light from a miner's helmet jump around in the blackness of one of those tunnels like a firefly flitting in the night.

First thing I thought was: *What if I get lost? What if I lose the group? There's miles and miles and miles of tunnel under here.* I caught a whiff of the air. It didn't smell like air up top. It smelled used. You could taste the salt. *I'm suffocating,* I thought. *I can't breathe this shit.*

I hadn't much liked the cage but this was worse. When I was in the shaft I knew there was a patch of sky over my head with a few stars in it and clouds and stuff. But all of a sudden I realized how deep we were. How we were sort of like worms crawling in the guts of some dead animal. Over us were billions, no, trillions, of tons of rock and dirt and mud pressing down. I could imagine it caving in and falling on me, crushing my chest, squeezing the air out slowly, dust fine as flour trickling into my eyes and nostrils, or mud plugging my mouth so I couldn't even scream. And then just lying there in the dark, my legs and arms pinned so I couldn't even twitch them. For a long time maybe. Crazy, lunatic stuff was what I started to think right on the spot.

My old man gave me a nudge to get out. We were the last.

"No," I said quickly and hooked my fingers in the mesh.

"We get out here," said the old man. He hadn't caught on yet.

"No, I can't," I whispered. He must have read the look on my face then. I think he knew he couldn't have pried me off that mesh with a gooseneck and winch.

Fred, the cage operator, lifted his eyebrows at Pop. "What's up, Jack?"

"The kid's sick," said Pop. "We'll take her up. He don't feel right." My old man was awful embarrassed.

Fred said, "I wondered when it'd happen. Taking kids and women down the hole."

"Shut your own goddamn hole," said the old man. "He's got the flu. He was up all last night."

Fred looked what you'd call sceptical.

"Last time I take you any place nice," the old man said under his breath.

The last day of school has always got to be some big deal. By nine o'clock all the dipsticks are roaring their cars up and down main street with their goofy broads hanging out their windows yelling, and trying to impress on one another how drunk they are.

Dad sent me to look for Gene because he didn't come home for supper at six. I found him in the poolroom playing dollar-a-hand poker pool.

"Hey, little brother," he waved to me from across the smoky poolroom, "come on here and I'll let you hold my cards!" I went over. He grinned to the goofs he was playing with. "You watch out now, boys," he said, "my little brother always brings me luck. Not that I need it," he explained to me, winking.

Yeah, I always brought him luck. *I* kept track of the game. *I* figured out what order to take the balls down. *I* reminded him not to put somebody else out and to play the next guy safe instead of slamming off some cornball shot. When *I* did all that Gene won—because I brought him luck. Yeah.

Gene handed me his cards. "You wouldn't believe these two," he said to me out of the corner of his mouth, "genuine plough jockeys. These boys couldn't find their ass in the dark with both hands. I'm fifteen dollars to the good."

I admit they didn't look too swift. The biggest one, who was *big*, was wearing an out-of-town team jacket, a Massey-Ferguson cap, and shit-kicker wellingtons. He was maybe twenty-one, but his skin hadn't cleared up yet by no means. His pan looked like all-dressed pizza, heavy on the cheese. His friend was a dinky little guy with his hair designed into a duck's ass. The kind of guy who hates the Beatles. About two feet of a dirty comb was sticking out of his ass pocket.

Gene broke the rack and the nine went down. His shot.

"Dad's looking for you. He wants to know if you passed," I said.

"You could've told him."

"Well, I didn't."

"Lemme see the cards." I showed him. He had a pair of treys, a six, a seven, and a lady. Right away he stopped to pocket the three. I got a teacher who always talks about thought processes. Gene doesn't have them.

"Look at the table," I said. "Six first and you can come around up here," I pointed.

"No coaching," said Pizza Face. I could see this one was a poor loser.

Gene shifted his stance and potted the six.

"What now?" he asked.

"The queen, and don't forget to put pants on her." I paused. "Pop figured you were going to make it. He really did, Gene."

"So tough titty. I didn't. Who the hell cares? He had your suck card to slobber over, didn't he?" He drilled the lady in the side pocket. No backspin. He'd hooked himself on the three. "Fuck."

"The old man is on graveyard shift. You better go home and face the music before he goes to work. It'll be worse in the morning when he needs sleep," I warned him.

"Screw him."

I could see Gene eyeballing the four. He didn't have any four in his hand, so I called him over and showed him his cards. "You can't shoot the four. It's not in your hand."

"Just watch me." He winked. "I've been doing it all night. It's all pitch and no catch with these prizes." Gene strolled back to the table and coolly stroked down the four. He had shape for the three which slid in the top pocket like shit through a goose. He cashed in on the seven. "That's it, boys," he said. "That's all she wrote."

I was real nervous. I tried to bury the hand in the deck but the guy with the runny face stopped me. He was getting tired of losing, I guess. Gene doesn't even cheat smart. You got to let them win once in a while.

"Gimme them cards," he said. He started counting the cards off against the balls, flipping down the boards on the felt. "Three." He nodded. "Six, seven, queen. I guess you got them all," he said slowly, with a look on his face like he was pissing ground glass.

That's when Duck Ass chirped up. "Hey, Marvin," he said, "that guy shot the four. He shot the four."

"Nah," said Gene.

Marvin studied on this for a second, walked over to the table and pulled the four ball out of the pocket. Just like little Jack Horner lifting the plum out of the pie. "Yeah," he said. "You shot the four."

"Jeez," said Gene. "I guess I did. Honest mistake. Look, here's a dollar for each of you." He took two bills out of his shirt pocket. "You got to pay for your mistakes is what I was always taught."

"I bet you he's been cheating all along," said Duck Ass.

"My brother don't cheat," I said.

"I want all my money back," said Marvin. Quite loud. Loud enough that some heads turned and a couple of tables stopped playing. There was what you would call a big peanut gallery, it being the beginning of vacation and the place full of junior high kids and stags.

"You can kiss my ass, bozo," said Gene. "Like my brother here said, I never cheated nobody in my life."

"You give us our money back," threatened Marvin, "or I'll pull your head off, you skinny little prick."

Guys were starting to drift towards us, curious. The manager, Fat Bert, was easing his guts out from behind the cash register.

"Give them their money, Gene," I said, "and let's get out of here."

"No."

Well, that was that. You can't change his mind. I took a look at old Marvin. As I said before, Marvin was *big*. But what was worse was that he had this real determined look people who aren't too bright get when they finally dib on to the fact they've been hosed and somebody has been laughing up his sleeve at them. They don't like it too hot, believe me.

"Step outside, shit-head," said Marvin.

"Fight," somebody said encouragingly. A real clump of ringsiders was starting to gather. "Fight." Bert came hustling up, bumping his way through the kids with his bay window. "Outside, you guys. I don't want nothing broke in here. Get out or I'll call the cops."

Believe me, was I tense. Real tense. I know Gene pretty well and I was sure that he had looked at old Marvin's muscles trying to bust out everywhere. Any second I figured he was going to even the odds by pasting old Marv in the puss with his pool cue, or at least sucker-punching him.

But Gene is full of surprises. All of a sudden he turned peacemaker. He laid down his pool cue (which I didn't figure was too wise) and said: "You want to fight over this?" He held up the four ball. "Over this? An honest mistake?"

"Sure I do," said Marvin. "You're fucking right I do, cheater."

"Cheater, cheater," said Duck Ass. I was looking him over real good because I figured if something started in there I'd get him to tangle with.

Gene shrugged and even kind of sighed, like the hero does in the movies when he has been forced into a corner and has to do something that is against his better nature. He tossed up the four ball once, looked at it, and then reached behind him and shoved it back into the pocket. "All right," he said, slouching a little and jamming his hands into his jacket pockets, "Let's go, sport."

That started the stampede. "Fight! Fight!" The younger kids, the ones thirteen and fourteen, were really excited; the mob kind of swept Marvin and Gene out the door, across the street and into the OK Economy parking lot where most beefs get settled. There's lots of dancing-room there. A nice big ring.

Marvin settled in real quick. He tugged the brim of his Massey-Ferguson special a couple of times, got his dukes up and started to hop around like he'd stepped right out of the pages of *Ring* magazine. He looked pretty stupid, especially when Gene just looked at him, and kept his hands rammed in his jacket pockets. Marvin kind of clomped from foot to foot for a bit and then he said: "Get 'em up."

"You get first punch," said Gene.

"What?" said Marv. He was so surprised his yap fell open.

"If I hit you first," said Gene, "you'll charge me with assault. I know your kind."

Marvin stopped clomping. I suspect it took too much co-ordination for him to clomp and think at the same time. "Oh no," he said, "I ain't falling for that. If I hit *you* first, you'll charge *me* with assault." No flies on Marvin. "*You* get the first punch."

"Fight. Come on, fight," said some ass-hole, real disgusted with all the talk and no action.

"Oh no," said Gene. "I ain't hitting you first."

Marvin brought his hands down. "Come on, come on, let fly."

"You're sure?" asked Gene.

"Give her your best shot," said Marvin. "You couldn't hurt a fly, you scrawny shit. Quit stalling. Get this show on the road."

Gene uncorked on him. It looked like a real pansy punch. His right arm whipped out of his jacket pocket, stiff at the elbow like a girl's when she slaps. It didn't look like it had nothing behind it, sort of like Gene had smacked him kind of contemptuous in the mouth with the flat of his hand. That's how it looked. It *sounded* like he'd hit him in the mouth with a ball-peen hammer. Honest to God, you could hear the teeth crunch when they broke.

Big Marvin dropped on his knees like he'd been shot in the back of the neck. His hands flew up to his face and the blood just ran through his fingers and into his cuffs. It looked blue under the parking-lot lights. There was an awful lot of it.

"Get up, you dick licker," said Gene.

Marvin pushed off his knees with a crazy kind of grunt that might have been a sob. I couldn't tell. He came up under Gene's arms, swept him off his feet and dangled him in the air, crushing his ribs in a bear hug.

"*Waauugh!*" said Gene. I started looking around right smartly for something to hit the galoot with before he popped my brother like a pimple.

But then Gene lifted his fist high above Marvin's head and brought it down on his skull, hard as he could. It made a sound like he was banging coconuts together. Marvin sagged a little at the knees and staggered. *Chunk! Chunk!* Gene hit him two more times and Marvin toppled over backwards. My brother landed on top of him and right away started pasting him left and right. Everybody was screaming encouragement. There was no invitation to the dick licker to get up this time. Gene was still clobbering him when I saw the cherry popping on the cop car two blocks away. I dragged him off Marvin.

"Cops," I said, yanking at his sleeve. Gene was trying to get one last kick at Marvin. "Come on, fucker," he was yelling. "Fight now!"

"Jesus," I said, looking at Gene's jacket and shirt, "you stupid bugger, you're all over blood." It was smeared all over him. Marvin tried to get up. He only made it to his hands and knees. There he stayed, drooling blood and saliva on the asphalt. The crowd started to edge away as the cop car bounced up over the curb and gave a long, low whine out of its siren.

I took off my windbreaker and gave it to Gene. He pulled off his jacket and threw it down. "Get the fuck out of here," I said. "Beat it."

"I took the wheels off his little red wagon," said Gene. "It don't pull so good now." His hands were shaking and so was his voice. He hadn't had half enough yet. "I remember that other guy," he said. "Where's his friend?"

I gave him a shove. "Get going." Gene slid into the crowd that was slipping quickly away. Then I remembered his hockey jacket. It was wet with blood. It also had flashes with his name and number on it. It wouldn't take no Sherlock Holmes cop to figure out who'd beat on Marvin. I picked it up and hugged it to my belly. Right away I felt something hard in the pocket. Hard and round. I started to walk away. I heard a car door slam. I knew what was in that pocket. The controversial four ball old Gene had palmed when he pretended to put it back. He likes to win.

I must have been walking too fast or with a guilty hunch to my shoulders, because I heard the cop call, "Hey you, the kid with the hair." Me, I'm kind of a hippy for this place, I guess. Lots of people mention my hair.

I ran. I scooted round the corner of the supermarket and let that pool ball fly as hard as I could, way down the alley. I never rifled a shot like that in my life. If coach Al had seen me trigger that baby he'd have strapped me into a belly pad himself. Of course, a jacket don't fly for shit. The bull came storming around the corner just as I give it the heave-ho. I was kind of caught with shit on my face, if you know what I mean?

Now a guy with half a brain could have talked his way out of that without too much trouble. Even a cop understands how somebody would try to help his brother. They don't hold it too much against you. And I couldn't really protect Gene. That geek Marvin would have flapped his trap if I hadn't. And it wasn't as if I hadn't done old Gene *some* good. After all, they never found out about that pool ball. The judge would have pinned Gene's ears back for him if he'd known he was going around thwacking people with a hunk of shatter-proof plastic. So Gene came out smelling like a rose, same suspended sentence as me, and a reputation for having hands of stone.

But at a time like that you get the nuttiest ideas ever. I watched them load Marvin in a squad car to drive him to the hospital while I sat in the back seat of another. And I thought to myself: *I'll play along with this. Let the old man come down to the cop shop over me for once. Me he takes for granted. Let him worry about Billy for a change. It wouldn't hurt him.*

So I never said one word about not being the guy who bopped Marvin. It was kind of fun in a crazy way, making like a hard case. At the station I was real rude and lippy. Particularly to a sergeant who was a grade A dink if I ever saw one. It was only when they took my shoe-laces and belt that I started to get nervous.

"Ain't you going to call my old man?" I asked.

The ass-hole sergeant gave me a real smile. "In the morning," he said. "All in good time."

"In the morning?" And then I said like a dope: "Where am I going to sleep?"

"Show young Mr. Simpson where he's going to sleep," said the sergeant. He smiled again. It looked like a ripple on a slop pail. The constable who he was ordering around like he was his own personal slave took me down into the basement of the station. Down there it smelled of stale piss and old puke. I kind of gagged. I got a weak stomach.

Boy, was I nervous. I saw where he was taking me. There were four cells. They weren't even made out of bars, just metal strips riveted into a cross hatch you couldn't stick your hand through. They were all empty.

"Your choice," said the corporal. He was real humorous too, like his boss.

"You don't have to put me in one of them, sir," I said. "I won't run away."

"That's what all the criminals say." He opened the door. "Entrez-vous."

I was getting my old crazy feeling really bad. Really bad. I felt kind of dizzy. " I got this thing," I said, "about being locked up. It's torture."

"Get in."

"No—please," I said. "I'll sit upstairs. I won't bother anybody."

" You think you've got a choice? You don't have a choice. Move your ass."

I was getting ready to cry. I could feel it. I was going to bawl in front of a cop. "I didn't do it," I said. "I never beat him up. Swear to Jesus I didn't."

"I'm counting three," he said, "and then I'm applying the boots to your backside."

It all came out. Just like that. *"It was my fucking ass-hole brother, Gene!"* I screamed. The only thing I could think of was, if they put me in there I'll be off my head by morning. I really will. *"I didn't do nothing! I never do nothing! You can't put me in there for him!"*

They called my old man. I guess I gave a real convincing performance. Not that I'm proud of it. I actually got sick on the spot from nerves. I just couldn't hold it down.

Pop had to sign for me and promise to bring Gene down in the morning. It was about twelve-thirty when everything got cleared up. He'd missed his shift and his ride in the cage.

When we got in the car he didn't start it. We just sat there with the windows rolled down. It was a beautiful night and there were lots of stars swimming in the sky. This town is small enough that street-lights and neon don't interfere with the stars. It's the only thing I like about this place. There's plenty of sky and lots of air to breathe.

"Your brother wasn't enough," he said. "You I trusted."

"I only tried to help him."

"You goddamn snitch." He needed somebody to take it out on, so he belted me. Right on the snout with the back of his hand. It started to bleed. I didn't try to stop it. I just let it drip on those goddamn furry seat-covers that he thinks are the cat's ass. "They were going to put me in this place, this cage, for him, for that useless shit!" I yelled. I'd started to cry. "No more, Pop. He failed! He failed on top of it all! So is he going to work? You got the boots ready on the back step? Huh? Is he going down in the fucking cage?"

"Neither one of you is going down in the cage. Not him, not you," he said.

"Nah, I didn't think so," I said, finally wiping at my face with the back of my hand. "I didn't think so."

"I don't have to answer to you," he said. "You just can't get inside his head. You were always the smart one. I didn't have to worry about you. You always knew what to do. But Gene..." He pressed his forehead against the steering-wheel, hard. "Billy, I see him doing all sorts of stuff. Stuff you can't imagine. I see it until it makes me sick." He looked at me. His face was yellow under the street-light, yellow like a lemon. "I try so hard with him. But he's got no sense. He just does things. He could have killed that other boy. He wouldn't even think of that, you know." All of a sudden the old man's face got all crumpled and creased like paper when you ball it up. "What's going to happen to him?" he said, louder than he had to. "What's going to happen to Eugene?" It was sad. It really was.

I can never stay mad at my old man. Maybe because we're so much alike, even though he can't see it for looking the other way. Our minds work alike. I'm a chip off the old block. Don't ever doubt it.

"Nothing."

"Billy," he said, "you mean it?"

I knew what he was thinking. "Yes," I said. "I'll do my best."

A Manly Heart

Hugh Garner

Graduation Day morning was cloudy, and it looked like rain. Through the narrow window that I shared with my roommate Archie Tomlinson I could see a corner of the quadrangle, grey-looking under the dark clouds that hung above the school. The sight of the threatening clouds made me happy, for if it rained they'd have to move the graduation exercises into the auditorium. It would be bad enough her being there, but not half as bad as if they held the affair on the Junior Playing Field, and she would be out there being stared at by all the other parents, and the masters too.

I could picture her walking around among the other mothers, dressed in her old velveteen dress with the pile worn thin in patches, her hat one of those silly-looking ones with the cloth flowers, ready to tumble any minute from its perch on her disarranged hair. Her ankles would bulge over the tops of her shoes, and she'd toddle around wearing a proud smile that the other parents would glance at but ignore. Her appearance would be bad enough, but worse still would be the way she'd chatter away to the other mothers, in a high giggly voice I'd been hearing for the past seventeen years, since I was born. The sound of it had come rushing back into my memory as soon as I received the telegram saying she was coming up to the school for the graduation exercises.

It all started when old Palgrave, the headmaster, had written to the parents and guardians of the graduating class, inviting them to attend the seventy-fifth Graduation Day Ceremonies at Rutland. Its full name is Rutland Preparatory School for Boys, but none of us ever call it that. It has quite a good history but only a so-so scholastic record. Old Palgrave always mentions the famous graduates in his speeches, but most of them were generals rather than scientists or famous men.

Even the weather was against me that day, for after lunch the sun came out bright and clear, and what I'd been fearing, happened: they held the ceremonies out on the playing field.

Old Palgrave began his speech in the same way he began his weekly sermons in the chapel. His opening words were spoken first in a whisper that was hard to hear three rows away from the platform, then his voice got louder and louder until the key word of every sentence (which he underlined in ink on his notes, according to Warner, M.L.) seemed to tremble in the air long after it was spoken.

"...is the greatest day of your life. Today a door is being opened to the world, and you are taking your first hesitant steps across the doorframe. Ahead of you lie the years that will be moulded and fashioned by your endeavours, by your application to your tasks, by your facing up to realities...."

Archie Tomlinson nudged me with his knee, and when I looked up he suppressed a giggle and pointed surreptitiously to a hole in the heel of Warner J's left sock, just above his shoe. I gave it a brief glance and looked away, ignoring Archie's tremors as he held his laughter. I thought, I wish I only had a hole in my sock. I wish I didn't have to worry about anything but that.

"...some of our illustrious alumni have etched their names on the memories of the citizens of this great land, and their deeds and accomplishments will live as long as these monuments of stone and mortar (he swung his arm around and gave a significant glance towards the school buildings) that make up the physical being of our school...."

There was a smattering of applause from the visitors' section, that was taken up half-heartedly by the boys in the forward rows of chairs. I took advantage of the interruption to steal a glance behind me. My mother was clapping her hands harder than anybody, and her fat face was flushed as she shouted—actually shouted— something into the ear of Mrs. Dorrance. I felt a tightening of my insides at the sight, and I turned away, hoping she hadn't told Mrs. Dorrance who she was.

For the next few minutes I tried to hide under the headmaster's words, hearing them but pushing them from my consciousness with the sickly shame that I felt. When Archie nudged me once again with his knee, I kicked at his ankle, and he glared at me in outraged astonishment, biting his lower lip with pain.

When Palgrave's words got through to my brain once more, he was nearing the end of his speech, and as I looked at him he seemed to be staring at me alone. "We have—done our best to prepare you for the game of life, and from now on you must carry the ball. The future is yours for the taking, so grasp the opportunities that university has to offer you. And in conclusion let me quote these words from the pen of

Henry Wadsworth Longfellow: 'Go forth to meet the shadowy Future, without fear, and with a manly heart.' God bless you all!"

As Palgrave gathered his gown about him and sat down between old Penfield and another man I'd never seen before, the audience broke into applause once again. Archie dug his elbow into my ribs and asked, "What's the matter with you, Martin? What'd you have to kick me for?"

"I don't know," I answered. "Forget it."

"You've been acting funny all day," he said. "Ever since Final Chapel—even before that—you've been acting funny."

I didn't answer him.

The crowd was getting to its feet, and the black-gowned figures on the platform looked like monks going through a bowing and scraping ritual as they shook hands with one another. All about me the boys were pushing their chairs out of the way and were running to join their relatives and friends. I noticed Fred Hartenby, who was in my form, being embraced by his parents. His father had a businessman's moustache and was wearing an expensive sport jacket. His mother was tall and slim, and she wore one of those wide hats that all women do at garden parties. She was smiling and nodding her head at Fred, and she seemed to fit into the picture as if she *belonged* in it. My mother, on the other hand, looked like the Hartenby's cook.

Just then she spied me, and came hurrying across the grass in my direction. I couldn't run for I knew she'd shout out my name and only draw attention to us. I waited for her, and when she came up and tried to kiss me I backed away a step and began to walk in the direction of the school, while she tried to keep up with me on her unaccustomed high heels.

"Where are you going, Donald?" she asked me, out of breath.

"Back to my room."

"But they're going to serve refreshments," she said.

"Half the parents don't stay for them," I lied. "Most of them will be drifting over to the school in a couple of minutes."

"I'm so glad the principal—"

"You mean the headmaster."

"Well, yes—the headmaster—I'm so glad he sent me an invitation to come up here. You sure have a fine school, Donald. Yes, and fine friends too. That Mr. and Mrs. Dorrance are very nice. What does he do?"

"He's in stocks and bonds or something."

"Has he got a lot of money?"

"A million or so, I guess," I answered, hurrying to get her out of sight.

"Imagine me talking to a real millionaire!"

Up ahead I spied "Slivers" Sleddon, the science master, coming towards us, and I steered her over to read the inscription on the war memorial. I'd have never been able to face "Slivers" again if he'd stopped to be introduced to her. After he passed, we went on towards the school.

Just as we were going through the South African War Memorial arch we ran smack into Mr. Johnson, the athletic director. He smiled and nodded to us, but I kept on going. Not my mother though; she stopped and said, "You're Mr. Johnson. I recognize you from the photograph that Donald sent me of the soccer team."

I felt the shame crawling down my back. I couldn't hear what he answered, for I was several yards away by then, but when I looked around they were shaking hands like old friends. Then Johnson gave me a queer look as he turned to go; I guess he was sympathizing with me.

I breathed a sigh of relief when we reached my room without meeting anyone else. Through the open window we could hear the talk and laughter from the Junior Playing Field, but she didn't seem to notice that we had the building to ourselves.

She began talking about how business was in the store, and of how she'd increased her ice cream and soft drink orders over last year. The last thing I wanted to hear about was the store, but she went on talking about it as though it was the biggest thing in our lives. It is one of those dinky little cigar stores stuck on a corner in a poor neighbourhood, and my mother even sells cent candies, for crying out loud. She's proud of it though, even if it does keep her on her feet from early morning till late at night.

"Your Uncle Willie called me up the other day," she said.

I thought of how I was probably the only student at Rutland to have an uncle called Willie.

"What did *he* have to say?"

"Nothing much. He said your Aunt May is recovering from her stroke, and he asked me how you were doing."

"What did you tell him?"

"I said that you were doing fine; that you were graduating today."

"I guess he was proud of that?"

"He was. We all are."

"Why does he have to keep on asking about me all the time?"

"Why, Donald, he has a perfect right to! After all, it's him that's paying your tui—your way here."

"I know, but that doesn't mean to say the old fool has a right to keep asking about me."

She gasped.

The words, "old fool" crept in before I had a chance to stop them. But that's what he is, an old fool of a garage owner, with no children of his own, who offered to pay my way to Rutland, and afterwards through college because he's my mother's brother. Nobody else in the school has a family like mine, storekeepers and garage owners. I just wish I had an uncle or two who were big businessmen or doctors or something.

"You have no right to call your uncle things like that!" she said to me. "He's been very good to us. I don't know what would have happened to us after your father left if it hadn't been for Willie helping us out."

"Don't harp on that again," I said, wishing the day was over and we were back in the city.

"Listen here, young man—" she began, but then the door opened and Archie Tomlinson came in followed by his mother and father.

"Oh, sorry, Martin!" he said, when he noticed we were in there.

"Come in, come in!" my mother invited heartily. "There's plenty of room."

I could have cried.

Mr. and Mrs. Tomlinson followed Archie in, and there were introductions all round. Mrs. Tomlinson is a sort of heavy woman too, but she is quiet and well-dressed, and sort of—educated. Mr. Tomlinson is thin with grey hair. He was wearing an Air Force blazer and flannels, and a Rutland tie. Archie had told me that his father was an Old Boy. He was the kind of parent you'd *want* to introduce to people.

My mother wore her usual grin, and she reached out and shook Mrs. Tomlinson's hand. Archie's mother pretended not to notice, but only smiled.

As soon as they had sat down my mother asked, "I suppose your boy's graduated today too?"

"Yes."

"Isn't it thrilling! You know, I've never been in a school like this before. It's a little posh for people like me; I just run a little cigar store. Donald wouldn't have been able to come here if it hadn't been for my brother."

"It was good of him to help Donald," Mrs. Tomlinson said.

I knew they were just being polite to her, and I wished there was somewhere to hide, or that the building would collapse, or something.

"Yes, my brother Willie's in the garage business. He started out fifteen years ago as a mechanic, and now he owns his own filling station. He employs five men—that's pretty good for a man with no education, isn't it?"

I could have died right here.

"It certainly is pretty good, Mrs. Martin," Archie's father said. Both he and his wife were smiling at my mother, and I knew it was only because they were too polite to laugh.

"What line of work are you in?" my mother asked, as if she were talking to one of the customers in the store. I turned and stared out of the window, wanting to jump through it, wondering what I could do to end the conversation.

"I'm a lawyer, Mrs. Martin."

"Oh, that's nice."

Nice! Ye Gods!

Mrs. Tomlinson said, "I suppose you're very proud that Donald graduated today, Mrs. Martin?"

"Oh, yes," she gushed. "Everybody on the street knows about it. I went around and told all the neighbours he'll be going to college next year. I can hardly imagine it; none of the rest of us got past public school."

I glanced around; I had to. Archie Tomlinson seemed to be enjoying it, and I remembered all the lies I'd told him about my family, like my father being an engineer and how we went South in the winter, all that kind of stuff.

Archie's mother said, "It would be nice if Donald and Archie went to the same university. They could room together again as they did here at Rutland. Archie has told us so much about your son."

"That's what I say!" Mr. Tomlinson added, too enthusiastically.

Couldn't she see they were just being polite and well-bred! I could imagine the laughs they'd have together later.

My mother kept on talking, while I sat in a corner and stared at the pile of luggage belonging to Archie and me. Thank God I was leaving Rutland. I would never be able to face anyone there again.

"...We were so proud of him down on our street when he used to come home wearing his blazer with the school crest on the pocket. Mrs. Lawrence, she lives above the store—we live at the back of it, used to say, 'Donald looks like a real rich man's son wearing that jacket.' He did too. Somehow though after he came here it seemed he didn't belong with us any more. It seemed as if he'd climbed out of the neighbourhood. I used to wonder about it sometimes, and once or twice I cried about it, but then I got to thinking that it was all for the best, and that we all lose our children sooner or later."

"Ma—mother!" I said. "Mr. and Mrs. Tomlinson don't want to hear all that."

Mrs. Tomlinson gave me a look that in other circumstances I would have thought was an angry one, but I knew she was sympathizing with me.

Archie's father, polite to the last, said, "Go on, Mrs. Martin."

My mother looked at me questioningly, and gave a wan smile to the Tomlinsons. "I guess there isn't anything else to say," she said.

Archie finally saved the day. He got up and said, "I guess we'd better be going."

His mother asked, "Did you come up here by train, Mrs. Martin?"

"No, by bus."

"We'd be more than happy to give you and Donald a lift back to the city in the car."

"Oh, that would be real nice of you," my mother said, grinning at them both.

"We've got plenty of room," said Mr. Tomlinson.

I could picture us driving down into our neighbourhood, and the Tomlinsons seeing the dump I lived in, while I was there. I would sooner have died than have that happen.

"I'm not leaving right now, Mr. Tomlinson, thanks," I said. "I promised the science master, Mr. Sleddon, that I'd help him pack some stuff in the lab."

"Oh, that's too bad," Archie's father said, fixing me with his lawyer's eye.

Archie turned from picking up his bags and stared at me in disbelief.

"You people go ahead and Ma—mother and I will take the bus later on, after I'm finished with Mr. Sleddon."

"But it's so good of Mr. and Mrs. Tomlinson to offer us a ride," my mother said. "Besides, the bus doesn't leave until late in the evening. This will give me a chance to get back to the store and relieve Mrs. Lawrence, who has her children to look after."

"It can't be helped," I said angrily.

Mrs. Tomlinson got up, and turning her back to me said to my mother, "If Donald *has* to stay here, you come along with us anyhow. He can follow in the bus."

"Certainly," agreed her husband, walking over to help Archie with his bags.

"Well, all right. But I did so want Donald to come home with me. I'd have been so proud to have walked down the street with him today."

Archie's mother gave me an awfully funny stare.

Archie and his father had the bags in their hands and were heading for the door, when there was a knock and old Palgrave and Slivers Sleddon walked in. There were the usual bustling introductions as there always are when people are leaving and arriving in a room at the same time. I wanted to rush between them and just keep running and running, right out of Rutland, right out of sight of everyone I'd ever known, and away from everything I'd ever been or was.

Old Palgrave said, "I'm sorry I missed you after the ceremonies, Mrs. Martin. That is why I dropped up here before you left. I'd have felt that you were snubbing me if I had missed you altogether. For me, one of the highlights of Graduation Day is meeting the parents of the boys."

"That was real nice of you," she said, shaking his hand.

"And that goes for me too," Slivers said, leaning down and taking her hand as if she was the Queen or something. They were sure a couple of great actors.

Everybody but me began talking at once, and my mother stood there grinning at everything they said. When they finally ran out of congratulations and stuff, Sleddon said to her, "Say, I could give you and Donald a lift into town if you like."

"It's nice of you to offer me a lift, but Mr. and Mrs. Tomlinson are driving me in. But I'm sure Donald would appreciate a ride, after you finish your work."

Sleddon looked at me, but I turned my head away. Archie's mother said, "I think it is mean of you, Mr. Sleddon, to ask Donald to stay and help you pack up your old retorts and test-tubes and things on a day like this."

I *had* to look at Sleddon then, and he must have seen that I was desperate.

"Well—of course—" he began.

"It's no trouble, Mr. Sleddon," I broke in. "Honest, I don't mind it a bit."

Mrs. Tomlinson said, "Come on, Dr. Palgrave," and before he could say anything she led him from the room.

My mother turned to me, and by the look on her face I could see she knew. She was trying to keep from blubbering as she said, "I'll see you later at the house, Donald."

"Yes. Sure."

Archie said, "So-long, Martin," but the others didn't even wish me goodbye. Sleddon followed the rest of them out of the room without a word, closing the door behind him as he left. I heard their footsteps retreating down the hall.

From the way they acted you'd have thought they were ashamed of *me*!

After a while I walked to the window and looked down into the quad. They were crossing it on the way to the car park beside the gym. My mother was dabbing at her eyes, making a big scene. Old Palgrave was holding her elbow, and was saying something to her; he was sure a great politician.

I sat down on the edge of my bed and tried to think things out. It wasn't my fault that they'd sent me to Rutland instead of the neighbourhood high school. It wasn't my fault that I had a family I was ashamed of. It wasn't my fault that Palgrave and Sleddon had come barging up to the room like that. I wished uselessly that I could rub out everything that I hadn't wanted to happen that afternoon.

I was so sick with the shame I felt that I began to bawl like a little kid. Then I remembered the closing words of old Palgrave's speech. "...and with a manly heart." I knew that it meant you should face up to embarrassments like I had had to face that day. It kind of strengthened me, and I wiped my eyes and lit a cigarette. When I knew the coast was clear, I carried my things down the back stairs, and left Rutland for the last time. I had a long wait for the bus, but I kept thinking of the line about facing the future with a manly heart. It seemed to mean something else, that I couldn't quite understand at the time.

Maiden Aunt

Patrick O'Flaherty

After a wait of an hour or two, sometimes longer if it had been raining and the roads were muddy or if icy weather had made them slippery, they would see the lights of a car on the highlands three miles away and Jimmy or Colin would race down the lane to tell the family she was coming. It might take the taxi another half hour to get to lower Long Beach, because there were sometimes important passengers to be let off in Northern Bay. But then the car would turn the corner by the graveyard and she would arrive: suitcases and parcels were tumultuously unloaded; Max Morris, her slave, was paid his fare for the hundred-mile trip; and the taxi, full of the exotic smells of leather, rum, and cigarette smoke, would head down the shore, leaving Jimmy and his brothers and sisters in darkness at the top of the lane. Down this narrow track, not innocent of cow dung and similar perils, they now had to conduct their Aunt Agnes in her high-heeled shoes and fancy clothes. The children surrounded her, each carrying a piece of luggage or a package, subdued in her presence. She had come only for the weekend, and they were excited that she had brought so much with her. Despite what experience had shown, they hoped most of it was for them.

"How's Ma?" Always her first question. Their grandmother lived in the Byrne house.

"Good."

"Your father?" He was her youngest brother.

"Number one."

"Your mother?"

"Ok, I guess," someone would say. Their mother sometimes got a bit cross when Aggie came to visit.

"Will John?" No answer. Though their uncle lived only a few hundred yards away, the two families hadn't been on speaking terms for years. It was a fraternal quarrel that went far back in the Byrne family history. Aggie knew this, but always asked about Will John anyway and made a point of going to see him on her visits. Jimmy hadn't been inside the other Byrne house since he was five, when his uncle had taught him to read from old copies of the London *Times*.

Aggie might then ask about one or two of her great friends from Gull Island.

Finally: "How are ye getting on in school?" They'd be at the gate by this point.

"Good."

The warm house then received them, where she distributed her gifts of candy, oranges, and sweet biscuits for the children, cigarettes and something stronger for the adults. It was on one of her visits, latterly when he was in grade ten, that Jimmy first saw gin. She drank it with hot water and sugar. It smelled like juniper berries. Even with sugar, he thought, it had to have a sour taste.

It was always better waiting for her than actually having her in the house. Not that she ever came without presents. But keeping watch for the headlights was the best part, no matter what she brought. Her gifts, moreover, were of a certain character; edible, never playful. Her relationship with the Byrne youngsters, Jimmy realized much later, was the formal one of duty. She didn't coddle them, and when she gave them things, she expected gratitude and quiet in return. Having children underfoot was not her vocation. At times she got their names mixed up.

It wasn't until he was older that Jimmy also came to see what cargo, beyond candy and liquor, she carried into their lives in the declining outport of Long Beach. But he had some sense of it even then. The sight of a middle-aged woman smoking, drinking, and holding her own in arguments with men—there seemed to be more of them around when she visited—made an impression on him. Her loud, husky, laughter reverberated through the house, whose old timbers were used to softer sounds. He noticed that her presence affected the status of their father. What he said wasn't the law, to her. She paid no heed to their taboos and grievances. As head nurse in the St. John's Sanatorium, she moved in a larger sphere, moved easily, on her own terms. To the children, her example was a shining one, extending the range of what was possible. Yet it was unsettling too, for it subtly loosened the ties that bound them to the familiar and available pleasures of their narrow world.

In Jimmy's first two years of high school, her visits were less frequent, and in his final year, she didn't come at all. He would hear his mother and father speak of her in low tones: she was travelling, with whom or for what purpose was not disclosed; she was sick, then better. Or was she better? Some doubt was expressed. Letters arrived from foreign places, letters not shared with the children. Jimmy knew she was pressing to have him and Colin go to St. Bon's College in St. John's to take grade twelve as boarding students. Neither one of them had been to the city before. Indeed, they had gone only once as far as Carbonear, twenty miles up the shore.

It was in their third week at St. Bon's that their aunt again entered Jimmy's and Colin's lives. They were now starting to get used to the harsh discipline of the Christian Brothers' school and the tough curriculum of the advanced grade. A boarder's life was grim, especially if weekend visits home weren't possible. Boys from Bell Island or Holyrood might escape; most wouldn't get away until Christmas. Before the third Spartan Sunday had to be endured, the head of the boarders, Brother Bowen, approached Jimmy one evening after rosary.

"Byrne, you got an aunt working in the San?"

"Yes, Bro."

"She run the joint?"

"Don't know, Bro."

"She wants you to go in for dinner Sunday, with that brother of yours. What youse people call dinner." Brother Bowen was an American in exile.

"Yes, Bro."

"That's against the rules. Boarders aren't allowed out for meals on weekends, unless it's to their own home. You know that?"

"Yes, Bro."

"If I change the rules for youse guys, I gotta change 'em for everyone. You know that?"

"Yes, Bro."

Brother Bowen looked at him sourly. Jimmy had got on the wrong side of him once already, by mispronouncing Chicago. "I hope you do, bud, I just hope you do. But I'll make an exception in this case. You and Colin have permission to go, every Sunday until the end of term. Unless you lose more than four points the week before. If you do, you can't go. I don't care if the prime minister phones up. Got that?"

"Yes, Bro." Every week the boarders were given cards with ten spaces, one or more of which was crossed and initialled by any Brother spotting a fault in their clothes or behaviour. Each point lost beyond four meant an hour taken away from the precious free time on Saturday and Sunday afternoons.

"Be back in time for the rosary, twenty to six. Y'hear, wise guy?"

"Yes, Bro."

"And there's no need to broadcast this to the other boarders. Ok, smart ass?"

"Yes, Bro."

The idea that the rules of St. Bon's were capable of being bent for any purpose had not occurred to Jimmy before.

And so a weekend custom was established that, in fact, lasted for the whole year. They would leave St. Bon's in time to get a Bowring Park bus at one o'clock, reaching the Sanatorium a half hour later or, if the bus was late, by two o'clock. Aggie would often be watching through the window of her apartment in the nurses' residence as they got out at Hamlyn's store, opposite the main entrance. She knew Mrs. Hamlyn personally; indeed, she seemed to know everybody in the west end of St. John's. At first, she would meet them in uniform, talk to them briefly, and then phone the hospital kitchen for plates of dinner. Big servings of turkey or beef with vegetables would be produced, together with glasses of milk and bowls of custard. Once there was lemon meringue pie, a special treat. Second helpings were available, a thing unheard of at St. Bon's. When they finished, another phone call brought someone to take the dishes away, and Jimmy and Colin would sit around reading her books until four o'clock, when they left to be sure to make it back in time for the rosary. On snowy or rainy days, Mrs. Hamlyn let them wait inside the store for the bus.

While they read her books, Aggie would leave to go on her rounds in the hospital. Different books would be laid out on the card table each week. It was in her living room—the bedroom they took to be off limits—that Jimmy first tackled A.J. Cronin's novels, *Thirty Days to a Better Vocabulary,* the *Imitation of Christ* of Thomas à Kempis, and Merton's *Seven Storey Mountain*. The last two were hard going. Aggie had scribbled notes on many pages.

A sense of her mastery was conveyed in the way her orders were promptly obeyed. The kitchen staff and nurses jumped when she said jump, and it wasn't as if she forced them to do what she asked; they wanted to do things for her. Though there was someone called Matron to whom she deferred on rare occasions, it was clear that she had great authority. She was surrounded by drama. Nurses rushed to her with questions. Phone calls would come through to her bedroom, announcing some trouble on the wards. On their first visit the phone rang a few minutes after their arrival. They could hear her. "Yes.... No! Too bad, I thought she'd last a bit longer, but there you are. We'll have to send her home.... No, she's got to have something decent to be buried in. There's nothing for her down north, where she's going. Remember, it's an outport, my dear. I've got a dress that's not too bad. Come over and get it. Shoes, too. Can you get me some stockings and underwear? ...No, there's nobody with me. Two boys, that's all.... All right. Phone for the casket, the cheap one, we'll get the money somewhere.... No, I don't want to do it, you do it." A nurse soon came in and went to the bedroom, leaving with a brown bag under her arm.

When they left each week she gave them two dollars each, to add to the modest weekly allowance they received from their parents. Jimmy saved the money and bought the *St. Joseph's Daily Missal,* greatly favoured over other missals by the Brothers. Colin generally lost his money playing poker. He was getting a reputation in the school. Once he borrowed the missal and, seeing that the mass for the day was that of "a virgin, not a martyr," went looking for one of a martyr, not a virgin. That was the one he wanted to read, he said. He spoke out a couple of times against the Latin mass in religion class. As the term wore on, he became less willing to go to the San, but the two dollars drew him. One weekend, Aggie treated a black eye he'd been given by a tough boarder from Placentia Bay, who'd lost a front tooth in the exchange. "I hope his gob is sore for a month," she said; then added, to Jimmy, "Colin's not so bad as he lets on."

On the first Sunday after the Christmas break, Jimmy went to see her alone because Colin had lost too many points. Aggie spent most of the afternoon on the wards and missed her calls. The telephone rang again and again. At last Jimmy, who was trying to read an article in the *Catholic Digest* on proofs for the existence of God—he was studying apologetics, and having a hard time with it—went into the bedroom, picked it up, and said "Hello." The bed was unmade. Books, letters, and prayer beads were spread over the sheets. Medicine bottles and other objects were on the bedside table by the phone.

A man's voice was on the line. "Ag, I can't make it tomorrow," he said. "The usual reason. Nothing special; you know I want to come, I just can't. Phone you next week when I get back from the north."

"I'm not Aggie," said Jimmy, miffed that someone had taken him for a woman.

There was a pause. "Who are you, then? What are you doing there?"

"I'm her nephew, Jim Byrne." He decided then and there to try to change his name to give it more of an adult ring. "I'm just in getting my dinner." Should he have said that? Was he allowed to be in here at all, eating hospital food? Was this an inspector he was talking to?

"Oh, sorry," said the man. "I'll call back." Then he hung up.

A half hour passed; still no Aggie. The phone rang again, and when Jimmy answered there was a click on the other end. On being told of the calls, Aggie said with a laugh, "It's nothing. Forget it. Now you tell Colin to watch his bobber and come in here next week to have a decent meal. I want you to know what good food is like." She had hurried back to see him before he left for the bus and was out of breath. He noticed she had lost some weight. She was a big woman, always dieting.

Three weeks passed before they made it back to see her. St. Bon's was playing the Feildians in senior hockey the first Sunday, a game they didn't want to miss. The Brothers urged all the boarders to come out and cheer for the team. It was more than just a hockey game, they said. Though behind 4-1 at the end of the second period, St. Bon's fought back and won 5-4. The following week they both lost too many points. Jimmy had been walking outside the boarders' common room, when Brother Caine met him and accused him of crawling through the window. He denied this, but the Brother scratched off the rest of his points anyway, confining him to quarters for the whole weekend.

After classes on Monday, Brother Bowen spotted him in the corridor just after he had written a rough test in social problems. He was doing his best to make sense of Malthusian theory and economic principles, but the subject was new to him.

"You didn't go to see your aunt yesterday, Byrne," the Brother said.

"No, Bro. I had to stay in. Brother Caine took off eight points for crawling through the common room window, and I didn't even do it."

"You sure you didn't?"

"Yes, Bro."

"Yes what?"

"Yes, I didn't do it."

"How many youse lost this week?"

"One. Somebody messed up my bed." Jerome McIsaac did it. Jimmy would find a way to get him back.

"Ok. Don't lose any more, y'hear, Jimbo? Your aunt called up Brother French." Brother French was the principal. He and Brother Bowen didn't get along.

"Yes, Bro."

"One more thing. If you lose more than four again, let me know. I might be able to do something. Not for Colin, just for you. Keep that to yourself, y'hear?"

"Yes, Bro. Colin's not so bad as he lets on, you know." But Brother Bowen shook his head and walked away.

The next weekend was free for both of them, but Colin won eight dollars playing Chicago on Saturday morning and didn't want to go in. "Tell her I lost ten points," he said. Jimmy did so, although he thought she'd find out. She was out of uniform this time and stayed with him, watching him eat. Her smoking made her cough. There were pill boxes and gauze bandages around the living room, and he had to put some of the gear on the table to get a place to sit down. When the phone rang she jumped up to answer it, and he listened: "Yes.... Oh, hello.... Just a second, before we get into that.... Now hold on, I've got something to say to you too. I have to close the door, hang on." She put the phone down and came out. "I'll be with you in a few minutes," she told Jimmy. With the door closed he couldn't hear anything, but he was reading a book called *The Green Hat* and didn't mind being alone. When she came out an hour later, her eyes were red and puffy. She had little to say to him before he left.

He missed the next week because he had special classes with Brother Murphy on calculus. Math was giving him and Colin a lot of trouble, but Colin wasn't one to worry and went off to see a girls' basketball game on Sunday afternoon, skipping the extra class. Jimmy had come fifth in his class at Christmas and knew that unless his math picked up he'd do no better in the finals. There was even a danger of dropping below fifth, if he didn't hold his grades in the subjects he was best at, English and French. The four ahead of him weren't slacking off, and Ears Kavanagh was starting to catch him.

Now came the retreat week for Lent. Brother Bowen caught him reading Llewellen's *How Green was my Valley* in study period.

"What's this?" he asked.

"A book, Bro." This slipped out.

"I can see that, wise guy. Is it part of your courses?"

"No, Bro."

Brother Bowen picked it up. "This a western?"

"No, Bro. It's about Wales."

"What about them?"

"Not the fish. The country."

"Oh. Where'd you get it?"

"My aunt loaned it to me."

"The one at the San?"

"Yes, Bro."

The Brother cleared his throat. "All right. Put it away. This period is for study, y'hear?"

"Yes, Bro."

Ten minutes later Brother Bowen was back. "You know something, big mouth? The whale is not a fish at all. It's an animal. You're not so smart."

"Yes, Bro."

"Yes, what?"

"I meant no, Bro."

"That's better. See me after. Colin too."

"Yes, Bro."

The discussion that followed was on the ten points that Colin said he'd lost two weeks before. Aggie had phoned Brother French about them. The cards were checked and the double lie easily discovered.

It was certainly a strapping offence. Brother Bowen merely grinned. "I'm not going to lay a hand on youse guys," he said. "Go and face your aunt on the weekend."

But when they went she was glad to see them. "Sure that's nothing, a few lies," she said, chuckling. "I've told hundreds myself, thousands. I'll let ye off this time. Hark now, don't do it again." They talked this over on the way back on the bus. Why hadn't they been punished? They couldn't figure it. "Bugger Bowen straps me if I don't piss straight," Colin said. Jimmy noted one other thing on their visit: the phone hadn't rung once.

Soon sports day rehearsals were taking up all their Sundays and, with that and the approach of the dreaded final exams, Jimmy didn't get to the San until two weeks before the end of term. She was in bed when he came in, and a nurse was looking after her. His meal was sent for once more. He did his best with it, but the food was no longer appetizing to him and he ate only half a plateful. She then came out of the bedroom in her nightgown, sent the nurse off on an errand, and sat looking out the window. She was drinking something from a cup. "Oh, bitter, bitter!" she said as she tasted it. Any kind of movement seemed to make her wince.

"Why don't you heat it up and put sugar in it?" asked Jimmy.

She smiled. "Oh, no, that's not the kind of stuff I got here. Wish it was." She took another sip, and grimaced. "I have to drink every drop in the damned cup." Then she sat back and looked at him with gentle eyes. "Don't be afraid, never be afraid," she said for no reason that he could see. "Now, my lad, you stay around for a bit and talk to me. I was here by myself the whole morning."

And he did stay, thinking it was his duty to do so. He talked until it was twilight. In the distance he could see the red sign light up on Hamlyn's store and the buses go by to the centre of town. It was well past seven o'clock when he rose and helped the nurse get her back to the bed. He said he would come again next Sunday, his last, and bring her something. His idea was to get her a flask of gin. Colin would know how to get his hands on one.

After he said goodnight, the nurse opened the door for him and started to explain how to get back to the school. He was a little scared at what he'd done, but then he thought, what the hell. "I know how to get there," he said. "Don't worry about me." He walked out towards the red light in the warm evening air.

Birds

Roger Aske

Three years is a lot of time and a lot of distance between brothers when you are growing up, and it was like that in the Marigold family. It's a funny name, Marigold. Other kids used to tease us about it: "Are you some kind of flower?" they used to say. Charlie just shrugged it off; he walked by it, his large feet carrying him in easy abstraction, smiling. Only when he heard the question thrown at me would he stop, threaten with his size, and move me away. Charlie would rarely fight. And if he did, he never hurt anyone; held them in his hands until his strength overwhelmed them, and then he let them go. Once he tackled a couple of girls, but he was too gentle and they pulled him into the ditch and scratched his face and tore his clothes so that he looked as if he had been tortured by the Chinese. When we were kids we thought all torturers were Chinese.

"A lot of help you were," he said to me on the way home as I kept looking at the blood on his cheek and the collar of his shirt hanging down his back. But they were girls with breasts and warm secrets under their clothes, sacrosanct, inviolable. Charlie told mother he had been playing in a rough scrimmage after school and she listened to him patiently, but mostly she watched him as I stood by her side trying to tell if his lies were any good.

"You'd better get that shirt off before your father comes home," she said when he had finished, and then turning to me: "Are you all right?" she said. Mother always seemed to be somewhere near the truth.

But most of the time Charlie didn't pay any attention to me at all. He didn't really have to, because I paid all kinds of attention to him. Most of the time he treated me like a dog treats a cat in the same household, ignored, sniffed at occasionally. And like a cat I watched him, eyes wide open, closing in tight ecstasy whenever I discovered a new truth about him, stretching to follow him.

At sixteen Charlie was smooth and muscular, and he spent hours in front of the bathroom mirror flexing his biceps and sucking in his belly. He combed his hair until the parting was an incision, and he squeezed the pimples on his face until they became small purple bruises. And all the time, he grimaced and posed, cocking his head at angles of reflection, searching for an image.

Dad used to "get at" him a little bit for that. He wasn't as tall as Charlie, but he was hard and he had no time for what he called "Charlie's fanciness." Dad was a sawyer at the lumberyard down by the river, below the bridge. He wore his wedding band on his right hand because he had lost two fingers on his left when he was an apprentice. He was a fierce, compact man, who worked hard at the lumberyard because he believed that was what he was there for. Younger men despised him for it, and he returned the favour with a brusque contempt. His tolerance for idle hours was very limited. When he was roused, his voice was like the saw at the yard as it whinnied and growled. He would hitch his leather belt about his middle with his good hand so that his chest and stomach were all one hostile curve, and he would cut away at his imaginary antagonists, office clerks, the pope, whatever government was in power, and Charlie.

Mother calmed him slowly. She sat in the chair that was hers, trying not to say anything except "Now George," as her fingers knitted rapidly, her head downward in listening patience. It was difficult to believe that such a meek and gentle person could have chosen to spend her life with such a man. But sooner or later he would look across at her as a "Now George" bluffed through his tangled words, and the whole steaming paroxysm would begin to slow down and then come to an end with a soft sigh.

If it was Charlie Dad was "at," he would be gone by then. Sometimes Charlie didn't come back until long after we were all in bed and asleep, except mother. I tried to stay awake for him, but I never heard him. He was always at the breakfast table, sitting heavily in his place at just about the same time Dad left to go to work. They looked at each other, but their eyes never met.

One Spring, when the Winter had finally cleared from the land and the sun released a new energy in us for the outdoors, Charlie discovered a way to catch birds. Using four housebricks, he made a rectangular cell, and he propped a fifth brick over it on a rig of sticks, one of which was flat and horizontal. On the inner end of the flat stick he placed a suitable bait so that when a bird went after it, its weight tripped the rig and the fifth brick fell down and imprisoned the bird inside the cell. It was simple, clumsy, and not very successful.

Charlie set a whole series of these traps at the bottom of the garden, and for days he tended them like a trapper. Every morning before breakfast he went there to set them in order and in the evening, after school, I would meet him coming away.

"There were feathers. I saw them," he said. "Two of the bricks were down. Must have been a fair size because all the bait was gone."

But I gave up hope sooner than Charlie; there were other things to do.

Then one night at the supper table Charlie was very quiet, pushing his food around his plate; the hungry action was missing. Dad was telling mother about a run-in he had had with the office clerk at the lumber yard. I was trying to follow the story and kept looking at Charlie to see if he was able to follow it. But Charlie wasn't listening. His eyes were still, his expression inward.

As soon as we had been excused and were clear of the kitchen, he grabbed my arm with a strength I had learned not to challenge.

"Paul?"

"Yes?"

"I got one."

"Really?" I said. He nodded and let go of my arm.

"Will you come with me, Paul?"

"Sure."

The evening was cool and half-dark. The sun had already gone behind low clouds. Charlie led the way to a small plywood shed Dad had built to store things in; the door never quite closed properly.

"Is it in there?" I asked innocently.

"Wait, will you," Charlie breathed impatiently. He disappeared inside and emerged a few seconds later carrying something under his jacket. "Come on, Paul," he said and I followed, but not very happily because I had guessed what he carried.

When we reached the trap, the one with the brick lying flat on the others, we stood looking down. It was a tomb, as overwhelming to my young heart as a new grave. Instead of a joyful sound of fluttering wings, some little creature trapped by a nice kid like Charlie, chirruping to be free, there was only silence. Instead of a trap there was a weight of red stone.

Charlie opened his jacket and passed me the BB gun.

"It's got a broken wing," he said.

"Won't it get better?" I could smell the oil on the gun-barrel, feel the cold weight of the stock in my small hands. Charlie didn't answer my question.

"You've got to shoot it, Paul."

"Shoot it?" Charlie faded to a vague silhouette as he stood by my side, a dark ghost; the bricks of the trap were blood red. My finger touched the trigger feeling its tension. The gun was loaded.

"Shoot it?" I said again.

Charlie knelt on the earth and put his hands on the trap and waited. Then he removed the covering stone, slid it away. The bird was a dry ball of brown feathers and dust, one wing spread like a pinned specimen, one visible eye, a polished bead. At first sight I thought it was already dead, but its beak opened, a minute image of terror.

"Shoot it, Paul," pleaded Charlie, and with his hands placed at each end of the trap he looked up at me. I knew then why I held the gun and not Charlie. Charlie was broken like the bird. If, at that moment, I had pointed the gun at his own temple, he would have offered no plea.

"Paul?" he said.

I held the front sight within an inch of the bird's head and pressed the butt of the gun hard against my shoulder; the end of the barrel traced loops in time to the beating of my heart. The bird's beak opened again, emitting a tiny, bleak cry.

"Jesus," Charlie said and turned his head away.

The quick snort of the rifle was surprisingly soft, but the power of the slug lifted the bird out of the trap onto a patch of weeds; there was no sign of blood. Charlie picked it up by its broken wing and threw it into the bushes before he kicked the trap apart with the toe of his shoe. Then he took off, his head down, like a kid that has just messed things up for the team. I stayed there for a long time, and then I carried the gun back to the shed and put it away.

At eighteen, Charlie was rugged; the pimples on his face had become scars, and he washed with great vigour and splashing, paying no apparent attention to his hair which grew in a wild thicket of black wool.

I kept watch on his progress. There were copies of *Playboy* and *Hustler* in his bedroom, carefully hidden from mother's eyes but searched for by my own. There was nearly always a case of beer hidden in the shed, although I followed the diminishing count without ever discovering where he drank it. His wallet contained a whole mess of treasures. There was a pass card to some club called the "El Galleon," which I imagined must have been crowded with dark, exotic people; a single contraceptive wrapped in tinfoil; a typewritten sheet of dirty jokes; a photograph of a girl that wasn't a school picture, someone rather underfed and ethereal, a row of X's and a capital P in a fading scrawl on the back.

Soon after he was nineteen, Charlie quit school. Mother didn't want him to quit, but he had missed a grade and Dad kept telling him how many years of work he had put in by the time he was Charlie's age. Charlie thought it would be easy for him to get a job at the lumberyard because Dad had worked there for such a long time, but when he went to the office and started to complete the application, the clerk leaned over the counter and read the name at the top. He pulled the paper from under Charlie's hands.

"Your name Marigold, is it?" the clerk said.

"Yes sir," said Charlie.

"There's nothing here for you then," the clerk said bluntly. He tore the application down the middle and dropped it into the waste-paper basket.

For a long time after that Charlie just hung around the house. His big frame and lack of response and communication made him a stuffed bear which Mother loved and at which Dad ranted. He went out at night, as much to avoid the tensions created by his own presence as to enjoy himself. Usually he came home early and went to his own room.

But eventually he got a job at the lime quarry. It wasn't much of a job, toting one-hundred-pound bags and stacking them in the warehouse, but they paid him well, and although he came home sweat-streaked and grey with dust, he gained a new confidence which father was less able to challenge. They were happier times. Occasionally the two of them went out for beers, and when they came home they were slapping each other on the back and talking loudly as if they had always been good friends.

Then one night, Charlie brought Nessie home. Mother had been urging him to bring her home for some time, on the supposition that she liked to have young people in the house. She said she was sure Charlie was "going" with a "nice" girl and wouldn't it be better if we all knew her. I think she really wanted to convince herself that Nessie was nice, but Mother had an instinctive judgement that was all Baptist, and Nessie was anything but that.

She was a little shy when she first came into the house. Perhaps that was because the front door opened right into the living-room, and we were all there waiting for her. Faced with such a curious and wide-eyed reception, she backed into the shelter of Charlie's shoulder, creating a picture of tenderness even as I wondered how anyone could be tender with Nessie; she was too much of everything.

Her anatomy wasn't a gift; it was a prizewinner from an exhibition. Her breasts were marvellous things, sculptured by a bra which showed a thin line of upward stress through the pink nylon blouse at her back; they were a season of melons. Her tight black pants revealed the outline of her bikini briefs, smooth to her shining haunches. She wasn't tall, a blonde with some original brunette showing at the roots, her face a little pinched in contrast to her figure, a gap between her slightly protruding front teeth.

"This is Nessie Allsop," said Charlie, touching her. "Nessie, this is my mother and Dad and my brother Paul."

"How do you do?" Mother said, more as a judgement than a welcome.

"Hello. What a nice place you've got," said Nessie, recovering from her shyness and taking two or three steps into the room. She turned like a fashion model: "You're a lucky fellow, Charlie Marigold, to live in a nice place like this. Isn't he, Mrs. Marigold?"

Mother smiled and blinked her eyes, and Dad sat down and shook the newspaper he had been reading, as if he were trying to bring the words into focus.

"Would you like a cup of tea, Miss Allsop?" Mother asked.

"Oh, I don't drink tea, thank you very much, do I, Charlie?" Nessie simpered, and she put her arm about Charlie's waist and pressed her hip into his. Her eyelids fluttered; Charlie's face reddened.

"We are going to the movies, Mother. I wanted Nessie to meet you."

"It's John Wayne, Mrs. Marigold. He's getting on now, but he's still gorgeous, isn't he?" Father's newspaper rustled audibly.

"I suppose he still is, really," Mother said. She rubbed her hands together nervously. "Enjoy yourselves then."

When they had gone, Mother stood looking at the closed door long enough for Dad to put down his newspaper and breathe heavily. "She'll be too much for Charlie," he growled. But Mother didn't say anything. She lifted the hem of her apron and gently wiped the brass of the door knob, as if to restore its bright polish, and went into the kitchen.

To me, Nessie was wonderful. She accented a femininity I had not known in our house, and as far as I was concerned she belonged to Charlie. Everything about her was shapely and painted and perfumed and exciting. Time after time I asked Charlie when he would bring her home again, but nearly always he ignored the question. All that summer he never brought her to the house. When I met them on the street, either by coincidence or design, I wanted them to stop and talk to me, to be a part of their intimacy, but Charlie was always reluctant, taking her arm, wanting her to go.

Then, when the fall set in and the evenings grew colder, things suddenly changed. Mother and Dad renewed their habit of going to the Legion every Thursday, and Charlie began to bring Nessie home. The visits were irregular in the beginning, but as the weeks progressed they became a routine. I was shy with Nessie, although she was much more relaxed than when she first came to our bungalow on Edith Avenue. She talked to me about the movies she had seen and about the people at the office where she worked as a receptionist, while all the time I tried to think of something to say to her, handicapped to a degree by Nessie's obvious body.

Charlie, on the other hand, was different. He sat in Dad's chair and read the newspaper or watched the television set, made trips to the refrigerator and ate bags of potato chips without offering them to anyone. He paid no attention to Nessie, until, when we came to the final impasse in our conversation she turned to him, her eyelashes fluttering, her voice rich with promise:

"Are you going to give me any time at all tonight, Charlie Marigold?"

Charlie would deliberately continue reading or watching, or whatever he was doing, while Nessie huffed and preened and I withdrew into silence and the awkwardness of the wait. When he finally came to her, he would kiss her in a wet and audible way and Nessie always responded quickly—very quickly, I thought, after so much neglect. Her arms were quickly about him, her red nails digging into his broad back, her skirt sliding higher up her thighs. It was a signal for me to go away, to leave them. From the loneliness of the rest of the house, I listened to their heavy breathing, and their whispered words, and their suppressed cries.

Like any routine, its cessation left a void. Charlie was restless and unhappy. That first Thursday evening, when I asked him why Nessie wasn't there, he paced the room and then went out, slamming the door. The following Thursday he was calmer, but he had been like a bear all week. He had even growled at Mother, which he rarely permitted anyone else to do, not even Dad. No one dared to mention Nessie. When the telephone rang for him, everyone knew it was Nessie, and the house tensed as we tried not to listen to Charlie's one word conversations and the long silences before the receiver was slammed down. Mother did occasionally mention "Charlie's young lady," perhaps hoping that he would respond, but Dad's eyes were stubbornly incurious.

Then, one night in early December, about six weeks after they had separated, Nessie came to the house again. Charlie and I were lying on the floor playing checkers—it was a game Charlie had always liked and one at which he consistently defeated me—and when she knocked on the door his head shot up like a dog awakened from sleep.

"Christ," he said, heaving himself upright. "If that's Nessie, tell her to get lost. Get her out of here. Understand?" I didn't say anything, but I waited until he had left the room before I opened the door.

Nessie was dressed in a brown mini-skirt and a white vee-necked sweater. Her hair was piled on top of her head in a shining spray-stiffened mass of new brunette; her lips were painted a thick and deep rust colour. Around her neck was a gold chain with a locket in the shape of a heart attached to it. One hand carried a large purse and the other was posed on her hip.

"Hello, Nessie," I said as warmly as I dared, bearing in mind the instructions from Charlie.

"Don't give me that crap," she answered. "Where's Charlie?"

"I don't know," I said, but the lie hung between us and I closed my eyes, unable to defend it.

"You don't know?" she shrilled.

"No."

"Really!" she said in a long breath of sarcasm. She knew I was wilting under her pressure. I shook my head feebly.

"Well, let me in to wait for him, will you? I've got a message for him. Besides, it's cold standing out here in this rig."

"You should have worn a coat, Nessie," I said, backing away from the door, surrendering to her.

"Your goddamn brother wouldn't know what a coat was for," she shouted as she entered. "Would he?" she yelled, turning her head so that her voice would carry better to the other end of the house. I hoped Charlie would be unable to resist the challenge thrown to him, but there was no sound. She paused for a moment and then went over to the couch. Even now, her walk was there, practised but a part of her, an equation of sight and seduction. She sat down with her knees clamped together, her hands folded in her lap, her eyes in motion.

"What's that?" she demanded, pointing a long-nailed index finger at the checkers board, gouging at the truth.

"It's a game of checkers," I said simply.

"Ha!" She threw her head back in triumph. "And you say Charlie's not here. Then I suppose you play with yourself, you poor fart."

The intent of her words was not lost and I was angered. I sat cross-legged by the board and picked up the pieces one by one, putting them back into the box, carefully and methodically, before I spoke to her again.

"Nessie...."

"Oh, tell your brother Charlie I want to speak to him, will you? I haven't got all night, you know."

"Nessie," I said again.

"What?"

"Nessie, if you have a message for Charlie, I will give it to him for you. Tell me what it is."

"Oh, for God's sake. You sound like the bloody minister. Just go and tell the bastard I want to see him. Tell him Nessie Allsop, the one he made all the promises to before he...."

"Nessie," I barked. "Stop it, Nessie!" Her face was flushed, the high spots on her cheeks, crimson. She looked down into the vee of her sweater and clutched it together with her fingers. Her eyes faded into a plea for clemency. She was waiting.

"Nessie," I began again, and she bowed her head as if sensing a blow. "Nessie, he doesn't want to see you. He told me to send you away."

Her face came up, her eyes glinting, her mouth open as if to release a stream of obscenities, but then, as suddenly, she collapsed. Her face crumpled and tears coursed through her make-up. She looked for a handkerchief in her purse and couldn't find one, so I gave her mine, but she didn't care about its torn, grey look. She threw herself down on the couch and blurted muffled words into the cushions, and her shoulders shook piteously.

I wanted to touch her, to comfort her, to tell her I understood, but a strange sense of loyalty to Charlie held me back. Charlie was still in the house and Nessie belonged to Charlie.

"Nessie. Nessie." I repeated her name again and again, until finally she sat up, her hands to her face, the tips of her fingers trying to rearrange the destruction of her tears. "Forget him, Nessie. Forget Charlie. He doesn't want you to go through all of this."

She took her hands away from her face and stared at me in bewilderment.

"But you don't understand. You don't understand," she sobbed. "Charlie—your brother—he's so beautiful."

Somewhere in the silence which followed her cry, Charlie closed a door, the click of the latch betraying him.

It took a long time for me to persuade Nessie to leave, but when she did, she was almost herself again. When I finally saw her to the door, I was unprepared for the hard check of her parting words:

"Tell the son of a bitch I haven't finished with him yet," she said. "Tell him that's my message."

I watched her walk down the concrete path, her hips swinging angrily in the pale light of the street lamp.

Charlie never discussed the matter with me afterwards. I didn't want to talk about it to anyone, especially Charlie, but the affair was back in the house sooner than I expected.

I returned from a bowling game in the city the following Saturday and walked right into it. Charlie was standing against the wall, feet apart, his expression one of anger and waning patience. Mother was knitting, her head down. Dad was moving about the room, jabbing with a finger, cutting through the air with the edge of his spoiled hand, hitching his belt, half crouched at times as he delivered his fury.

"And Mister Allsop," he shouted. "Mister Allsop of all people, comes creeping into my home. My home, not your home, Charles Marigold. Creeping in here like Judas, to inform me, not you, that a son of mine has wronged his bleeding daughter. 'Wronged Nessie,' he said. There was a better word than that for it when I was a kid. Mister mealy-mouthed Allsop couldn't pronounce it, I suppose, all sewn up that he is with his Jesus conversion. I can remember him, came right out of a rathole in the South End. Nothing but a digger of ditches until he got into the Union, then he kissed his way all up the line. And you, you boneless fish-head, take his daughter into the bushes, and God knows where else, just because she's got fat in the right places. Why don't you go and live somewhere else and do your dirty business on someone else's doorstep. Take the tramp with you and Mister Allsop too. He'd make a great bloody grandfather, he would."

I was standing in the kitchen when Charlie pushed by and out went the back door. Mother had stopped knitting then, and as Dad continued to rave, she kept saying:

"He's gone now, George. He's gone now. He's gone."

It was Mother's turn to do the worrying then. Charlie didn't come home that night or the next. She called the lime quarry on the second day, but they told her he hadn't shown up for work. Dad had the savvy to know that a nineteen-year-old youth could survive in the world, benefit perhaps, but Mother couldn't accept it. I watched her move about the house and worry and jump when she heard someone come to the door or when the telephone ring. She would stand in his room for long aching minutes as if looking for some way to make it more acceptable for his return. I think Dad began to worry about Mother as the days passed without Charlie.

The day he came back to collect his things, I was eating my supper. The door opened and there was Charlie, clean and well-dressed, a flushed half-smile on his face, a new vigour in his stance.

"Hullo," he said. I expected Mother to rush to him, but she just stood by the stove, unable to move, tears running down her cheeks. He shook my hand and then put his big arm around Mother's shoulders and hugged her.

"I'm not staying," he said. "Got a friend picking me up in ten minutes."

"Your Dad won't be home by then," said mother quickly, and they were the only words she spoke to him.

I followed him into his room and sat on the bed, watching him throw things into a bag: underwear, socks, shirts, a sweater.

"Have you found a place to live?" I asked.

"If you can call it that."

"Isn't it up to much?"

"The Queen thinks its all right."

"The Queen?"

"Yes. I've joined the army. Private Marigold, that's what I am now. They still call me flower, though," he laughed. "Yet it's not so bad. The sergeant is just like Dad."

"You're kidding," I said. "You must be kidding."

"It's the truth," he said.

"I don't believe it. Do you think you'll be happy?"

"I'll be all right. They don't care very much. At least I won't have to ask my kid brother to get rid of birds like Nessie."

"What will you do with them then?" I grinned.

"God knows," he shrugged. "Shoot them, I suppose."

"With a gun?" I asked him. He zippered the bag with a quick finality and stood up.

"They say they'll teach me how," he said.

Never Sisters

Aritha Van Herk

You would never believe that we are sisters. If you see us together, you might think we are friends or cousins, but never sisters. Unless you are perceptive enough to notice that we have the same hurried walk, the same unsympathetic way of speaking. But she is far more beautiful than I am, emanating a suggestion of wispy frailness that completely contradicts my stocky build. And in contrast to her dark hair and eyes, I am fair and freckled, without the clear olive tone of her skin. Or the decisiveness of her actions. Whatever I may seem like, I am not jealous. Although I will admit, as a child I worried that she would be forever beyond my grasp. Older, slimmer, always an edge of knowledge, her hands flying easily where mine fumbled. That is the advantage an older sister will perpetually have: she experiences long before you possibly can.

She is older than I am by eight years. An odd situation. I have a menage of brothers (four of them), but only this one sister. My brothers used to be important, but that has changed and now it is my sister who preoccupies me. I suppose we ought to be close. But somehow, in the patterns of years, we have admitted distance. Eight years is an enormous gap when you are young. And perhaps it was for the best. Throughout my childhood she was my second mother, a surrogate. Now that I am old enough to be called adult, there are those years between us so that we do not compete, there is no severing dragon of jealousy. Instead, time interfered. We are not close; I must say that. We never were.

I was ten when she left home. I stand at the window and watch the car drive away; Hannike sits very straight on the front seat beside my father. The picture has the clarity of illusion: she wears a creamy blouse and a wine-coloured jumper and in her ears are the pearl earrings my mother has given her that morning. In that instant I see only a flash of her fine dark hair drawn back off her forehead and then the car is gone.

In a certain sense, she ceased to exist, no longer the cool inviolable sister who moved among my brothers so effortlessly. And so unlike me. I fought and kicked and yelled, learned all of the boys' bad habits and none of the good. My mother often wished aloud that I had been born a boy so that she could treat me like one. Sometimes she even dared to ask me why I was not more like Hannike. I pretended not to care, but I felt hurt, secondhand.

Hannike and I shared the same bedroom. When the car turned out of the driveway, it was that I thought of, her sleeping beside me for as long as I could remember. For the first time, I would sleep alone. The idea paralyzed me—not that I would sleep alone, but that *she* would sleep alone far away in a strange bed while I had the comfort of our familiar room. And lying still and awake that night I cried for her more than for myself.

In bed. I suppose that was when we were the closest. After all, we spent little time together during the day. I was locked into my child's world of play while she had gone a step further into the labyrinth of chores and responsibility. It was her room. She was the oldest and she shared it with me, but it was still her room. There was never any question about that. I was tolerated. Still, there was an intimacy about it that I appreciate only now.

I was a pretender. I lie awake in bed until she comes upstairs and closes the bedroom door behind her. I lie perfectly still with my eyes shut until she thinks she is sure that I am asleep. I can peek through my eyelashes at her without her ever guessing that I am awake. She hesitates and stands at the window for a moment, looking out into the darkness. Then she turns back to the room, stilled and reluctant, almost compliant. I thought that she was cautious and quiet for me, but now I believe her stillness was something else.

She was the first naked woman I ever saw. My own nakedness was shameful and wretched—I had the straight body of a boy. Watching her step out of her skirt and shuck off her blouse to stand fragile and a little stooped in white panties and bra emphasized my inadequacy, how hopelessly far behind I was. I could have watched her for hours, the turns of her body as smooth and pale as those of a ceramic figure. And it was not her sexuality, the white cotton bra easily unhooked and flung onto the dresser, the panties kicked from around her ankles, that made me hold my breath, but the fragility of her bones, the angularity of her back and hips, her long slender legs moving in a blurred sibilance of lambent skin. I wanted to touch that skin, feel the texture of it, but I never did, knowing my grimy child's hand would be a kind of violation.

Propped against the pillows, with the book resting on her knees, she would read. I shifted closer and closer until through my eyelashes,

I could almost see the page. I didn't want to read her book, I only wanted to be close to her, to watch her read. But she sensed my awareness always, caught me immediately.

"Get over on your own side!"

I am instantly quiet as a shell, feigning perfect slumber.

"You can't fool me, Marikje. Turn over and get to sleep."

That was the year I could never fall asleep. I lay awake for hours, listening to the sounds the old house made around me. And always she was there, Hannike my sister, the sprawl of her dark hair, the fluidity of her body in sleep, even the smell of her faint and dark like thin-skinned oranges at Christmas.

If she was angry, she would shove me over, her hands pushing at my rigid and resistant body. I never said a word, as if I thought silence would confirm my innocence, that I wasn't really awake at all. She was never cruel. Rather, she used a form of practicality on me that was sometimes humiliating, sometimes comforting.

"Go to sleep. You'll be too tired to go to school tomorrow."

That was true. In the mornings I could not move; I had to be prodded and shoved and pulled at until I was walking down the driveway to the end of the road to wait for the school bus.

She was different at school, one of the older kids who moved smoothly between the separate circles of home and learning. For us they were still two isolated worlds, so radically different we could hardly think of them together, let alone merge them. The long and jolting bus ride divided them completely.

For her, there was no separation. Outwardly at least, she made the transitions easily. I am still envious that she could have become an adult before I was even aware that I was a child, or so it seemed to me. It was strange that she was old enough to be a babysitter and a stand-in mother, but young enough to have to listen to my parents. Her eight years superiority became my incessant preoccupation. When I'm as old as Hannike.... Of course, I will never catch up.

She will tell you that we were very different, but neither of us is remembering the way I used to imitate her, emulate her, wish to be her. To all outward appearances, I have given that up now and so the memory remains unjogged. But her shape was always there. My childhood has no memories that do not include her.

Did I say that she was an adult before I was even a child? She had to be. We were all younger than she; we were all her responsibility. I know she wishes she had been the youngest, had been absolved of our weight. But there it was; older children do what they have to do and then leave home.

When she was left with us she was the boss, we had to listen to her. Of course we were unwilling, disobedient, eager to imagine new forms of misbehaviour. Jan broke his ankle jumping out of the hayloft. Dad found the horse in the next county after we let her out. And always Hannike was stoic and responsible. I think she sometimes even took the blame.

The old bureau in the attic was full of pictures and books and boxes of letters. They were the leftovers of my parents' past; a lock of my grandmother's hair, a christening gown wrapped in tissue. We were allowed to play drum corps in the attic but were supposed to stay out of the bureau. I didn't open the drawer and find the picture of my father in a uniform, holding a gun, but we were suddenly fighting over it and then we tore it. I remember her lighting among the five of us like a hailstorm, yanking at us in a silent fury. Her small fists useless against us, she flashed away and in a moment was back wielding my mother's wooden butter paddle. How could she possibly catch us? We were Indians, monkeys, devils going in five directions at once. And she chased us all, furiously and frantically while we laughed and ran and whooped at her. It was only when she stomped back to the house with such anger written in every line of her body, the paddle dangling from her hand, that we stopped, sobered.

She locked us out of the house that afternoon. Locked all the doors and wouldn't open them for anything. Left us to our own devices as if she didn't care if we were dead, or would all kill ourselves. We slunk around the porch, hoping she would relent, hoping for anger rather than icy withdrawal. We knew only that she was crying, crying and crying with that helpless inevitability that we sometimes glimpsed in her. And we were terrifyingly ashamed.

And then there is the other picture. I stand at the end of the driveway with Hannike and my brothers waiting for the bus. The trees are heavy with frost, the bus is late, and we have been waiting for fifteen minutes. I am in grade two. I carry a lunchkit but no books. Inside my red mittens my hands are cold, so cold I am unable to hang onto the handle and I drop the lunchpail with a clatter. I curl my hands into fists but they only seem to be getting colder.

Hannike is looking down the road for the bus, squinting into the brilliant ice-sun as if she would challenge it. Her boots scrunch the snow and she is standing beside me. "Are you cold, Marikje?"

I nod, huddled inside my coat like a turtle.

"Stamp!" she says.

I stamp my feet hard on the ground so that needles of fire race through my legs.

"It's my hands."

"Put them in your pockets."

I shove them into the pockets of my coat but still they feel stiff and bloodless.

"Are they still cold?"

I nod, miserable. "Isn't the bus coming?"

"It's probably stuck." She takes my mittened hands in hers, rubs them absently. Suddenly she turns her back to me. "Here. Take off your mitts and put your hands under my coat."

I drop my stiff mittens at my feet and shove my hands under her coat, into the warmth trapped there.

"Is that better?" she says over her shoulder.

"Yes." My hands are still curled into fists.

"Put them under my sweater."

I fumble with the layers of clothing, the suddenly acute sensation of rough wool on the backs of my hands in opposition to the smoother crispness of her blouse on my palms and fingertips. And suddenly I am afraid, afraid of touching her. I pull my hands away from her blouse, her body underneath it.

"Marikje, you're letting all the cold air under my sweater!" She is suddenly ruthless, authoritative. "Look, put your hands under my shirt and on my back and stand still."

For an instant I am petrified, then slowly, slowly I obey her, moving deeper under the cocoon of her clothes, my fingers stumbling onto the incredible softness of her warm skin. Entranced, I open my hands and touch her, lay my spread palms on her. It is as if I am touching some magical source of heat that thaws my fingers immediately, but more, leaves them with a tingling ache of sensation. Her skin is like warm water, perfectly still and smooth, unshrinking. Under my fingers I can even feel the shape of her ribs. I marvel at that now, the intimacy of it, the liberty she allowed me, my cold hands warming themselves on the flush of her skin. That was my sister.

When I am twelve, she comes home on weekends. Now she is totally beyond me, a woman from another place who does not belong here anymore. She even laughs with me. She is free of having to protect me, free of having to punish me. I am fascinated by her. She is free of my parents too; free as I know I will never be, too young and malleable to tear myself away. The turn of her head and the fine line of bone along her chin have left us behind completely, another transition accomplished. While she has grown more graceful, I have become clumsy and awkward. I break dishes and stumble; my hair is lank and colourless.

She still sleeps in the big bed with me and now she talks to me before we go to sleep. About the residence and about going to university and about taking courses and becoming a teacher. I want to do exactly what she is doing; I want to retrace every step she makes. Her life seems as perfect to me as mine is not. She falls asleep before I do and I lie staring at the sloping ceiling above me and wishing I could be her, free of having to wait, waiting for everything. Beside me her body is restless and suddenly she turns over.

"No," she mumbles. "No."

I am instantly motionless. "What? Hannike?"

"Mmmn."

She is still asleep; her voice comes out of the depths of her dreams. I am suddenly frightened, something somewhere has leapt beyond me.

She flings out her arms. "No. I don't want to."

I sit up and stare down at her. Now I am even afraid to touch her, to waken her.

She mumbles something else and then is quiet.

I sit frozen upright, not wanting to hear; yet I cannot stop myself from listening and I cannot bring myself to wake her.

She stirs. "I won't," she says clearly. "I hate them all. I won't take care of them anymore."

"Hannike, Hannike." I shake her shoulder hard. "Wake up. Don't you feel well?"

She opens her eyes for a moment, then sighs and turns her back to me.

"Go to sleep, Marikje," she says. "Go to sleep. You have to go to school in the morning."

I lay awake beside her then, trying to fit the pieces together. Her endless stooped endurance, the oldest of the six of us, the liberties she allowed us, the gleam of her creamy skin in the light. And I knew that she had made a transition that I would never even get to, let alone make, a spoiled child with an older sister.

When Hannike was married, two years later, I was fourteen. I was her youngest bridesmaid; I wore a yellow dress and carried pink flowers. But what I remember most is her standing in her bathrobe before she put on her dress, standing lost and defenseless as if she would cry, as if there were no hope or escape. I was dispassionate. I didn't want to be like her anymore. I would never marry and have children. I had decided.

And I remember that my father cried, that he stood beside my mother and the tears slipped down his brown face. He never cried when

I got married, eight years later. I know because I watched him. I wanted to see if he would. That was the difference between Hannike and me.

A year later she was heavy and awkward with her first child, as if she had never denied anything, only affirmed it. She had slipped away from me. At fifteen I did not understand pregnancy and I did not like small children. Her body seemed to be a gross intrusion on her small, light frame and I was afraid for her. She did not want my fear. She was happy, she said, and the corners of her mouth tilted upwards.

Now everyone says that her daughter looks like me when I was a child. I do not see the resemblance. She seems to me to look more like Hannike. But then, I do not see her often. Only often enough to remind her of my strangeness and that I am a disinterested aunt. Hannike and I live in the same city but we are far away from each other. She has four children now. I have none.

When we are home together, my father sometimes asks me when will I have a child and I smile and say, "Not yet, Dad." And Hannike looks at me very quickly out of the corner of her eye, but she says nothing.

Friends and the Peer Group

Growing Up Rosie

Lesley Krueger

I

The first time Rosie realized she was getting breasts was at the Stardust Roller Rink. It was Saturday; Rosie had come skating every Saturday for a year now, until all the coloured lights and shadows ate down into her bones. The Stardust was a whirling, flashing, carnival place of shouting kids and bubble gum. It made her smile; she smiled now as she stood at the gate and waited for an opening in the rolling crowd. The announcer had called reverse skate, so everyone was going left-left-left, ankle-over-ankle around round corners. Rosie looked sideways after them, looked up at the mirrors, looked down. And it was when she was looking down that she first saw the two bulges in her powder-blue, turtleneck sweater. Look at that, she marvelled. I've got tits. Then she stuck her chest out toward the whirligig crowd instead of sucking it back in like a proper girl. Which sealed Rosie's fate from that moment on.

"Hey Rosie, come on. Hurry up." Mary and Christobel were skating left-left-left going by her. Then there was an opening and Rosie plunged out in the crowd, catching its beat and rhythm before she caught her friends. But then she was with them and they skated hand-in-hand, three abreast and giggling, talking. Small boys crouched and sped by like hornets while bigger ones went faster even than that. They sprayed through the slow kids, blue and red and white in denims and checked shirts. They had crewcuts, they were like bullets. The girls watched and giggled as they passed.

"I've had enough of the reverse skate. I want to do a special skate," Mary said. "Partners."

"Or the bunny hop," Christobel added.

"Where's Rhonda?" Rosie asked, craning her neck between them. Christobel was the quiet one. She just sank into herself when Rosie asked, but Mary nodded her head significantly toward the railing. Rosie looked over and saw Rhonda skating slowly alongside Glenda Wickham and Doris Straight. Oh.

Glenda Wickham and Doris Straight were the Right Girls. No one ever called them that: Part of being Right was that no one ever called you anything, they just answered when you spoke. But at the same time there wasn't a soul alive who didn't know exactly what they were. Everyone watched Doris and Glenda, copied them and called it style. But who could copy them now? They wore little short circle skirts and matching leotards, cute bright weskets done with braid and *their own* skates, not rented. Who could afford that? (Because part of being Right was that Glenda's father was the English teacher at the Collegiate and Doris Straight's was the dentist—Dr. Straight Teeth, Rosie would say, if not for his daughter—and they could afford all the little extra things while everyone else still concentrated on the big ones.)

There was no way Mary or Christobel was ever going to be Right. To be Right you couldn't be too anything, and they were just too ordinary. Rosie wasn't—in fact she was downright pretty. She had curly blonde hair and Alice-in-Wonderland wide blue eyes, but the known fact was that she was stupid. Her report cards kept scraping the bottom and one teacher had even come right out and said it in front of the class. Said it not in anger either, but in exasperation, which was worse. Because funnier. And mean-mean-mean. Rosie had taken a lot of guff because of that one comment. If you were Right, you didn't have to take a lot of guff. But then if you were Right there was no reason to give it to you, either.

Rosie had known Mary and Christobel since the year dot; them and Rhonda Kastner. Rhonda was the one skating so earnestly now after Glenda and Doris. She was pleasing and compact; rather athletic. In gym class she turned neat somersaults just like the Right Girls. She *was* just like the Right Girls except for her father and what he did, and what he didn't do. Rhonda's father had been hurt in an industrial accident. What he didn't do was work. What he did was drink, and that was the shame of their working man's neighbourhood. They were too far east for central-city shiftlessness, too far south for rich north-central eccentricity, too long settled for the immigrants with their strange and unpredictable customs. So aside from Archie M'Closkey, the bootlegger, Rhonda's father was the neighbourhood shame. And why she could ever hope to be Right was a cipher to Rosie.

"Special skate," the announcer called.

"Special skate," Mary said excitedly. The lights flashed off and on, darkness and day.

"Couples' skate," the announcer called again, then played the Blue Danube organ record across the loudspeaker. Rosie looked over to see

Glenda Wickham and Doris Straight join hands against Rhonda, who had to dog over to her three old friends. Rosie offered her an arm, generous Rosie, but generosity wasn't what Rhonda wanted just then. She tugged Rosie across the floor like hell on wheels, not stopping to watch the Right Girls watch her, not stopping to think as Rosie did that if they weren't Right, then at least they weren't Wrong, either.

The first day that Rosie wore her new brassiere to school just happened to be gym day. After recess the girls' gym teacher marched into their classroom and marched them all out again, two-by-two down the stairs to the change room. The corridor walls were off-yellow, the floors sprinkled red and grey linoleum, but when you got to the change room it was all concrete. The floors were smooth poured concrete and the walls were concrete blocks; it was a bomb shelter too, impervious to radiation but musty, sweaty. Everyone had a little wire locker for their gym strip, and it was a disgrace if you didn't take your bloomers and blouse home once a week to wash them. A couple of girls didn't and you tried not to be seen with them. They smelled.

Rosie opened her locker and took out her gym strip. She shook away the creases, then started to change rapidly. There was a formula for taking off your shoes, socks, slipping bloomers under school tunic and then casting off the rest to stand free inside your undershirt. Today, however, Rosie couldn't help remembering that she didn't have an undershirt. That had made her proud this morning, but now she blushed a bit and turned her back on all the other girls. They won't notice, she thought. But of course they did: Rosie had forgotten about the back straps that stood out white as clouds for everyone to see. A silence dribbled slowly across the room as the girls turned toward her one by one.

"You're not wearing an undershirt anymore," someone commented. Rosie turned self-consciously. And look—it was Doris Straight speaking in her neutral and mannered voice. She might have used it to congratulate someone on getting a high mark, or to introduce the band at a school concert. Or Rosie knew too she might have used it to say: You're growing a third foot.

"I can't wear an undershirt anymore," Rose said, not knowing what else to answer.

"You're the first one in the class not to," Doris concluded, turning her back. Everyone else stared at her for a moment, then turned theirs too. So now she knew. Rosie was Wrong. And all her pride trickled out of her like old sweat.

What should have happened next was that Glenda Wickham would talk about something in her own muted voice. Then everyone would begin to chatter again, and change, and line up by the door. But instead everything stayed quiet because of a long, wicked laugh.

"You're just jealous," a voice said afterward. Who? Everyone turned and saw Jill M'Closkey laughing in the corner. It's the bootlegger's daughter. Quick. Ignore her. But Jill kept up her wicked little laugh, her wicked little kid's body slipping into her clothes. Rosie stared hard at the figure until thick tears rose slowly to her wide blue eyes. Jill M'Closkey had stuck up for her. And for Jill M'Closkey to stick up for you was the worst thing anyone could imagine.

All through gym class Rosie watched Jill do her exercises. She was such a pert little thing, so tiny she could wear last year's clothes. (So poor she probably had to.) But no one could say she wasn't clean: Her strip went home every Friday. And no one could say she wasn't smart, either. She was almost too smart. She knew all of the answers and a few of the questions besides. You'd come across her sometimes in the district library, then some other times on the edge of the playing field, shooting marbles with the boys. Now she was off in a corner on her own, running across an upturned bench like it was a highway instead of thin as a thumb. She balanced like a circus girl, that one. Some people said she was half gypsy anyway, what with her straight black hair and olive skin. Others thought it was a touch of the tarbrush, or tomahawk—anything that was Wrong, it was said about Jill. Not that she couldn't answer back. She had the sharpest tongue in Christendom, and used it too. Shame on Jill M'Closkey. Shame on Rosie, to find herself placed on Jill M'Closkey's side.

The air was full that day of little girls on parallel bars, on rings, doing cartwheels and somersaults across the mats. Rosie was usually one of the flying ones, but today she felt all arms and legs and tits: She started off in one direction and ended up somewhere else entirely. Mary and Christobel stayed by her and clucked sympathetically, but Rhonda was off after the Right Girls again. She'd left her old friends and got into the somersault line directly after Doris, then went across the mats with them one-two-three. They were all as neat as pins, there was nothing to choose between them (except that Glenda and Doris hadn't pushed into line and Rhonda had). Rosie watched them admiringly, then mussed it when her turn came. She went over crooked somehow and landed on one shoulder, coming up pained. Surprise: If you weren't careful the bra straps bit hard into your shoulder. She rubbed her hand along the path of the strap, then saw she was being watched and smiled. The watching girls didn't smile back. They just turned and walked away, leaving Rosie feeling puzzled and apologetic somehow, as if she'd been caught in a boast or a lie.

The class seemed to last an age that day, but finally the teacher whistled them to a stop. Little girls jumped down from the parallel bars, up from the mats, then filed into the change room to strip and shower. You went four people to each shower cubicle, unless you were Glenda Wickham and Doris Straight and found your cubicle held only two. The Right Girls were modest like that. They also had big towels, which they first held up as screens for each other, then draped about themselves and discarded only after disappearing into the shower. Rosie just stripped. She always had, she never thought about it, she just carried her towel in her hand as she crossed the concrete floor. Except—

"She doesn't need a bra. I don't know what she goes around wearing one for." Someone was whispering loud enough to hear. *Rhonda* was whispering, standing near the showers and directing her voice toward the Right Girls, if not exactly to them. She looked so hopeful. But, of course, her remark was in Bad Taste and they just ignored her. Rhonda always had trouble telling Good Taste from Bad, her father being a drunk and all. Rosie felt sorry for her exposing herself that way. Poor Rhonda, she thought. Poor us. Then Jill M'Closkey laughed again.

That laugh. That wicked, observant, old little laugh. It echoed through the concrete change room and followed Rhonda into the showers. It didn't matter how she walked, it didn't matter that she held her towel around her like Glenda Wickham and Doris Straight. Rhonda was naked. Jill M'Closkey laughed and everyone saw through her like the water collecting on the floor.

After school that day Rosie started home alone. Usually she walked with her three old friends, but today Rhonda had given her a dirty look and they'd disappeared before she even got her coat on. Rosie knew that Rhonda didn't like her anymore. She'd been the cause of Rhonda's humiliation, although it wasn't her fault, none of it was her fault. She couldn't help it if she was the first one in the class to grow tits. And so what if she had, anyway? They were just jealous, just jealous, were were were.

Rosie started skipping down the sidewalk to the rhythm of her complaint. It was autumn, and red-green-gold leaves made it slippery, made it hard to see the cracks and lines so you could (step on a crack, break your mother's—) avoid them. But she skipped and stepped and avoided, all alone, going home, until there was a small blackness growing up beside her.

"You want to come to my house to play?" Jill M'Closkey asked, skipping to her side. Rosie turned. This was the bootlegger's daughter inviting her to the bootlegger's house.

"I can't," she said, then remembered politeness. "My mother said I had to come right home after school today."

"Then I'll walk home with you," Jill M'Closkey said. "It's on my way." Rosie was trapped, tried not to look trapped, looked over to see that Jill M'Closkey was smiling. Why the mean little creature. She knew that Rosie didn't want to be seen with her and she was coming along anyway. She was vengeful, that's what she was. (Or maybe just lonely.)

"Tell me a story," Jill said.

"Story?" Rosie asked. She kicked the red-green-gold leaves and thought, for some reason, that Jill was three months older than her. "I can never remember any stories."

"Then make one up." But making up stories was the worst homework Rosie could get. How I Spent My Summer, by Rosie Cox. Except how did she ever spend her summers? Rosie's mind ran blankly along empty tracks until Jill laughed, although not meanly. "I'll tell you one then," she said.

People passed them on the street. Rosie tried to make herself invisible as Jill walked along beside her, head bent, thinking. Maybe Jill could be the invisible one. Maybe Rosie could roll her up in a little lump and bounce her down the street like she was something ordinary, a rubber ball instead of the bootlegger's only daughter.

"Once upon a time," Jill started, then paused. "Once upon a time there was a maiden named Rosie of the Morning. She had hair of gold and a cloak of velvet and a kirtle made all of gossamer and lace."

"What's a kirtle?" Rosie asked suspiciously.

"It's a dress," Jill replied. "So anyway she had a cloak and a kirtle and she lived in a high, high tower with spikes along the wall tops to keep invaders at bay." Then Jill told her tale of the maiden Rosie, her prince, her dragon and the Queen of the Elves—a small queen, a dark queen, a queen of remarkable familiarity. There were a great many secrets in Jill's tale, and more chases. They went over hummocks, down vales, through mysterious barrows. They had adventures you couldn't imagine in words you'd never heard. And Rosie was entranced. Her mouth hung open all the way down the block, until they reached her house and the tale was suddenly, magically over. Then Jill was gone (Queen of the Elves, dark hair bouncing, light feet stepping) before Rosie had a chance to not invite her in.

II

Two months later Rhonda Kastner's father died. Their teacher told them the next morning, her voice all dressed in black. Children, she said. Mr. Kastner passed away last night. Rhonda will be away from school for two weeks, and I hope you'll show her every consideration when she returns.

"He was so drunk he just lay down in the middle of the road and got run over by a car," Jill claimed, when her path crossed Rosie's after school. But Rosie was with Mary and Christobel (for once) and just gave Jill the same look they did. Speak no ill of the dead. And whose liquor was he drinking, anyway?

It was their first death, and Mary and Christobel discussed it as solemnly as undertakers. He'll lie in the chapel for two days before going on his final journey, they said. There'll be floral tributes from the friends and bereaved. Rosie just thought about run-over cats, some of them flat-out dead, some of them crawling up afterwards and shaking their heads until they shook themselves forward and died. You weren't supposed to say that though, about run-over cats. It was Bad Taste. So Rosie asked instead whether they should go visit Rhonda in her hour of need. Mary shook her head no. Then she and Christobel hunched over in the way they did recently, like they were protecting a secret. Rosie knew what it was, and watched them later when they zagged off at the bottom of her street later when they were supposed to be on their way home. She hunched into herself like they did, and the secret she was protecting was a secret hurt. But then the bra straps bit into her shoulders again and Rosie had to smile. So who needed kids for friends anyway? she asked. (Aside from her.)

Everyone talked about Rhonda for the next two weeks, but it ended up that Rosie only saw her when she finally got back to school. She was pale, pale like she'd washed her face in lemon juice and pitiful as can be. Of course everyone was considerate toward her just as the teacher said. And of course Glenda Wickham and Doris Straight were the most considerate of all. They talked to Rhonda in their neutral and mannered voices, twice shared their cake at recess, once were seen walking her home. She sobbed a bit and thanked them, which made Rosie, watching, plain out mad. She probably *was* washing her face in lemon juice; she'd hated her Dad. But Rosie bit her tongue and didn't say it. No one could say anything bad about Rhonda these days, what with the protection of the Right Girls. You could only say: Poor little fatherless thing. So brave. Such a sad birthday she's got coming too. She won't feel like having a party, they said, although it's kind—so brave.

Because, of course, Rhonda Kastner was having a party. The rumours went round that she and a few select friends would go for a quiet afternoon's skate at the Stardust Roller Rink. Rosie looked on disgustedly. All she could say was that Rhonda was lucky her birthday was six weeks after the funeral. Good Taste demanded that you wait at least six weeks before looking happy again, and she was just getting in under the wire. Who did she think she was fooling with that bereaved act, anyway? Phony reluctance, phony tears. (Sitting between Glenda and Doris, flitting to Mary and Christobel, her old friends—so loyal—but never to Rosie. Oh no, never to Rosie, the 34 double-A certified class freak.) Who did she think she was, anyway?

Rosie had half a mind not to go to her stupid party. She had half a mind to march up to Rhonda and say: Crocodile tears, Rhonda Kastner. You're crying crocodile tears. Then she'd tear up the invitation while everyone looked admiringly.

Except she didn't get an invitation.

She hadn't been asked.

Oh, humiliation.

Rhonda had invited Mary and Christobel, all right, old friends, so loyal. But the only other people going were Glenda Wickham and Doris Straight. She'd bagged the Right Girls. And Rosie walked home disconsolate.

It was a snowy winter day. The wind froze through your clothes the way Rhonda Kastner's stare did when you weren't being invited. It blew through your leotards the way it blew through the Poor houses, the Wrong houses. Because Rosie was really Wrong now, there was no getting away from it. She was like the crazy lady down the block who covered herself in cellophane to keep the germs out. She was like Gord Hamilton, the strike-breaker's son. And she was like Jill M'Closkey, the final, the foremost, the freakiest freak. Who'd been hurrying down the sidewalk for the past five minutes trying to catch up with her.

"Hello," Jill said finally, pulling alongside. Rosie kept quiet and stared straight ahead until Jill laughed. "You'd think it was your father who died," she observed, sliding on the ice.

"Oh go away, Jill M'Closkey," Rosie replied. She walked on faster.

"It's a free country," Jill said, catching up again. "I can walk anywhere I like." So she walked beside Rosie down the snowy path. She was wearing those black rubber boots that boys wore, the kind with the red line running around the top. And her coat was bigger than she was, bought to grow into and quilted, bundled-up and blue. "I wasn't invited either," she said, and laughed her keen laugh as Rosie looked over. Had she expected to be? "And you didn't even invite me to your party last November."

Rosie slowed down and stared at Jill. It was true, she hadn't even thought about it. But why should she? "I'm sorry," she said, not meaning it.

"Want to come to my house and play?" Jill asked.

"No," Rosie yelled. It was loud, it was rude, and Jill edged away.

"I was only asking," she said. Her voice was hurt, and this time Rosie really did feel sorry.

"I didn't mean—" she said, "I mean—I mean—I mean sure. Why not?" She was Wrong now. Who cared who she played with anymore? Rosie turned and started to walk toward the street where she knew Jill lived.

"We should go to your place first," Jill said. "You'll want to tell your mother." Rosie stopped, surprised. It was as if Jill always did herself.

"She doesn't care so long as I'm home for dinner," she said. "I don't ever have to tell."

"Well, so what if you want to stay for supper? I mean I'll have to ask my mother—"

"Then I can phone," Rosie shrugged.

"We don't have a telephone." Oh. She was going to a place where they didn't even have a telephone. She was going to the bootlegger's. Who cared about Wrong? She was talking about dangerous. Rosie walked the rest of the way home trying to think of some way to get out of it. Maybe her mother would forbid—

But her mother didn't forbid. She didn't even seem to recognize Jill, just sat in her chair, tired as ever, and nodded. So they went outside again, and Rosie faced the more immediate problem of what you said to someone like Jill. What did you say to anyone? Mary? Christobel? (Rhonda?) Blank.

"Tell me a story," Jill said. Then Rosie remembered.

"No, you tell me one," she replied. Jill paused, dreaming, tramping through the snow. Then she started to tell how Rosie was a figure skater, famous and furred. She travelled to all the foreign capitals and performed before presidents, lairds and kings. Around her neck were royal jewels, and on her fingers, rings of ice—for Rosie was an elf queen, come to judge the men who thought that they judged her. It was a rippling, flashing story. It made the snow soften underfoot until it became light fairy furs, the pelts of unicorns. It made Rosie marvel. And Jill laughed to see her, laughed and built words gleefully with her scratchy, ancient, storyteller's voice. Then they were at her house and she finished it, the second end appearing as mysteriously as the first. Rosie pinched herself so she could come back down to her regular life, where snow was snow and cold at that. Then she saw that they faced the bootlegger's house and her heart plummeted inside her. They had to go in there?

Jill led Rosie up the path toward the house. It was a clear straight path, the bottom lined with tamped-down snow and sanded lightly for traction. Rosie didn't like it. She thought of the bad kings Jill had thrown across their path, then pictured men piling late late out the bootlegger's door and dropping dead drunk on the new-fallen snow. *They* were the ones who cleared the path, their falling bodies tamping it down so smooth it was hard against your feet. Rosie walked along it reluctantly. She knew in this day and age being a bootlegger didn't mean having a still like a hillbilly. It just meant buying booze from the liquor board and selling it after-hours from your own house. But did that mean men actually drank inside? Did it smell? And how did Jill get to sleep at night, anyway?

"We're supposed to take off our boots and leave them on a newspaper here," Jill said, leading the way inside. Rosie followed her, and the next thing she did was sniff. No, it didn't smell. You couldn't detect pee or beer, just warmth and steam and noise. Kids and kids ran everywhere—of course, Jill had five little brothers, everyone knew that. Or six? Now they raced around Jill and Rosie, upstairs, downstairs, countless little kids with black black hair. But they were all neat. It was a neat place, clean and warm. Rosie could almost feel at home here, until a strange foreign voice called out from the kitchen and Jill, going foreign, called back.

"My mother's from Quebec," she explained. Then a tiny woman appeared in the doorway and started rippling odd sounds over at Rosie. "En anglais, Mamman," Jill interrupted quickly. The woman paused.

"I said you're welcome to stay for dinner, Rose," she said then, wiping her hands on her apron. She spoke perfect English, although she did something extra to the 'r' in Rosie's name that made her feel disoriented.

"Thank you," she answered, but Mrs. M'Closkey was already gone. She was quick like her daughter. Tiny and dark too, although harder. Sharp, you thought. Stone.

Rosie's mother, the big one. Sitting in her chair with knees spread to hold her weight. Tired lines cracking her crepey face. Rosie was the youngest, the only one at home. She said: "Ma, I need a bra."

"You need a what? Come here and let me look at you." Rosie got up from the table and shied herself over to her mother's chair. Mrs. Cox held her at arm's length, then seemed to slump under the weight of her cares, her amusement and her own huge breasts. "Those?" she asked. Tears grew behind Rosie's eyes.

"*Ma,* I need a *bra,*" she repeated piteously.

"Well, Lord, child," Mrs. Cox said, sighing. "I don't know. I just went out the other day and bought you a load of undershirts. I don't know where we're supposed to find the money for all these clothes of yours, I just don't know." The lines deepened on her tired face, then she looked again at Rosie's young one and a quick tremor of something passed through her body. "You could probably get your father to buy you one," she said, awake now, and spiteful. "You could probably get your father to buy you the whole world, if it was for sale."

"I don't want to ask papa," Rosie said, horrified.

"You don't want to ask your old papa what?" Mr. Cox yelled through from the living room. Mrs. Cox yelled back.

"She says she wants a bra, Alf."

"Ma." Sheer horror, a moment's pause.

"Well then for God's sake woman, get her one."

But Jill M'Closkey's mother, you'd never catch her just sitting in a kitchen chair. She moved moved moved. She ordered you around every which way. You could see obeying her too, the way the kids did. When she called supper they came quietly to the table, sat quietly with their hands folded on their plates.

"Richard," she said, "you will please give us grace."

"Inthenameof—"

"Say it properly,", she demanded.

"In—the—name—"

"Properly."

"In the name of the Father, the Son and the Holy Ghost, amen. Bless us, Oh Lord, for these thy gifts we are about to receive from thy bounty through Christ, Our Lord, amen."

Two amens. Rosie kept her head bowed in case they were going to throw a third one at her, but that seemed to be it. She looked up from her plate in time to see a red-headed man sit down at the table.

"Good evening, children," he said.

"Good evening, father," everyone answered. He nodded, then looked over at Rosie.

"Father, this is my friend Rosie Cox from school." Rosie bobbed her head as Jill introduced her.

"Good evening, Rose," the man said, nodding back, "you'll be Alf Cox's daughter then."

"Yes sir," Rosie answered. She was scared stiff. Part of it was because she was scared of everyone else's father on principle, part because he was the bootlegger, and part because he seemed to know her father. You had to wonder how. And then, too, you had to resent Jill coming out boldly like that and daring to call you "friend."

"Michael, how did you do on your spelling test today?" Mr. M'Closkey said now, turning.

"Ten out of ten, father," Michael replied. Rosie would have got ten out of ten too, if she was him.

"Spell 'ancient.'"

"A-n-"

"My father doesn't come down until after grace," Jill whispered under the covering noise. "He's not a Catholic and he says it's all right popery. He's an atheist, like me." Catholic? Was that—

"Gordon, can you give me the order of the planets?"

"Mercury, Venus, Earth, Mars, Jupiter, Saturn, Uranus, Neptune, Pluto." Rosie would sure have known the planets too, boy. She was quaking in her boots, here at the bootlegger's house. It was also too different. You looked at everything the first time and it all seemed normal. Then the second time you looked it had all gone strange. There was Mrs. M'Closkey's foreign language, the double-barrelled grace. And now there was Mr. M'Closkey too. When he first appeared you thought he was a normal father, stocky and punchy with greying red hair. But then you looked one more time and saw that he only had three fingers on each hand.

"My father got hurt in the war," Jill told Rosie later. By this time they were upstairs and lounging around in Jill's bedroom. She seemed proud of having a room of her own, which Rosie thought was funny until she learned that Jill used to share with a couple of her brothers. Imagine having to share a room with your brothers. Rosie had to giggle when she thought about it, but giggle with a sort of awed fright. It was like when she passed a freak show on the midway, or when she was young and a boy said if she'd pay him, he'd show her how he pee'd. But truth to tell, Rosie'd always wanted to pay the boy or the barker to get an inside look. So, she shrugged. Now she was inside. And knew if she let herself relax she might even enjoy it.

"My father was in the war too," Rosie commented. "He was in England and Italy and North Africa."

"My father was at Dieppe," Jill said. "He got his fingers blown off by a machine gun." They went quiet for a moment, to honour the casualties of war.

"What do you think of Miss Winters?" Rosie said then, referring to their teacher.

"Winters is an old gas bag," Jill replied. "I liked Hawthorne better." Miss Hawthorne was their last year's teacher, who used to put Jill's compositions up on the class bulletin board.

"Tell me a story," Rosie said, running her fingers down the bedspread.

"I've already told you enough stories for today," Jill answered. "Someday I might show you my novel though."

"Your novel?" Rosie asked. But Jill clammed up, holding her small face tight before the blue-painted wall. It was quiet for a moment, since Jill seemed determined to be dramatic and Rosie couldn't think of anything else to say. But finally Jill sighed into the silence.

"I'm going to be a writer," she said. "What are you going to be?"

"I don't know," Rosie answered vaguely.

"Well, are you going to get married then?" Jill asked. "I'm going to marry someone rich."

"I'm going to marry someone handsome," Rosie said eagerly. Then she remembered that she and Rhonda used to talk like this, and tears filled her eyes.

"What's the matter?" Jill asked.

"You know what I'm not going to do?" Rosie said. "I'm not going to go to Rhonda Kastner's birthday party."

"I'm not either," Jill said firmly, like it was her choice.

"But I was her friend," Rosie wailed. "She and Mary and Christobel were supposed to be my friends, and now they don't even want to see me anymore."

"Well, I'm your friend now," Jill answered. "And the more fools them." Rosie looked at her reproachfully. Are you calling my friends fools? she thought. And are you calling yourself my friend? But then a wave of fatalism and self-pity flowed through Rosie's body and she knew that Jill was right. They weren't her friends anymore. And Jill might as well be. (NO. Kids'll laugh. They'll sing:

Jill and Rosie sitting in a tree
K-I-S-S-I-N-G—)

"I can't help it if I was the first person in the class not to wear an undershirt," Rosie wailed again.

"The first one in the class to start wearing a bra, you mean," Jill corrected. "They're just jealous."

"Oh Jill, you shouldn't ever have said that," Rosie protested, her wet eyes widening.

"Why not? It's true. And maybe I'll go out and get a bra myself and see what they say about that." Rosie had to giggle at the picture: Jill was built like an eight-year-old kid.

"It'd just ride up under your arms," she said, wiping her eyes. "There's nothing to keep it down."

"I'd use kleenex," Jill replied. "I'll bet Glenda and Doris get bras and start doing that. Changing behind their towels. Silly girls."

"Don't say that," Rosie pleaded, then started to cry again.

"Why not?"

"Because they're Rhonda's new friends." And she prefers them to me so they have to be something special, or what am I?

"They're Rhonda's friends for now," Jill said in disgust. "But for how long? They're just silly girls."

"They're not."

"They're the silliest girls I know. They think they're better than everyone else. I'd like to know what makes them think they're any better than me."

"Oh Jill," Rosie said. "But they do. Everyone does."

"Well, they're wrong," Jill replied, standing up quickly. "I'm smarter than they are and you're prettier, as far as that goes."

"Do you think so?" Rosie said hopefully.

"Sure," Jill said. "Just wait till we're in high school, then they'll see."

"What'll they see?" Rosie asked, her eyes widening once again.

"They'll see the boys are after you, not them, prissy little Glenda Wickham and prune-faced Doris Straight. Just wait and see how pretty you'll be. And I'll be the class valedictorian."

"Pretty," Rosie whispered to herself. "And we'll get little circle skirts and weskets and *our own* skates and go to the Stardust every Saturday." Jill looked over quickly and frowned. She could seldom afford to rent skates, much less buy them. But beyond that she knew instinctively that if you let other people set your standards, then you'd never measure up. Because no matter how well you did they'd always know some hidden rule and end up doing better. The only thing to do was pick your own goal, something possible, and go after it with everything you had. People might hate you for it, but at least they could never call you second rate.

"I went up a bra size the other day." Jill looked over and saw that Rosie had dried her eyes, lost her complaint. She was sitting there calmly and smiling at Jill with a look of vague friendship.

"Yeah?" Jill replied. "Maybe if I'm lucky I'll grow out of my boots before Christmas and be able to get a new pair."

"Thirty-four A," Rosie said. Then she shrugged her shoulders inward till the straps bit again, tearing a satisfying pain across her nice, first, round, bulging breasts. "Thirty-four A," she repeated. And grinned gloriously.

The Immortals

Ed Kleiman

For days in the fall of forty-nine, St. John's High had buzzed with rumours about whether or not Torchy Brownstone would be allowed to play in the football game on Friday. Torchy was our first-string quarter-back, a two-year veteran with the school, and if we were to have any chance of beating Kelvin—our arch-rivals from River Heights—then the team could not afford to see him sidelined with a knee injury. The injury had been sustained in a practice session last week when a second-string linebacker had gotten carried away with enthusiasm and tackled Torchy just as he was coming around the end on a double reverse. So one of our own players had done what the rest of the league would have been trying to do all through the fall.

What hurt most was that Torchy should be sidelined when we were playing Kelvin. The game itself didn't count for anything. It was an exhibition game, a warm-up before the regular season began. But what did count was that this was a contest between the North and South Ends of the city. And that was no small matter.

The North End consisted mainly of immigrants from Eastern Europe, labouring classes, small foreign-language newspapers, watch-repair shops, a Jewish theatrical company, a Ukrainian dance troupe, small choirs, tap-dancing schools, orchestral groups, chess clubs and more radical political thinkers per square block than Soviet Russia had known before the Revolution. The South End—or River Heights, as it is more fashionably called—was basically what that revolution had been against. The mayor, most of the aldermen, the chairman of the school board and many of the civic employees—not the street sweepers, of course—lived in River Heights.

Actually, when you think about it, they had chosen a curious name for their end of town. If you've ever passed through Winnipeg, you'll realize that it rests on one of the flattest stretches of land in the world. In fact, I read in the school library once that the land falls at the rate of no more than two feet per mile as it extends northward towards Lake Winnipeg. So the Heights, you see, can't amount to much more than six or eight feet, at the most. But people there like to think of themselves as living on a plateau overlooking the rest of the city, as in a sense they do. For the heights they've attained are built on political and economic foundations that give them a vantage point of something more in the order of six or eight hundred feet.

Another way of distinguishing between the two parts of the city is by looking at the street names. In the North End, you'll find such names as Selkirk Avenue, Euclid Street, Aberdeen, Dufferin—names steeped in history, names which suggest the realm of human endeavor, anguish, accomplishment. But if you look at the street names in River Heights, what you'll find, with few exceptions, are such names as Ash Street, Elm, Oak, Willow. Vast expanses of velvet lawns, well-treed boulevards—the area looks like a garden, a retreat from the toil and anguish everywhere visible in the North End. The two cultures meet downtown, where the South End gentry immediately head for the managerial offices, and the North End rabble file past the company clocks with their time cards. After work countless numbers of expensive cars sweep grandly across the Maryland Bridge back into Eden, while street cars and buses pass northward beneath the C.P.R. subway into a grim bleak underworld of steel fences, concrete walls, locked doors, and savage dogs that seem capable of looking in three directions at once.

But at the Osborne Stadium in the fall, the traditional roles can be reversed for an evening. There, on Friday nights, the North End may once more experience the heady hours of triumph it knew during the 1919 Strike, when it seemed the World Revolution might begin right here in Winnipeg. So, you see, the fact that Torchy Brownstone had injured his knee in football practice was of major concern to us all.

And then to add insult to injury, the English teacher Mr. Rockwood caught our star tackles, Norm Mittlehaus and Sam Margolis, in Room 41 the day before the game and tried to have them disqualified from playing on Friday. Room 41 is Goldman's Drug Store—just across the street from the high school—and kids are always sneaking across during the day to have a soda, read a magazine, or have a smoke. And Rockwood is always catching them. Rockwood is about five foot two and weighs about a hundred and eighty, so he's a fairly stocky little guy with huge shoulders and a neck like a bull dog. Needless to say, Rockwood lives in River Heights, and he would have still been teaching at Kelvin if he hadn't swatted one of his pupils one day—the son of a school trustee, as it turned out—and since then he's been our affliction. He often tries to have kids expelled, banned from writing exams, or disqualified from playing football—which drives the football coach, Mr. Powalski, wild. It had always seemed to us that Mr. Rockwood would have been much happier, would have felt more free to express himself, and would have achieved a greater degree of fulfilment if he'd been a guard at Auschwitz.

Anyway, as soon as Mr. Powalski learned that Rockwood had disqualified our star tackles Mittlehaus and Margolis from playing the next night, he rushed up to the principal's office and threatened to resign—again, for what must have been the tenth time that year—if they weren't reinstated.

On the Friday night of the game, the stands were packed. Would Torchy play? And what about Mittlehaus and Margolis? Even I came to the game that night, and I rarely go to football games—or any kind of sports event for that matter. As usual, I was intensely preoccupied with the finer things in life, with art and poetry, and all my evenings then were taken up by an epic poem in hexameters I was working on. But the whole school was caught up in the game that night, and Nate Samuelson, my bench partner in physics lab who had just been elected student president, finally persuaded me that I couldn't stay behind.

So there we all were, glaring across the field at the River Heights stands, where, sitting shamelessly among the staunch supporters of the opposing team, we could make out Rockwood; Peg-Leg Dobson—our physics teacher; Mr. Atkinson—our chemistry teacher and Mr. Clearwater—the principal. Still, Kleinberg, Schultz, Rasmussen and Pollick—all loyal North Enders—had stationed themselves prominently in our end of the stadium.

Rumours abounded. Kelvin was supposed to have all-new football equipment donated by the president of a huge department store. Their new sweaters, it was claimed, were no longer the school colours, cherry and grey, but a regal purple and gold. It was also whispered that the team had been practising secret plays to be unveiled that night. They had a new fullback—a huge two-hundred-pounder, who would make mincemeat of our line. And, most ominous of all, there was talk that the chief referee had bet five dollars on the River Heights team.

But each new rumour of impending doom simply sent our spirits soaring higher. We shouted taunts across the field, blew up Sheiks and let them float skyward, unveiled posters that displayed a hammer and sickle, beneath which were the words, "Workers, Arise!", bombarded the officials with over-ripe tomatoes and rotten eggs which we'd saved especially for the occasion, and flung rolls of toilet paper into the playing area. Until an exasperated voice in an Oxford accent that had obviously just been acquired that summer asked us all to stand for the National Anthem.

Then the whistle blew, and we kicked off to Kelvin, and, to our horror, that two-hundred-pound fullback really did exist because he caught the ball and ran over three of our tacklers for a touchdown. Less than sixty seconds after the game had started, they had a converted touchdown—worth six points then—and we had three injuries. Suddenly our players in their ripped sweaters and torn pads looked like a pretty shabby lot compared to that Kelvin team, which moved with such military precision in their new uniforms and shiny helmets.

On the next kick-off, our star runner, Cramer, caught the football, and was promptly tackled by their two-hundred-pound fullback, whose name, we learned, was Bruno Hogg. When Cramer finally managed to get up, he was limping. A mighty groan escaped from the North End stands. Jerusalem had just been taken and we were all being marched off to captivity in Babylon. We could see Torchy, down on the sidelines, pleading with the coach to let him in—knee injury and all—but Powalski sent in Marty Klein instead.

When they first caught sight of Marty, the military discipline of the Kelvin team threatened to disintegrate. Marty's all of five foot two and can't weigh much more than 125, so his appearance caused first titters, then guffaws. Of course they didn't realize that Marty uses his size to advantage. He's the sneakiest player you'll ever see.

Right away, Marty calls a plunge by the fullback. But when they peel the players off our boy, he doesn't have the ball. Then the Kelvin line pounces on the two halfbacks, but they don't have the ball either—and so they throw them away and begin looking around with murder in their eyes for the tailback. By the time they start looking around for Marty, it's too late. He's waving to them with one hand, the ball in the other, from behind their own goal line. Marty had jumped right out of harm's way once the ball had been snapped, and then he strolled off down the sidelines while the Kelvin team pounced upon one player after another in their frantic search for the missing football. Somehow we managed to finish the quarter with a six-all tie.

But in the second quarter, disaster struck. We'd managed to hold Kelvin in their own end of the field until they had to kick on third down. Out of their huddle they marched in that military precision of theirs, and we knew right away something tricky was up. Three of their backfielders pranced out to one side behind the kicker, who booted the ball no more than fifteen yards, and those three ballet stars danced away with the ball while we were left looking like jerks, with our coach hastily thumbing through his handbook to see what it was all about. When Kelvin tried the same stunt a few plays later, all three of their ballerinas were immediately flattened. But that was strictly *verboten*, according to the officials, and we were penalized fifteen yards. Then that two-hundred-pound fullback of theirs got the ball again, and we were behind another six points. But at last Powalski found the section in the rule book dealing with on-side kicks and brought an end to that particular gimmick.

When we finally got the ball again, Marty Klein called another plunge by the fullback, but now the whole line piled on top of poor Marty, and so the fullback—who did have the ball this time—had already bulldozed his way more than half the length of the field when his bootlace came undone, and he tripped over the loose end. Of course Kelvin recovered the fumbled ball, and we were lucky to finish the half only six points down.

During the intermission, more rumours swept through the stands. A doctor had been seen racing down to the stadium from the North End with a special drug and a set of splints that would enable Torchy to play in the second half. This was immediately contradicted by another rumour: the same doctor had warned that Torchy would limp for the rest of his life if he played that night.

Someone else hinted that there was a special reason for those Kelvin players moving about with such stiff, jerky motions and spastic gestures. All that talk about military precision and strict training was a bunch of nonsense. Nate Samuelson had sneaked into the Kelvin dressing room before the game and sprinkled red pepper into every one of their jock straps. A little later somebody spotted Nate sitting beside me, and soon a couple of dozen people were cheering their new student president. None of us suspected then that twenty years later, long after he had become a doctor, gotten married and had two children, he would take an overdose of drugs and walk off the MacIntyre Building smack on top of the early morning traffic jam. Nate stood up in the stands that evening, smiled in that sly way of his, and waved his hand to the cheering crowd.

Later still, a few students from the Grade Twelve Industrial Class stormed across the field to pick a fight with some of the River Heights fans, but they got thrown out of the stadium by the police for their efforts. Afterwards, we heard that they had peed in the gas tanks of all the posh cars parked around the stadium—cars which after the game that night were seen to be lurching and stalling through the streets leading back into River Heights.

Then the players came back on the field, and that two-hundred-pound fullback of theirs got the ball, and now we were behind twelve points. It was during the third quarter that they really began to grind our team into the turf. They seemed to be getting stronger by the minute while our crew looked shabbier than ever. We couldn't understand it. It didn't make sense. Unless perhaps they'd discovered the red pepper. From the way they paraded and strutted across the field, it was clear they'd be prepared for any contingency. We couldn't put anything past them.

When calling plays, they didn't huddle, as we did. Instead their team would line up in two rows, with their backs to us, and their quarterback would stand facing them and bark out the number of the play. They couldn't have cared less if we overheard or not, they were so confident. Then the centre would march out and crouch over the ball, while the rest of the team moved with just as much military precision to their positions. The ball would be snapped and—Quick March!—they had fifteen more yards, while, as likely as not, we had a few more lumps.

Just as we were getting used to the fact that they weren't trying anything fancy now—that this was going to be one of those bruising games where each side tries to pound the other into the earth—their two-hundred-pound fullback started to come round one end, then handed the ball off to the tailback, who scooted round the other end on a double reverse. And we were eighteen points behind.

The mood on our side of the stadium became grim. On the field the game was turning into a rout. Marty Klein, who was playing safety, as well as quarterback, got creamed when he intercepted a Kelvin pass on our one-yard line, and the Ambulance Corps had to carry him off the field. Down on the sidelines, Torchy Brownstone was still pleading with the coach to let him in.

I guess we should have known when Torchy appeared on the bench dressed for the game that the fates had decreed he would play that night. We knew it was crazy, but on to the field he limped with the first-string line: Norm Mittlehaus—a savage tackle who was later to sing with the Metropolitan Opera and eventually become a cantor; Marvin Zimmerman—who'd recently met a bunch of pretty nurses at the General Hospital and was playing with the reckless abandon of someone determined to break a collarbone at least; Sammy Margolis— who never quite came up to expectations, and who, when he was sent to Los Angeles to study dentistry, married the daughter of a clothing manufacturer instead; and Sheldon Kunstler—who later moved to New York and got rich by inventing a machine that bent, folded and stapled computer cards. Across the field they moved, as the voice on the P.A. system announced that Torchy Brownstone was playing against doctor's orders, and we all cheered mindlessly.

St. John's huddled behind their own goal line. A couple of Kelvin linemen—huge Goliaths that seemed to have just wandered in from the battle plains of Judaea—let long thin streams of spit slide from between their teeth to the grass. Their team-mates looked no less contemptuous.

Then the St. John's huddle broke, and Izzy Steinberg, who'd played the Lord High Executioner in *The Mikado* the year before, marched with an exaggerated goose step to his position as centre. About him the rest of the team marched with stiff, jerky steps to their places also. Dressed in their torn sweaters and oversize pants, held up by bits of string and old suspenders, they turned smartly to salute Torchy, who promptly returned the salute, and then as one man they all whirled about to give a "Sieg Heil" to the members of the Kelvin team. As the full impact of the caricature was taken in by the spectators, laughter began to gather within the North End stands until it washed over the Kelvin fans.

The laughter and noise quietened into an expectant hush as Torchy began to call signals. Everyone in the stadium knew that Torchy had the largest sleight-of-hand repertoire of any high school quarterback in the city. Consequently, once the play began, anyone who could conceivably get his hands on the ball—backs, ends—all were immediately flattened by those Kelvin behemoths that came roaring through our line. Which meant that nobody laid a hand on Torchy as he limped down the field, paused briefly to fish the ball out of the hole in his sweater, and then crossed over the River Heights goal line. The quarterback sneak had travelled the whole length of the field.

While the Kelvin players were still complaining to the officials, we could see Torchy calling the St. John's team into a huddle. I don't know what he said, but after the kick-off, our players charged down the field as if they'd been transformed. In the fading sunlight, their torn uniforms looked like golden armour, ablaze with precious stones; their helmets shone with emeralds and sapphires; and they moved with a grace and power that was electrifying. That two-hundred-pound River Heights fullback—who was playing both ways—caught the ball and was promptly hit by Sidney Cohen in the hardest flying tackle any of us had ever seen. After that tackle, Sidney, who had always impressed us as something of a Momma's Boy, was Papa's Boy forever.

The Kelvin fullback had fallen to the earth as if he were the Tower of Babel crumbling beneath the wrath of God. The ball bounced into the air, and Torchy...Torchy was where he always is during a fumble. He would have scored touchdowns if he had had to go down the field on crutches. The same, I'm afraid, could not be said of the two-hundred-pound fullback. Bruno Hogg lay unconscious on the field, dreaming strange, alien dreams of knishes and gefilte fish, and blissfully unaware that, for once, he'd met his match and been vanquished utterly. Now we were only six points behind.

During the fourth quarter, the Kelvin line started tackling Torchy on every play. You'd see him out there, limping away from the action of the hand-off, holding up both arms to show everyone he didn't have the ball, and still they'd tackle him. So then Torchy started throwing passes—that way the whole stadium could see he didn't have the ball. But neither the Kelvin tackles nor the officials seemed to care. And that was when Torchy sent word to the bench that it was time for Luther Johnson to come out.

Luther was our secret weapon. Just recently, his family had moved up from a black ghetto in Chicago, where Luther had played end for the city high school champions. He was a lanky six foot five, could lope along for miles faster than most people could sprint, and caught passes thrown anywhere within shouting distance.

Before vanishing in a melee of purple Kelvin sweaters, Torchy managed to get away a twenty-yard completion. On the next play, Luther caught a thirty-five yarder. Suddenly those River Heights players didn't seem to be strutting about so much. From the way they kept pointing, first to one player on our team, then to another, you could see that they were puzzling who to go after. Torchy might just choose to go limping across the goal line for the tying touchdown himself.

Our team wasn't sure, either, what to do next. You could hear them arguing about it in the huddle. Once Norm Mittlehaus's deep baritone voice could be heard demanding that they call a trick play and throw the ball to him for a change. Finally...finally...they came out of the conference, but before they could line up, one of the officials blew his whistle to signal they'd lost the down. Too much time in the huddle. So back they went to argue some more.

They were still arguing when they came out for the second down. Torchy looked pretty small out there as he limped into position behind the centre. Even without the limp, though, we would have recognized him by that hard whiplash voice of his, the black hair constantly falling down into his eyes and the fluid way he managed to move once the ball was snapped—hurt leg and all. He was like a particularly graceful predatory bird that's injured a wing.

Again the ball was sent arcing through the air, and again Luther was running along in that lope of his—this time across the Kelvin goal line. Everyone on the Kelvin team seemed out to intercept the pass, and all the possible receivers were immediately encircled by River Heights players. The ball, which was soaring a good two feet above everyone's hands, kept rising still, and looked as if it would fall uncaught in the end zone.

Luther didn't need to leap or spring to reach the ball. Suddenly he was just there—his black face a good three feet higher than the distraught white ones looking up at him in disbelief. At that moment, with the players all frozen together in a portrait of triumph and defeat, Luther must have looked—to the Kelvin team—like the Black Angel of Death himself. They hung there for a moment, Luther's eyes ablaze with laughter, his white teeth flashing savagely. Then they all broke apart and tumbled to the ground, and the roaring from the stands broke over them.

As both teams lined up again for the kick-off, Torchy moved toward the sidelines, his limp worse than ever. Though only five minutes remained, now that the score was tied, not a spectator there doubted for a moment that we would go on to win the game. Standing at the bench and looking at his team-mates lining up, Torchy seemed a magician who had just worked a miraculous transformation. The fumbling rabble of players who had dragged out on to the field two hours before now looked like a company of young gods come to try their prowess on the fields of Olympus.

But that was when the Kelvin team began their incredible march down the field. It all started after the kick-off with the referee claiming that we had roughed the receiver. When Mittlehaus objected, he was promptly kicked out of the game for unsportsmanlike behaviour, and the team given an additional penalty of another ten yards. On the next play, Kelvin's pass was incomplete, but we got called for being off-side. A few minutes later, and they kicked a single point from our thirty-yard line.

After a moment of doubt and disbelief, a few cheers broke, halting and uncertain, from the River Heights stands. Yet almost immediately a feverish silence gripped the stadium, preventing even the outraged protests of the North End supporters from gathering momentum. Furiously, the St. John's team gathered about the ball. There were only two minutes left in the game, barely enough time to set matters right. Torchy began calling signals, the players snapped into formation, the ball was hiked, and now they were all in motion. Every line in their bodies, the practised way in which they moved, spoke of an assurance and competence toward which they'd been building throughout the game. The fullback slashed into the line. Three yards, maybe four. Again the players gathered about the ball and signals were barked. Ends criss-crossed over the goal line, players blocked, changed direction, faked. And then the fullback—on a delayed plunge—slashed into the line again. But the Kelvin players held as fast as the walls of Jericho before they finally came tumbling down. Five yards.

For the third down, Kelvin didn't even bother sending back receivers. The play began as another plunge, with the two lines clashing and then becoming still for a moment. Suddenly Torchy began fading back, arm raised to throw—as deadly as a cobra—while Luther burst into the open, shifted to his left, and raced downfield. Torchy waited till the last possible moment as the purple sweaters converged upon him; and then the ball was soaring free out of that jumble of players—as straight and true a pass as any receiver could hope for. Luther loped effortlessly toward where the ball would arc downward into his waiting hands, and we cheered with enough energy to split the stadium apart and bring the walls of that Philistine temple down upon our enemies' heads. And about us, the city shone as if made of molten glass—aflame in the radiance of the setting sun—gates garnished with pearls and gold and all manner of precious stones.

In the dazzled eyes of the frenzied North End fans, Luther, in his dented helmet, torn sweater and baggy pants, was already a figure of glory. But suddenly a look of alarm and disbelief crossed Luther's face as he was brought up short in his tracks, then pitched down, face forward, into the turf—his outstretched arms empty—the ball arcing downward to bound mockingly across the Kelvin goal line, just beyond his fingertips.

His own disbelief was mirrored in the faces of the fans. He had been upended, not by a Kelvin tackle, but by a pair of snapped suspenders which had suddenly catapulted his pants violently downward so that they now hung about his ankles. As the stands erupted in catcalls, laughter, boos and cheers, we glimpsed what looked like a white flag signalling defeat. And then the whistle blew to end the game.

It was right, I suppose, that we should have lost. Anything else would have been a lie. Afterwards, as we pushed and elbowed our way out the gates, we were only too aware of the outraged glances being directed at us by our teachers from across the field. While behind us, in a mighty crescendo of triumph, rose the voices from the River Heights stands:

Send him victorious,
Happy and glorious,
Long to reign over us,
God Save the King!

Those voices followed us right out of the stadium, and once out of high school, we fled in every possible direction. Marvin Zimmerman raced back to the General Hospital and eventually married one of those pretty nurses; Sam Margolis got his father to mortgage the house and send him to college in Los Angeles; Nate Samuelson, who planned to become a famous heart surgeon, actually entered Medical School; Marty Klein became a delivery man for a local dairy; Luther Johnson got taken on by the C.P.R. as a sleeping-car attendant; and Torchy Brownstone just dropped out of sight. As for Mr. Rockwood, the short, heavy-set English teacher who was the terror of Room 41, he was at last allowed to return to Kelvin—after his years of penance in the North End—but almost immediately he was forced into early retirement when he swatted a grade ten student he caught sneaking out to the drugstore on Academy Road. Most of the others—players, teachers, friends—I'm afraid I've lost sight of over the years. But often, when I'm least expecting it, a familiar face that really hasn't changed all that much will stare out at me from the eleven o'clock t.v. news, or from the society pages of the *Free Press*, or, even occasionally now as the years pass, from the obituary columns. When that happens, I fill in a little write-up of my own beneath a photograph I keep filed away in my memory.

But not only have familiar faces disappeared, familiar landmarks have vanished also, and during the last twenty-five years it has become more and more difficult to keep track of the city I once knew. The Royal Alexandra Hotel, where we held our graduation dance, is gone. Child's Restaurant at Portage and Main, where we'd all meet after a play or movie—no more. Even Osborne Stadium, where we played our football games, has vanished, replaced by a huge, expensive insurance company. Do the shouts of former high school battles ever echo within those heavy stone walls, I wonder, or have they been filed away, along with such names as Norm Mittlehaus, Nate Samuelson, Marvin Zimmerman and the rest, as insurance statistics in grey steel filing cabinets?

With the passage of time, the North End, too, has changed. So final has its defeat become that it has even had thrust upon it a suburb with such street names as Bluebell, Marigold, Primrose and Cherryhill. Over the years, that two-hundred-pound fullback has managed to race clear across the city to score a touchdown right here in our home territory. Now we also have our false Eden.

In an attempt to exact some small measure of revenge, I bought a house in River Heights a few years ago and let the lawn go to seed, allowed the back gate to fall off the hinges, let the torn screens on the veranda go unrepaired, and filled the garage and backyard with old furniture and junk from my grandmother's house. But even I know that this attempt to plant a bit of the North End in the heart of River Heights doesn't begin to restore the balance.

The only time we ever came close to holding our own—and, better still, maybe even winning—was that night years before when a lone figure with a hard whiplash voice and black hair falling into his eyes came limping on to the field for part of a football game. He was one of those figures who, at the time, are filed away in a special place in your memory and are then, unaccountably, forgotten—unless, awakened by some chance occurrence, they spring to life again.

It was just a few days ago, as I was passing a downtown parking lot early in the evening, that I heard a familiar voice barking out directions to some motorists who'd managed to snarl up traffic and block both exits at once. The dark figure of the uniformed attendant moved with a fluid grace that I was sure I had seen somewhere before. There was something familiar about that limp and the way he jerked his head to glance over the lot—like an athlete assessing a new and difficult situation. Back and forth he darted among the honking cars as he signalled some forward, others backward. Until, with a flair that—under the circumstances—was really quite surprising, he had managed to untangle them all.

In the darkness, as he started back toward the booth at the entrance to the parking lot, he seemed to merge with the figure that had limped along the sidelines of the stadium so many years ago and shouted encouragement to a grumbling rabble of players. That night, for almost thirty minutes, under the stadium lights, he had discovered to us all a grace and a strength that flashed electrically from one player to another. And then they were no longer a grumbling rabble of players. They became timeless, ancient, a group of immortals caught up in trials of strength that would never end, Greek athletes who had just come to life out of stone. That night, while we all watched in wonder, the city had flashed about us with sapphires and emeralds, jasper and amethysts. And how we had longed to believe that the city could stay like that forever.

Death of a Nation

Ernst Havemann

In my boyhood every small white boy on a farm in Natal had a black companion, an "umfaan." The umfaan was usually three or four years older than the white boy, so that he could take care of his charge and carry him piggyback when necessary. My umfaan was called Fakwes. His real name was Ukufakwezwe, "The Death of the Nation," because he was born at the time of an epidemic that killed a great many people, including his father.

He was ten or eleven when he came to work on my family's farm, which meant that he had had five or six years as a herdboy, spending all day every day in the veld with thc other boys of his family. He knew the name of every bird, every little animal, even every insect we came across, and he knew what one should do about each of them—which bees sting and which merely buzz, how to salute the praying mantis, and what to cry out to the nightjar when it suddenly flies up and then flops down invisible in deep shadow. (You say, "*Savalo, savalo,* milk for my people.")

We collected quails' eggs, flying ants and small white tubers and roasted them on the lid of a cast-iron pot. We hunted cane rats and lizards and helped herd the cattle. Sometimes we went with one of Fakwes' relatives to visit the native reserve adjoining the farm. We took salt, tobacco and matches as gifts, and perhaps a beer bottle of lard, liquid in the heat. We were received ceremoniously, like adults, and when Fakwes' grandfather took the tobacco, he invited us into his hut, which was very special because of his spears and his big oxhide shield.

An exciting thing happened on one of those visits. On our way home we heard a shout from very far away, then a louder one close by from a man high in a tall tree. He was shouting, "The goats are in the field!" In a moment we saw a boy scramble up the rocks to the top of a little hill and heard him scream, "The goats are in the field!" Fakwes ran to a big tree, climbed up and shouted the same words. Someone picked up the message, and we could hear it repeated from the next hilltop and then the next, far away.

"Where are the goats?" I demanded: "Shouldn't we run and chase them?"

"You will see the goats in a little while,"he said. "They will be riding horses and carrying revolvers."

Some time afterward—I think we had ridden more than a mile—the "goats" appeared. They were two policemen on horseback. Fakwes said that by the time they reached the kraals all the men who did not have passes or poll-tax receipts would be hiding in deep bush, together with all the unlicenced dogs.

"You have seen a secret thing," he said. "You must never speak of it." He knew that if he said it was secret I would not tell, just as I did not tell when we killed the prize rooster with our catapults. I never did tell, though I felt guilty and anxious whenever a policeman looked directly at me, in case he knew.

My first few school years were in a one-roomer a few miles from our place. I rode a pony to school; Fakwes walked or trotted alongside. Out of sight of adults we both rode, or Fakwes rode and I tried to keep up. When we reached the school, I went into the playground while Fakwes joined the other umfaans and the ponies in the school's field. The umfaans played games of guessing how many pebbles there were under which condensed-milk tin, breaking off to listen to our singing lessons. When we emerged, they would break into "John Peel" or "Land of Hope and Glory," rendering it loudly and perfectly but with a distinctive African flavour.

On the way home I regaled Fakwes with what I had learned that day. After lunch we usually went down to the reservoir to draw in the soft mud left by the receding water. (There must also have been times when the water was rising, but I don't remember them.) There were long, flat, absolutely smooth stretches of yellow ooze. Whatever one scratched on it stayed put while the mud dried and finally cracked into big flat pieces like gigantic slabs of chocolate. Fakwes drew bulls with enormous horns and genitals and cows with long teats. I drew faces and wrote letters. He laughed when I wrote FAKWES and said it was his name. In response he scratched zigzag lines and said they were my name, but after a while he took writing seriously and began to copy letters from my books. He was quicker and neater than I was. He wanted to write his whole, long, real name, but I could not cope with long words and we had to abandon it. He drew one of his fearsome bulls and said, "Let that be the writing for my name."

We had trouble with other Zulu words, because I did not know how to write the click sounds. The teacher said that Zulu was not made for writing, it was for savages, but by the time I left the one-roomer to go to Big School in the village, twenty miles away, Fakwes and I could both read the Zulu on the packets of baby formula at the trading store. It said that baby formula was better than milk.

Once I was at Big School, I saw Fakwes only when I came home on weekends. Though only fifteen or sixteen, he received a full man's wages, because he could read and write figures and work out piecework tasks and things like that. I brought him a Zulu New Testament, which was the only Zulu book I could find. He was ecstatic. "I shall be as clever as a preacher! I shall know all that he knows, from this Believer's book. But I will not be a Believer." He wrote me a careful letter of thanks in Zulu and signed it with one of his drawings of a bull.

The New Testament was full of place names—Nazareth, Bethlehem, Rome, Ephesus. But where were they? We went through my school atlas. What really gripped him in the atlas was England. He scoffed at the idea that such a small red patch could be England that had defeated the Zulus, the Boers and the Germans. His grandfather liked to tell how *his* father had fought at Isandhlwana, where the Zulus wiped out Lord Chelmsford's column, and at Ulundi, where the British broke the Zulus. The withered old man had a deep respect for British soldiers. "They were all heroes," he recounted. "They died without flinching. And they killed without flinching. Like Zulus." He enjoyed the little red-coated lead soldier I brought him, and attached it to the end of a spear.

Fakwes shared his grandfather's admiration for British soldiers but deeply resented settlers. "One day we will take back all this land," he declared. "We will burn the sugarcane and take the horses and cattle and sheep. The farmers will load their trucks and go, go to the south, away from us. I will be a great man in the council of chiefs, and I will live in Armstrong's house." Armstrong, the storekeeper, had a place in the East Indian-colonial style, with little turrets and fretwork lattices, painted what we called coolie pink. "On letters to friends I will draw a bull. And you, my brother"—he put his arm around me—"you will be our adviser. The great chiefs always had a white man to tell them the thoughts and deceits of the English. We will give you many wives and red Boer cattle with their horns swept back, and a little band of warriors to guard you and greet you with praises. Which house would you like?"

One weekend when I came home, Fakwes was not there. No one knew where he was, and the police were looking for him. A youth with whom he had quarrelled at a beerdrink had been found unconscious by the roadside, with a head wound. If he died, the police would probably charge Fakwes with murder. My father let it be known that we would arrange a lawyer if Fakwes turned himself in, but that proviso was unnecessary. The wounded youth recovered and refused to make a complaint—it was a fair fight, he said—and so no charge was recorded against Fakwes. Fakwes nevertheless stayed away. We heard rumours that he had been seen in Durban, and then in Cape Town. About a year after Fakwes disappeared, I received a card with a London postmark. It had a picture of a red-coated soldier. There was no message, only a drawing of a bull with big horns and genitals.

About five years ago I had a visit from Benny Miller. He was, and is, an undistinguished lawyer with a drinking problem. Most of his clients appeared to be shopkeepers charged with minor breaches of municipal bylaws, but he had also, surprisingly, appeared in two or three African political trials.

He phoned me one evening at my house. "I didn't want to be seen coming to your office," he said. "Your friends might think you were involved with one of my clients, and that wouldn't do, eh?"

"What do you want?" I snapped.

"I'm representing an old friend of yours. You may be able to help."

I agreed to see him, and within twenty minutes he arrived through the backyard servants' entrance. He was a plump, sallow man with curly grey hair and a practiced, self-deprecating smile. He accepted a drink, looked around the room and remarked, "Nice place you have here."

I waited, not concealing my dislike.

"Do you know a man called Mkize? Big fellow, around 40."

I could not recall a black acquaintance by that name.

"He says to tell you the goats are in the field."

"Oh, Fakwes!" I exclaimed. I had forgotten that his clan name was Mkize. "Fakwes. Sure. We grew up together, but I haven't seen him for years. Where is he?"

"In jail. Forged papers and possession of an offensive weapon. But that's just to hold him until they get to the red meat. I think the prosecution is after conspiracy or sabotage or worse. He was abroad a long time and he speaks fluent Portuguese and French."

"French! Fakwes speaks French?"

"Quite educated French, as far as I can judge. He seems to have got around."

"Portuguese and French, eh?" I could not believe it. "Well, how can I help?"

"Perhaps you can't help at all. But if there's no concrete evidence against him, just suspicion, then they might go for detention without trial. In that case character evidence may ease his lot. Someone like you—upright, prosperous, right-wing—could carry weight, perhaps pull a string or two. I understand you have friends in government circles. Well, we all have our weaknesses. I should warn you, though, a dossier is bound to be opened for anyone who's connected with him."

"I'll think it over," I said.

He took it as a refusal. "I don't blame you. Things are never quite the same once you've been mixed up in one of these affairs."

"I'm not mixed up in anything," I protested.

"No? Consider this: you're a friend of a subversive character. He sent you a coded message through me, which you obviously understood. Perhaps on your trips abroad you stopped over in Nairobi or Lourenço Marques or Marseilles, where he also happened, just happened, to be at the same time. Adds up. So you're probably wise to turn your back. Boyhood pals across the colour line is one thing—touching, in fact—but in adults it's suspicious."

He rose to go, putting his glass down noisily. I held it up and looked inquiringly.

"I thought you'd never ask," he said, sitting down.

"Can I see Fakwes?"

"How naïve can you get!" He threw up his hands. "The man doesn't say 'Can I see the accused?'—or Mkize, or anything like that. No! He uses some kind of pet nickname! How do you suppose you would sound in court? What does it mean, anyway?"

"Fakwes is short for Ukufakwezwe."

"I see. Does Uku-whatever mean anything?"

"It means 'The Death of the Nation.'"

"Christ!" he exclaimed. "Imagine what a prosecutor could make of that in a subversion case! Imagine. The Death of the bloody Nation! 'And which nation were you planning the death of, Mr. Mkize?'"

"Can I see him?" I repeated impatiently.

"I wouldn't advise it," he said seriously. "It would tar you a bit. In case you change your mind, I'd prefer you to stay remote. It would be better for you, too."

"Can I do anything else? Clothes, cigarettes, money? Your fees?"

"Since you ask, since you ask, I'll tell you. I earn my living helping small businessmen who make mistakes. Clients like your friend usually don't have a penny. I handle them *pro deo*. Naturally, I try to avoid incurring expenses. But even so, there's stationery and postage and official fees. And tobacco for the poor bastards. I try to look after things like that, and perhaps get a wife in from the country to see her husband for the last time. It costs. Of course, it's a mitzvah." He assumed a mock Yiddish manner and spread his palms. "You know vot is a mitzvah? A credit up there." He jerked a thumb at the ceiling. "Mitzvahs I got like Job had boils. But can you mit a mitzvah buy a bottle visky?" He reverted to normal. "You stock an excellent spirit, by the way. Not like some cheapskates, who put away the Black Label and bring out the Japanese when they see me coming."

I refilled his glass and took out my wallet. I like to carry a reasonable amount of cash, and that afternoon I had drawn an extra sum because my wife and I were going to the races the next day. There were always races in Durban on Wednesday afternoons. I took all there was in the wallet and gave it to Benny Miller without counting it.

He weighed it in his palm. "I wish I had a boyhood chum like you," he said. "It's understood that this is an unconditional gift? I use it as I choose, and I don't account for it?"

"I don't know what happened to the money," I replied. "It must have slipped out of my hip pocket in the street when I was tying my shoelace."

He put the money in his pocket. "Okay. But remember what I've said. Once you've done something like this, things are never quite the same. As the rabbi says, one mitzvah leads to another." He drained his glass and left.

My wife was horrified when I told her what had occurred.

"You've always told me of your wonderful Zulu friend, the David to your Jonathan," she jeered. "And now, when he might be in jail for the rest of his life and you might get a chance to speak for him, you'll think it over. Think it over! I'm ashamed."

"You'd be more than ashamed if the police came and turned the house inside out, looking for God knows what," I retorted.

I kept telling myself that I didn't owe Fakwes that much. I would have owed him if he had been just an ordinary, or even a rather special, black man, like those I met on the Bantu Welfare Committee. With his brains and a bit of help he could have got more education and perhaps become a teacher, or my head clerk, which would pay better. We would have remained friends. He would come to dinner from time to time. My European friends would recognize that they were being given a special treat if they were invited when he and his wife came. But as it was.... He had nearly killed that youth years ago, and now it seemed he wanted to take the land back from the settlers. Fancy his learning French! I wondered what he looked like. Was he the same person that I had known 25 years ago? I was guiltily certain that if I were a fugitive, he would risk his life for me. Or would he? Several kids with whom I had been friendly at school were now only distant acquaintances, whom I might see at Rotary but not otherwise.

At the races the next day my wife ostentatiously put all her money on Bosom Friend at 50 to one and won. Someone assured us that Beesknees was a certainty for the main race. I backed him without excitement. Fakwes and I used to rob wild bees' nests. We got up early, because in the cold dawn bees huddle together, more or less inactive. We collected twigs and leaves, made a smoky fire and blew smoke into the nest, which was usually a hole in the ground or in a hollow tree. The smoke stupefied the bees, Fakwes always made me stand some distance away while he chopped and dug to get at the honeycombs. He was often stung. I was occasionally stung too, but I learned not to cry out: one of Fakwes' rules was that one was never allowed to cry for pain. I was always the one who carried the honey home, like a conquering hero, while Fakwes stood by, waving an insect-repellent herb and describing how we had located the nest by following the flight of bees from a flowering tree or by listening to the bee-eater. The bee-eater has a very pronounced swallow tail and....

"Wake up, dreamy Daniel!" My wife shook my elbow. "When you come to the races, you're supposed to care which horse wins." She pointed to the board flashing BEESKNEES 12-1. He had won by three lengths.

The next day I phoned Benny Miller. As soon as he heard my voice he said, "I'll ring back" and put down the receiver. Ten minutes later he called from a pay phone.

"My office phone is tapped," he explained. "What's on your mind?"

"I've decided I will be available as a character witness, or do whatever else you think may help."

"Congratulations. Or perhaps you're psychic. Your friend escaped from custody last night. There is the usual loose talk about venal guards. Anyway, I don't suppose you'll see your pal again unless you rendezvous abroad. Well, so long."

About a month afterward I received a postcard from Spain. It showed a black bull, its shoulder bristling with lances, kneeling on a bullfighter. That was all. No message, just the wounded black bull triumphing over its adversary. I burned the card. It is not the sort of thing one wants to keep around.

Benny Miller was in the news a couple of times during the next year. A technicality saved him from conviction on a charge of corrupting a Customs officer, and he was knocked down the court-house steps by women protesting against his defense of a black girl who had organized a union of nursemaids.

He called me soon after my return from a visit to Europe. He spoke from a phone booth. "Did you have a good trip? See all the old friends you wanted to see? Look, a fund you know of has developed a deficit like the national debt. Would you care to perpetrate a mitzvah?"

We met in a bar. We did not drink together or greet each other, but he picked up an envelope that I left on the counter.

Eight or nine months later he phoned again, soon after the African bus riots. "Miller here. I'm sure you know why I'm calling."

I hesitated, and he said urgently, "Look, man, the bloody goats are in the field, man."

"Okay," I said. "The Four Seasons bar. Tomorrow at six."

"Bless you," he responded. "Thank God for boyhood chums, eh?"

He phones once or twice every year. He now announces himself as "Benjamin" (that is what his friends call him, he explains) and always asks what news I have from abroad. I always answer "Nothing," but he enjoys teasing me with the suggestion that I am connected with an underground movement. I inquire after his health and may refer to a trial in which he is appearing. Then I mention goats, and he makes a little joke about my accumulation of credits "up there." A good act qualifies as a credit even if it is not entirely voluntary, he says.

In a War

Mavis Gallant

When Lily Quale was fourteen, stockings were hard to come by, because we were in a war and factories were dressing soldiers. She coloured her bare legs with pancake makeup, some of which always rubbed off on the edge of her skirt. Recently she had taken up with a Polish girl, a few years older, twice expelled from convent schools. She taught Lily how to draw a fake seam with eyebrow pencil and explained a few other matters usually left obscure in Catholic Quebec.

Lily's mother showed a cold face to the girl who knew such a lot. She didn't think well of me, either, although I knew hardly anything that might interest Lily.

"You and Lily are too big to be natural company for each other now," her mother said one Saturday afternoon, when Lily and I were sitting in the Quales' kitchen, on the excuse of doing homework. I was a year ahead, writing an essay on how railways helped the Industrial Revolution, while Lily tried to disentangle the reasons for the American Civil War. We barely knew that Canada had a history. "She ought to be with a girl her own age," Mrs. Quale went on, "and you, Steve, you'd be better off with another boy. And I don't want the two of you going upstairs to study in Leo's room unless I'm in the house."

That was how adults saw things then: simply. Catholic-Protestant stories, all bad luck, lay strewn around us, the rocks and bricks of separation. Why let anything go too far between two kids who were bound to separate? The town we lived in straggled along both sides of the Châtelroux River. There was no core to the place except a huddle of stores around the French church, with its aluminum-painted roof and spire. The Quales were in bungalow territory, Catholic and English-speaking—everyone's minority. The last thing they looked for was trouble. My aunt had a house on the opposite shore, facing the river. We had a dock and a rowboat and a canoe. We had French-Canadian neighbors, working a strip farm, and English-Canadian acquaintances living in houses like ours, farther down the road, toward the bridge and railway station. We had a wide lawn and an enclosed back yard, and a low hedge of shrubs with red berries, and a covered gallery running around three sides of the house. We did not keep a cat, because my aunt thought cats were hypocrites, and we gave up keeping a dog after Snowy drowned and Rex was poisoned. My parents were Anglican missionaries in China; my Aunt Elspeth was bringing me up.

I knew even then that Mrs. Quale was mistaken about Lily. She could never have wanted a close girlfriend. The Polish chum was just a handbook she studied for expertise. Lily kept a large pond stocked with social possibilities, nearly all boys, and thought nothing of calling me on a Saturday if some other happy chance had let her down. My aunt, hearing my end of the negotiation, would dub me a human jellyfish; but one of the things adults forget is how complete younger people seem to one another, how individual and clearly defined. It is the grown person who looks evasive and blurry, who needs to improvise. Lily to me was without shadow: I took it for granted she worked her arrangements with hook and reel. My easygoing response was more toughly snobbish, and so more injurious to Lily, than my aunt could guess. Probably, I thought well of myself for letting Leo Quale's little sister get away with murder.

Before that time, when I was still in seventh grade—in those days known as Junior Fourth—my aunt remarked that it would be good for someone like me, raised by a woman, to have a stalwart figure of some kind to look up to. I thought about Lily, and the scale of her nerve, and how she learned the uses of gall from watching her brother Leo, and I said, "You mean like Leo Quale?"

"Leo has certain qualities," said my aunt, as if he had barely escaped hanging. "It was more a gentleman I had in mind—say, like Mr. Coleman."

She was defining a stage of growth as well as a caste. It is true that at fifteen Leo was too advanced to make a friend of me, but he was still too immature to offer paternal advice about sexual prudence and financial restraint. (My aunt actually believed fathers can do this.) She began to think well of him later that year, after running out of other models for me. To my aunt the male nature was expected to combine the qualities of an Anglo-Canadian bank manager and a British war poet, which means to say a dead one. Folded inside the masculine psyche there had to be a bright yearning to suffocate face down in a flooded trench, to bleed from wounds inflicted by England's enemies, even to be done in by a septic flea bite, if a patriotic case could be made against the flea.

Leo showed that eagerness to perish: enlist, ship overseas, never be heard from again. He was heavy and blond, a kind of Viking, one of the thick ones, out of dark small parents, Glasgow Irish on both sides. It had taken him six years to flounder through his last three grades, and he was now becalmed in eighth. He could read, he could even work complicated sums in his head, but he could not write a complete sentence. My aunt blamed his school, which also happened to be mine: Leo should have had Catholic teachers. All these years he had felt bewildered, unwanted, could not focus his intelligence. A memory of Leo—placid, sleepy, too big for his desk—stands next to my aunt's appraisal.

After school and all day Saturday he delivered groceries to English customers, on both sides of the river. Sometimes he made four or five trips along the same street—particularly Fridays, when there was a rush on beer. Quebec was the only part of Canada where beer could be sold by a grocer, instead of in a government liquor store. We owed the privilege to the twists and snarls of Catholic morality, said my aunt, who drank only sherry.

Leo and my aunt were expecting a war, well ahead of world leaders. "Ah, it'll come, all right," he would assure her, lowering a box of provisions from his shoulder to the kitchen table. "And we'll be in it. Don't you worry, Mrs. Cope. We need a good old war to sort us out."

"I'm afraid you're right, Leo. War brings out the best in men and nations, but we have to remember the fallen and the missing, and sometimes there is injustice, too."

"It's them or us," said Leo. "England forever!" He sounded a bit crazy. He couldn't have heard it at home: his father hated the English.

What did my aunt mean by "missing," I used to wonder. How did you know you were missed? I had never missed my parents, and their letters showed no longing to see me but simply told me to be good. People in Châtelroux, when they talked about the last war or the next, said, "You've got to die sometime." In St. George's Anglican Church my aunt and I droned in unison that we believed in the resurrection of the body, though common evidence spoke against such a thing. Leo may have seen a brief future in the Army as an improvement over the immediate prospect, stuck in a classroom where he was a head taller than his teacher. Perhaps he was just exercising his native talent for saying whatever might appeal. He once boasted to my aunt that, at thirteen, he had tried to join the Mac-Paps—the Mackenzie-Papineau Battalion, the Canadians fighting Franco. It was no more preposterous than his father's claim to have played rugby for Ireland: Mr. Quale was built like a jockey and had never been outside Quebec.

You expected people like the Quales to be undersized. They descended from immigrants known to other British incomers as "Glasgow runts." The term has vanished: it takes only two generations, no time in real time, to acquire strong teeth and large hands and feet and a long backbone. Only aversions and fears, the stuff of racial memory, are handed down intact.

To recall the Quales around their supper table, with the radio turned right up, three or four saucepans bubbling on the stove, everyone eating something different, Mr. Quale yelling back at the radio during the news broadcast, laying down the law on England, or Quebec politics, or the Spanish Loyalists ("Every last man a louse" did for them all) is to see in deep perspective the Gorbals of Glasgow, where their parents had started out, and farther away, thin on the horizon, the trampling of Ireland. Mr. and Mrs. Quale belong to the first race of Irish, black-haired, driven underground, their great gods shrunk to leprechauns. Leo is the Norse marauder, hopelessly astray in the dark. Lily seems delicate, at least to the eye, with pale fine hair: a recent prototype, if you count in centuries.

Weekdays Mr. Quale got up at five and took the train to Montreal, where he was a plainclothes officer on the police force. He did not know French but could cause the arrest of people who did not understand English. Usually he came back in the middle of the afternoon and sat on a bench outside the railway station reading the Montreal *Star* until about five, the Quales' suppertime. Their neighbors said Old Lady Quale gave him no peace to read the crime news at home. She thought a husband was supposed to keep moving, emptying the water pan under the icebox, examining for short circuits the loops of wiring that hung in fronds all over the house.

She had eyes that were fierce and round, and with her flat face and little beaked nose made me think of an owl. She screamed at children who walked on her lumpy, dried-up flower beds, at drivers who parked delivery vans in front of her door; but there were days on end when she had nothing to say, and peered out of some private darkness to the light. Then, all at once normal again, in whatever degree any Quale normality could amount to, she would start to predict the family future. It was as if she had been granted a vision during her silent trance. Lily was going to be in trouble at an early age. ("In trouble" meant unmarried and pregnant. As Lily was believed not to know how pregnancy started, the prophecy had to be left to drift, like a canoe with nobody in it.) Leo could expect a career of panhandling in downtown Montreal. Mr. Quale was sure to be fired from the police force, for inertia, while Mrs. Quale was promised an old age of taking in washing.

Hearing it, the children went on eating their supper, unmoved. Family conversation usually slanted in a single direction. "You'll see I was right!" and "Believe you me, one day you'll wish you'd listened!" and the shadowy, the mysterious "Remember me when the time comes." Unlike most parents on their street, the Quales did not beat their children, but they kept saying they ought to, and that the kids were asking for it. Any day now Mrs. Quale would take the broom to them and Mr. Quale start swinging the buckle end of his belt. Leo believed it might happen, though he could have knocked his father down with a shove; Lily, who was intelligent, did not.

Mr. Mitchell Coleman, elected by my aunt to be an example for me, had to resign from the prep school in Montreal where he taught English and art. She passed on the news in a cluster of baffling remarks: it was a great shock to his friends, he had betrayed a trust, he had to live with his conscience, only God could judge, and he would never set foot here again.

I thought he had pilfered something. It was the worst I could imagine as adult bad behavior. My aunt had a friend who borrowed small objects. (We never said "stole.") Her husband would go through her handbag at night and find an ivory carving, a butter knife, a china soap dish. I was not expected to have opinions about grown people. Once, I had imitated Mr. Coleman's way of standing in front of a bookcase, reading titles in an undertone, and my aunt had reproached me for mocking a man of moral worth, whose very friendship confirmed our own decency. Now she was in a close predicament, needing to let me know he had fallen and at once describing and concealing the nature of the fall.

Dilemmas of upbringing were often referred to my father, whose delayed seaborne answer was likely to be "Have it out with him." Having it out terrified her. She gave me a glass of ginger ale and three squares of cocoa fudge on a bread plate and made me sit down in the parlor, facing her but at a distance. I ate the fudge, then the crumbs. Meanwhile she said that Mr. Coleman's badness was an example of reality. Until now, "reality" had meant having no money. In her way she was as deft at dealing out a bleak future as any parent across the river. Poverty and high principle seemed to occupy the same terrain—to my mind, a vacant lot. I knew some of the discourse by heart: my father was unlikely to amass any capital out in China; one day I might have nothing to fall back on but a clean reputation. Better to run out of worldly goods than the world's good opinion, she said, never having been faced with the choice.

What was she trying to tell me? She knew, but wished she had a man there to take over the notes and deliver the lecture. It was for my benefit that she invited so many inspirational male figures to meals. Her generation of women attached no secondary meaning to "confirmed bachelor" or "not the marrying kind." Some men got along without a wife. English novels were full of them. Occasionally one of those bluff and taciturn heroes got tired of eating cold suppers and let himself be overtaken by a fresh-faced, no-nonsense country girl. That was fiction: in the real world homosexuality was a criminal offense, liable to a sentence in a penitentiary. For that reason, scores of thoroughly unmarriageable men had to let themselves be seen as a catch, without getting caught. My aunt was a social godsend, for she was attractive and kind, a widow who did not want to remarry ("Steven wouldn't like it"), and, apparently, bleached of desire. At least, she sent none of those coded messages over the female telegraph, meant to be deciphered only by selected men. Or, perhaps she sent explicit signals and was puzzled because no answer came. Or, owing to the amazing boundlessness of ambiguity, may have received more replies than anyone guessed.

At the time I am telling about, she was calm and cheerful, wore her glossy hair parted in the middle, had a supply of single acquaintances described as brainy, therefore harmless, masculine by denomination and ego, willing to take the train or drive down from Montreal, receive one glass of dark sherry, eat a well-done roast and Yorkshire pudding, and put up with me.

Boyd McAllister arrived in a roadster that had the shine and colour of a new chestnut. I climbed into the rumble seat, by way of a step the size of a piano pedal, and he took me for a spin along the river. My aunt shamed me by calling, "Don't fall in!" Ray Archer turned up slightly drunk, wearing a kilt, and got just his food: no sherry. Later, my aunt said he had no right to a clan tartan, not even on his mother's side. Herbie Dunn, just back from London, had seen Jack Buchanan singing and dancing, wearing a top hat. He gave my aunt a Buchanan record, "I'm in a Dancing Mood." We played it on the gramophone and he showed us some steps.

"Now, Steven, watch Mr. Dunn," my aunt said, as if this, too, were part of a virile education.

But the pleasures of adults are unbecoming. I looked out the parlor window, to the road and the river. More people walked than drove. There were French-Canadian boys dressed for Sunday, stiff and buttoned-up, and a few Anglos throwing sticks for their dogs. The English had on comfortable weekend clothes. To the French, they looked like hand-me-downs. "If you didn't know who they were, you'd hand them a nickel," our farmer neighbor once said. The river was the colour of thin maple syrup. On the far side, in a spread of bungalows, was my Protestant school and the deep Catholic mystery of Lily and Leo.

In those days people owned just a few clothes, no more than they needed. A garment was part of one's singularity. Our teachers put on the same things day after day—the same dress, the same shoes, the same crumpled suit. Leo *was* his plaid shirt and navy-blue sweater, Lily her red coat and knitted leggings. She pulled the leggings off when she got to school, revealing white cotton stockings, and draped them over the radiator, along with other snowy outfits. We were four grades to a room; the smell of the class was of wool drying. Whenever Lily tore her white stockings or got them dirty her crazy mother would scream, "I'll whip you, Lily Quale, I swear to God!", but Lily took no notice.

Mitchell Coleman came to Sunday dinner in blazer and flannels, a white shirt, and a striped tie, gray and maroon. He probably had been cautioned from childhood to be neat and clean, even where it didn't show, in case he got knocked down by a streetcar and had to be carried to the Royal Victoria Hospital and undressed by strangers. With his exactly combed sandy hair, his jacket and trousers uncreased even after a train ride, he was ready for every kind of accident except the one he ran into.

I make him sound set and congealed, but he was in his early twenties, a local poet of the schoolmaster breed. He offered my aunt stapled, mimeographed editions of his work—long spans of verse in which Canada sprawled forbiddingly (nothing enticing about the national posture) between two bleak alternatives, the United States and the frozen North. I realize now that he was an early nationalist, a term that would have been as meaningless to my aunt as "reality" was to me. Her Canada was a satellite planet, reflecting the fire of English wars, English kings and queens, English habits and ways. My uncle had been killed at Ypres. The men she summoned to dinner matched in age the young officer in the sepia photograph in her bedroom.

Alone with me, in mock after-dinner conversation, Mr. Coleman looked elderly and oppressive. My aunt would leave us so that he could tell me about ideals heritable by men—apparently a richer legacy than any endowed on women. I could hear her in the dining room, clearing the table. She would not come to my rescue until it was time for Mr. Coleman to catch a train back to Montreal. He lived in a two-room apartment in the basement of a stone house on Bishop Street. His windows were just under the ceiling: looking up, he could watch the boots and shoes of strangers going by. It cost him twenty-two dollars a month, which my aunt said was high. That was all we knew about his private arrangements.

The instant she left the room he would stand up, facing the bookcase, with his back to me.

"Read Dickens?"

"Aunt Elspeth reads '*A Christmas Carol*.'"

"Aloud, at Christmas?"

"Yes, sir."

"Read Kipling?"

"When we have to."

"At school?"

"Yes, sir."

"You've read the Henty books, I suppose?"

"We've got some that used to belong to my uncle."

"Good. They're good stuff. Read any poetry?"

"When we have to."

"What do they make you read? British? American? Any Canadian?"

"I wouldn't know, sir."

He told my aunt that bringing civilization to children was like throwing rose petals at a moving target.

"Some of the petals stick," she said. "I'm sure some do." She looked at me, as if wishing I would stop dodging.

If optimism is the prime requirement for teaching, she was a born educator. Mr. Coleman seemed to attract defeat and may have been in the wrong line altogether, on several counts. For one thing, whatever the scope of his personal adventures, he absolutely hated small boys. But when my aunt unfolded his disgrace, or thought she had, small boys were on her mind. She wanted to know if he had ever made a clear, coarse suggestion while standing in her parlor, reeling off names of authors. I did not know what she was getting at, and was merely thankful to hear he was never coming back. Her assurance that his failure was God's business meant that one more fragment of disorder had been added to the mess in Heaven.

"It may be for the best that it has come to light," she said, encouraging me to speak up. It was her second attempt, after the dead try over cocoa fudge. This time I was pushing a lawnmower around the back yard, earning my allowance. She sat on the back step, on a straw cushion usually kept in the hammock.

"Are you just as glad?"

"What about?"

"About not having to see Mitchell Coleman anymore."

I was just as glad, which condemned him. On his last visit he had sneered at her taste in books.

"She's reading Depression novels," he had said. "And now this thing." He pulled it off the shelf. "'*The Case of Sergeant Grischa*.' Not a lady's book. I'd like to know how it got here, right next to"—he paused to make certain—"'*To the Lighthouse*.'"

"Leo Quale read it," I said. "He says it's the best book anybody ever wrote."

"Do you know what it's about?"

"Yes. He told me. They shoot him."

"Your friend Leo?"

"No, the sergeant. He's supposed to be a deserter, so they shoot him."

"Don't take it to heart. It's only a story. Most of us die in bed."

He sounded simpler, easier—too late. My side of the exchange closed down. It was all right with me if we hated each other, as long as my aunt didn't know.

Better a reticent kid than one suddenly cold. He sensed the change—he was not a teacher for nothing—and began to speak at random, as if we shared the same tastes and the same age: "Arnold Zweig. I wonder if he and that other Zweig are brothers, like the two Manns." Did he really think I could tell him? "She's read it, too, " he said, showing me how the book fell open in his hands.

Later on, I discovered it opened to passages that my aunt, or Leo, may have liked in particular. The core of her mind, or Leo's, contained more anxiety than anyone guessed. One of the two had lingered over the short truth that death means dying. Only someone with great denseness of spirit needs to be reminded, so I suppose the steady reader to have been Leo.

Released from eighth grade, Leo became free to carry groceries full time. He set a box down in our kitchen and made the remark that we seemed to live on cereal. His habit of uttering one pointless thing after the other had my aunt believing he had plenty to say but lacked a sense of direction.

"Your parents must be paying Catholic-school tax, Leo," she said to him. "Why weren't you in a Catholic school?"

"You have to take a bus. My sister Lily pukes in buses."

"There are two Catholic schools here in the town."

"They're both French."

"What of it? It isn't too late for Lily to change. She could learn French, and she'd be with her own kind. We often see the little Chartrand girls going by, wearing their uniforms. They look so sweet, all in black."

Leo stared at the demented lady who did not know there were Catholics and Catholics. He made a stab at saner conversation, and asked if this was an old house.

"Fairly old," said my aunt, smiling. She did not want to make the tenant of a raw bungalow feel ill at ease.

"About a hundred years?"

"Perhaps more."

"Did you always live here?"

"It was a summer home," said my aunt. "But when I had Steven—I mean when Steven came to stay with me—I decided to bring him up in a house instead of an apartment."

"We move a lot," he said—I think with pride.

The Quales were not rich or poor enough to stay put. They kept packing and unpacking their bedsteads and their chamber pots and the family washtub. Each move was decided for the better, but they still had to pump cold water and cross a back yard to a privy. There was the same glassed-in cube of a veranda around the front door and storm porch at the back. The storm porch, a storage shed made of unpainted planks, was meant for brooms and pails, old newspapers, overshoes, rubber boots, stray scarves and mittens, jam jars without lids, hockey sticks. It was the place where the Quales shed snow from their outdoor clothes and where Leo sat down on a broken chair to take off his skates.

Sometimes when he got up in the morning, Mr. Quale would find a hobo sleeping on the floor, under a strip of carpet. "God alone keeps tramps from freezing to death," he would say aloud, as he heated the rest of last night's soup for the man. No one was ever turned away: the magic of retribution could transform any working man into a vagrant. While the stranger drank his soup, Mr. Quale pretended to sort newspapers, so he wouldn't make off with the bowl. If Lily came out, with her nightgown stuffed inside her woollen leggings, and her coat around her shoulders, on her way to the privy, Mr. Quale would order her back to her room until the man had disappeared. Sitting on the edge of her bed, she could hear them exchanging neutral opinions about good and bad times. The only thing Mr. Quale ever offered, other than soup, was a pair of old skates that hung by their tied laces from a rusty nail.

"Can you use these skates?" he would ask.

"I don't think so. Thanks all the same."

In every Châtelroux household there were skates that seemed to have arrived on their own, and that no one could wear. Ours were attached to the lock of a shutter. Every so often my aunt unhooked the skates and examined them. "Steven, are you sure they aren't yours?"

"They're miles too big."

"Well, they certainly don't belong to me."

"Somebody must have left them behind."

"I suppose so. I wish he'd come and take them back."

She tried to fob them off on Leo. He took one look and said, "Gurruls'."

"Girls' skates, Leo? Are you sure? Perhaps your mother could try wearing them, or Lily. Lily would have to grow into them, of course."

"Lily doesn't wear black skates. Only white."

Another day, she tried to get him to take home an assortment of piano scores, and seemed astonished to hear the Quales had no piano.

"Why not, Leo? Don't you like music?"

"My dad likes that Gershwing," he said, after a pause.

It is the only time I can ever remember my aunt's seeming foolish to me. She was pink in the face, ready to lead him by the hand through Gershwin to Bach. I bring to mind her flushed forehead and the excitement in the room, tension I was still too young to be able to measure, generated by the presence of the town dunce, unteachable and dying to go to war. Mr. Coleman had been right about her reading; Leo entered her imagination on the same wave as the Depression. For a while she decided the poor were to be joined, or imitated, rather than tided over. Leo was not offended; he did not know he was poor. The Quales were better off than most of their neighbors.

My aunt began to say that a taste of family life, of the warm, untidy kind that Leo surely enjoyed, might be good for me. She often sent me to the Quales' house with a grocery list for Leo, when she could as easily have called the store. A sheltered boy had much to learn from a brave, older boy already making his own way, she said; but all I learned, tagging after someone too big and too different, was that I had it in me to resent my aunt. I couldn't hate her. She wasn't a mean woman, not even strict by nature. She was trying to make up for the absence of a man's firm guidance.

Their family life seemed to me fierce and mournful. Between Leo and his mother lay something cold, like cold poison. On one of her dark days I watched Mrs. Quale putting Leo's plaid shirt through the hand wringer, clamped on the edge of the sink.

"On top of that," she said, perhaps to herself, not to me, "he had to take his time getting born. Arse first, as if he had all the leisure in the world. In no hurry. Didn't care about *me*. They said, 'Come on, Mrs. Q., make an effort, you don't want him to strangle.' He was blue in the face, when they finally saw he had a face. Didn't get oxygen. That's why. No oxygen. Nurse said, 'So don't be surprised if he stays pretty dim from the neck up.'"

Pursuing his cultural awakening, my aunt led Leo past the dining room, where he stopped to stare at an engraved portrait of Sir Walter Scott, but before he could ask who it was, and his age, she ushered him through to the parlor, showed him books, and said, "You may borrow anything."

His hand went straight to "*The Case of Sergeant Grischa,*" which he may have taken to be a detective story. He kept it, I think, about three months, returned it, then asked to have it again.

Much later, Lily told me about the first time he brought the book to supper and propped it in front of his plate. He had been reading it some five weeks.

"What're you wasting time on now?" said his mother.

"Let the boy read," said Mr. Quale. "It's education."

Mrs. Quale had nothing against that. She believed in education but was not sure how it was obtained.

"Well, what is it?" said Mr. Quale. "Answer your mother when she speaks to you."

"Book I borrowed from Mrs. Cope."

"Take it back," his father said. "They'll be saying you stole it."

"Tell me, Leo," said Lily. "Tell me what it's about." She was so crazy about reading that she read the stuff on calendars. "I'll read to you, Leo. I've finished eating. Do you want me to read to you?"

Lily was the favorite: they didn't mind letting her read. When she could not pronounce a word, she skipped the whole line. The radio news, tuned to the pitch of Mrs. Quale's voice when she raised it, ran alongside Lily's tone, which was soft and unsteady. Mrs. Quale soon grew sick and tired of hearing Lily, and she could not figure out what sort of army the sergeant belonged to. Mr. Quale became impatient, too. He shouted that in his day deserters were stood up and shot, and that was the end of it. They didn't drag their existence on for dozens of pages. Mrs. Quale said it would do Leo a lot more good if he read to Lily. They did try it that way, several evenings, but he didn't enjoy it, and for the others he was too slow. He finally finished the book, on his own, and was the only one in the family who knew the deserter was stood up and shot.

Leo had his tonsils and adenoids out and walked home an hour later, bleeding into a towel. His small mother was with him, holding on to his sleeve. The cuts became infected, and he nearly died. When he was said to be out of danger, my aunt made me go and see him. She sent two jars of grape jelly, wrapped in leftover Christmas paper, and a note of encouragement, signed, "(Mrs.) Elizabeth B. Cope."

My first surprise was that they were humbly glad to see me—the shrimpy parents, and Lily, wearing just her petticoat, her hair all suds. (Rumor had it that Catholics never washed.)

"Get some clothes on you," her father said. "There's company."

Leo was getting royal treatment, propped up in his parents' double bed with an embroidered pillow stuffed behind his neck. A number of unsorted social facts were shed from my person as I accepted his invitation to sit down at the foot of the bed.

He said, "Well, sport," in a husky whisper, and moved his legs to allow me more room. I hardly dared look at him—I was not sure how to deal with my advancement to family friend—and stared instead at the pattern of daisies and asters on the pillow case. On a table next to the bed was a white enamel basin with a towel over it. He said they were giving him emetics, so he would throw up the rest of the infection.

"Well, sport," he said again, meaning, I think, that extra conversation was up to me. The room was dark, ferociously heated by a kerosene stove. A stylized design of birch leaves, or sunflower petals, had been carved in the stove lid, to serve as vents. The heat and brilliance of the flame had turned the stove into a magic lantern: the whole ceiling was covered with ornamentation, hugely magnified, in quivering red and blue. Lily came in and sat down, combing her wet hair. She had buttoned on a gray cardigan belonging to her father, which fitted her like a coat. She said, "You're fine, Leo," because she still thought he might be dying.

Leo changed the position of his feet. I took it for a hint and got straight off the bed. He said, "Come again, sport," and that rounded off the visit.

In March he put his clothes on, and found that everything he owned was short in the legs and sleeves. He had to duck under the frame doorway between the kitchen and storm porch. He did not return to work at once but did odd jobs around the house, getting his strength back. My aunt had a new delivery boy, Doug Bagshaw. He kept his tips, coppers and nickels, in a baking-powder tin. He liked to weigh the tin in his hand and make the coins jingle. My aunt did not try to draw him out, and never once said he or the Bagshaws might be good for me. When she referred to the old days, before Leo was taken so ill, it was to mention Herbie Dunn and his kind gift of the Jack Buchanan record. She recalled other Buchanan songs—"Two Little Bluebirds" and "A Cup of Coffee, a Sandwich, and You"—which she hummed for me. Buchanan was so tall, and his top hat made him so much taller, that he had trouble finding suitable dance partners. Saying this, she drew herself up, even straighter than before.

"I'm the general, you can be Grischa, the rest of you are soldiers." That was Lily, marshalling her troops of little girls on the soggy spring lawn. There had been a freeze, then a thaw, then a new fall of spring snow. The game was a mixture of hide-and-seek and tag, with two teams drawn up, as in red rover or run sheep run. Anyone on the wrong side, the army that wasn't Lily's, could be shot on sight. "Grischa" was leader of a team, the equivalent of being a general. The victims lay down and got their coats wet.

Leo had been sweeping the front walk. Now he stood leaning on his broom, eating jujubes out of a paper bag. There was only one other boy, Vince Whitton, aged six. His sister, Beryl, wasn't allowed to play in the street unless she agreed to take him with her.

Vince said, "One other time, I was over here and some person gave us some jujubes," but Leo never made a move.

My aunt had sent me across the river after school to find out if Leo was ever going to work for the grocer again; it would be her last show of interest in the Quales. I stood, neither claimed nor discarded, doing nothing in particular, watching Lily in her red coat.

Just then Mr. Quale came along the street and up the walk Leo had cleared of snow. He wore a wool cap and a long gray scarf. He said to Leo, "How do you stand all that jabbering?," meaning the little girls, excited and shrill.

Nothing is so numbing as an unexpected audience. The soldiers started to pick lumps of snow from each other's coats. Mr. Quale nodded his head, as if it were on a wire spring, and took his cold pipe out of his pocket. He pointed the stem at the girls, then at us, and said, "And bear this in mind, lads. You can't ever do a bloody thing with them."

Now Mrs. Quale appeared on the doorstep. She held up a white stocking so we could see the hole in it, and called, "I'll thrash you, Lily Quale—I swear to God!"

Vince Whitton started to wail: "Beryl, I want to go home."

"Go home, then."

"Not without you."

"Glory, wouldn't I be glad to see the last of you," his sister said.

When the war came Leo waited to be the right age; then he enlisted and left Châtelroux. His mother baked coconut biscuits and marble cake, which she posted to him in a tin box. He brought the box back empty when he came on leave. They talked about different things to eat. She had an old, stained, illustrated cookbook they looked at together, and Leo would pick out what he wanted for supper. No more of everybody eating something different: the others had to settle for Leo's choice.

Lily and I commuted to high schools in Montreal. We took the same train in the morning but did not sit together. Girls sat with girls, boys with boys. Sometimes in the afternoon we saw each other in Windsor Station. The Quales had moved to a two-story, semi-detached house made of orange brick. A steep, narrow staircase rose out of the living room. It was the first thing you saw when you came in. Mrs. Quale waxed the steps and kept them very clean, and never missed a chance to say "upstairs." There was a bathroom and an indoor toilet. They were buying the house inch by inch.

Leo's room contained a large bed with a candlewick spread and a varnished desk, in case he had something to write. The desk and the counterpane were the first things Mrs. Quale ever had delivered from Eaton's. No sooner were they moved upstairs than he went away, leaving behind his civilian life and his life altogether. On that wartime Saturday when I sat doing homework with Lily, Leo had gone to Halifax with his regiment and was waiting to embark. His bed was always made up, Lily told me. Mrs. Quale, who now loved Leo best, had heard about embarkation leaves that occurred twice, sons and husbands who came back after having said goodbye. She thought she might see Leo, late at night, under the light in the porch, carrying his kit. Some women dreaded any hitch in the slow process of separation. It was impossible to speak the same brave words twice. Some said they would as soon face a ghost as a man seen off back a few days later but somehow different in look and manner, already remote.

When Mrs. Quale would let us, we used Leo's desk. In the kitchen our books got stained, because Mrs. Quale kept wiping the table oilcloth with a soapy rag, part of an old undershirt of Leo's. Upstairs we were obliged to sit at opposite ends of the desk, so our knees wouldn't touch. Mrs. Quale would look in, bringing us something to eat or drink, or just making sure we hadn't stirred from our chairs. Once, I remember, she said, "Who's winning?" as though "education" were another of Lily's games, one for which Leo had never found the knack.

Lily tried again: "How about letting us work in Leo's room?"

"You heard me. Not unless I'm in the house."

"You are in the house."

Mrs. Quale replied that we were to keep away from the stairs altogether. She was here, yes, but not for long. She sounded as if she had finally decided to quit her home and family, but she was just taking an embroidered tray runner over to Mrs. Bagshaw's, because of next day's Sodality sale. The sale was for the benefit of Catholic missions: my father's rivals.

"Steve," she said, "either you go home right away or you promise you'll stay where you are, by the window, where the neighbors can see you."

In their new kitchen hung a mirror with a frame of grained pitch pine—just for decoration. No one had to wash or shave in the kitchen sink. Mrs. Quale pinned a blue feather to her hat, then stared at it.

"Keep the feather on, Mum," said Lily. "It looks lovely." But Mrs. Quale could not decide.

Five minutes after her mother had gone out the front door, Lily said, "It would be better upstairs. We can't even spread our things out here—there's so much stuff on the table, ketchup and mustard and that. And I hate the noise of that kitchen clock. It's like a hammer."

"She said to stay near the window."

"Dad stops work at noon Saturdays, but he never gets in before five. Mum will be having tea with the other ladies."

"She might want to come back, just to see where you are," I said. "She may change her mind about wearing the feather."

"No, not now. She'd have done it right away." The clock was a china plate with a pattern of windmills. The arms of the tallest windmill told the time. She looked up; we both did. "Don't bother to bring all your books," she said. "Just what you'll be needing."

Upstairs we started one thing, then another. There wasn't much to it; we never got beyond high fever. I wanted to pull down the blind, but Lily said it would draw the neighbors' attention. She folded the bedspread—her mother's pride. She must have made a mistake about the family timetable, for we suddenly heard Mr. Quale at the front door. We were on our feet and presentable by the time he reached the kitchen and dropped something—a newspaper, probably—on the table. He got a bottle out of the icebox and poured himself a beer, capped the bottle, put it back. There was a moment of silence: he may have picked up the blue feather lying on the drainboard, wondering what it was doing there. Or he may have noticed the books we'd left behind, or heard us moving around, talking in whispers. He plodded to the foot of the stairs and called, "Who's home?"

Lily pulled the coverlet over the sheets and smoothed it. We started down the staircase and met him, almost at the top.

"Want me to get your tea, Dad?" she said.

"I'm all right." He did not acknowledge me.

Lily collected the rest of my books from the kitchen. I held them flat on my chest, like a shield. She came with me along the river road, up the wooden steps to the bridge, and about halfway across. The Montreal train rushed by and the whole bridge shook; we had to stop and hold on to the railing. As the noise faded, in a thinning mist of steam and soot, she said, "Leo's gone for good. I've said goodbye to him. I know it. Dad's already starting to say I'm all they've got, and Leo isn't even overseas. I'm not all they've got. They've got their new house."

When Lily arrived home her mother was waiting in the doorway. She smacked Lily's face twice, and Mr. Quale came running out of the kitchen, shouting something. He stopped to unbuckle his belt. Lily thought, God in Heaven, is he going to take all his clothes off, and she backed off and went down the front step and stood in the street. Her father came no farther than the veranda, because of the neighbors. He had his belt in his hand and looked as if he had just got up. They stared at each other, with the length of the front walk between them. Then he threaded the belt back on and said, "Have I ever laid a hand on you? But just you keep out of my way, now. Stay out of my way. That's what I want to tell you." His voice was so steady and quiet that Lily began to cry.

He had looked in Leo's room and seen nothing—and he was a policeman who later became a detective, specializing in divorces and evidence of adultery. When his wife came home the first thing she did was turn back the bedspread, and she found makeup from Lily's bare legs all over the sheet.

The Quales came to my aunt's house that night, carrying a leather grip. My aunt, sensing something, told me to go to my room. I was too big to be ordered that way, exactly, but I went upstairs and lay on the floor and listened through the iron grille of the hot-air register. I could hear Mrs. Quale telling my aunt how I had played them false and destroyed their daughter.

My aunt made an astonishing reply: "You have let that girl run wild. It's a wonder nothing worse has ever happened. She roams all over town on Leo's bike, talking to strangers. She has been seen near the highway, talking to men in cars. She has been seen with a gang, Lily the only girl, throwing stones at people in canoes."

The stone-throwing incident had occurred when Lily was eleven. My aunt was not trying to excuse me but simply was upholding the tradition that made girls responsible for their own virtue. I was guilty of having disobeyed Lily's mother—nothing more.

"Put that thing away," my aunt said, sharply, next.

The Quales had opened the leather bag and were attempting to unfold the evidence. "It's the sheet," said Mr. Quale—his only remark.

"I believe you. Please put it away."

"Don't you look down on us," said Mrs. Quale. "We've got our only son in the service. Lily's always been head of her class. We own most of the home we live in. My husband has an honored position on the police force. Mr. Quale has never walked a beat."

Did my aunt smile? Something made Mrs. Quale break into full-throated weeping—nothing like my aunt's rare, silent tears. It was a comic-strip bawling, Katzenjammer roars of "Wah!" and "Ooh." My aunt said, "I know, I know," and offered to make tea. Soon after that I heard the Quales leave.

My aunt did not let me think I was innocent. The only reason she did not send me away to school, as she wanted to, was that my father could not afford the fees. She was saving her own money to put me through university. In the meantime, it would be good if I were to show common sense and gratitude. I had never heard her say I was supposed to be grateful for anything: for a time, it put a wall of shyness between us. The Quales, stretching their means to the limit, shut Lily up with nuns, in one of the places from which her Polish friend had been expelled. I went on commuting, but without a sight of Lily.

Windsor Station was full of soldiers, and there was a brownish, bleak kind of light on winter afternoons. Once I saw Lily's Polish friend. She was a tender blonde, dimpled, with small blue eyes—something like Leo's. I noticed her wedding ring, and said, "Is your husband going overseas?"

"Oh, no," she said. "Morrie's got a heart. I mean, he's cardiac. I'm not here for anything in particular. I just came over with my girlfriend." I had shot past her in height. She had to look up, as Leo's mother did to Leo. Her girlfriend, talking to a knot of airmen in the shadows of the station, was unknown to me. Lily's friend seemed to be weighing the advantages of spending any more time in my company, but she must have spent more than I remember: it was she who told me what happened after Lily got home that other afternoon. She was a good-natured girl but restless, as if nothing had yet been settled, in spite of the wedding ring. She wrote me off, abruptly, and turned away. I took that for a good sign. I would not have known how to end the conversation. Something in my manner spoke for me, and would always ease me out of awkward times. So I thought.

"Aren't you Steven Burnet?" Mitchell Coleman looked wholly different as a soldier: younger, for one thing. The lumpy uniform, the thick boots, the close-cut hair, brought him near to Leo in age and manner. Even in the unprepossessing uniform he seemed neat and spruce, still ready to be knocked unconscious and undressed by strangers—all that was left of his former self.

He gave me a slow look and probably surmised, correctly, that I had known him at once but would never have approached him. "I barely recognized you," he said. "You're twice your old height. But there's still a look—a family look, I suppose. More of an expression than an arrangement of features." I did not know what to make of a personal observation of that kind. I wondered if he meant to criticize my aunt's appearance, or mine. "How old can you be now?"

"I'm still going to high school."

"They tried to teach me how to make Army training films," he said. "But documentary movies are a string of lies. I decided not to sit the war out." He did not ask for news of his old friend, the trusted friend who had dropped him, without a word of explanation, without hearing his side of the case. "Well," he said. "For King and country, eh?" and there was not a hint or a glance to let me know whether he was being ironic. He shouldered his kit, and we shook hands.

He's only a corporal, like Leo, I said to myself. At his age he should at least be a captain.

When she was playing at war, Lily made medals out of silver paper. Her soldiers, pronounced dead, got up to receive a decoration. They said, "I've got mud on my coat. I'm going to catch it at home. Somebody, help me get the mud off."

In that war, or one like it, Vince Whitton begins to whine: "Beryl, my feet are getting cold. I'm hungry. I have to go to the bathroom."

"You can pee your pants, for all I care."

He stops snivelling for a minute, and moves closer to Leo; leaves the girls to be with the men. Mr. Quale points the stem of his pipe, that time or another, and says, "You can't do a bloody thing with them." The players freeze. They stand, hardly breathing, small creatures in an open field, hoping they have become the white of the snow around them and the hawk will leave them alone.

Leo's death made two of the English newspapers in Montreal. My aunt sent Mrs. Quale a note. Looking back, she felt that the Quales had never been suited to the occasion; in short, they had done me no good whatever. I had learned nothing from Leo or his family—"poor Leo," he had become. In a sense, they had ceased even to be a family, with Leo gone and Lily away from home, under close surveillance. Once, she said, "The worst mistake I ever made was when I let you chase around after Leo"—which shows how blameless her life must have been.

Loss of Innocence

To Set Our House In Order

Margaret Laurence

When the baby was almost ready to be born, something went wrong and my mother had to go into hospital two weeks before the expected time. I was wakened by her crying in the night, and then I heard my father's footsteps as he went downstairs to phone. I stood in the doorway of my room, shivering and listening, wanting to go to my mother but afraid to go lest there be some sight there more terrifying than I could bear.

"Hello—Paul?" my father said, and I knew he was talking to Dr. Cates. "It's Beth. The waters have broken, and the fetal position doesn't seem quite—well, I'm only thinking of what happened the last time, and another like that would be—I wish she were a little huskier, damn it—she's so—no, don't worry, I'm quite all right. Yes, I think that would be the best thing. Okay, make it as soon as you can, will you?"

He came back upstairs, looking bony and dishevelled in his pyjamas, and running his fingers through his sand-coloured hair. At the top of the stairs, he came face to face with Grandmother MacLeod, who was standing there in her quilted black satin dressing gown, her slight figure held straight and poised, as though she were unaware that her hair was bound grotesquely like white-feathered wings in the snare of her coarse night-time hairnet.

"What is it, Ewen?"

"It's all right, Mother. Beth's having—a little trouble. I'm going to take her into the hospital. You go back to bed."

"I told you," Grandmother MacLeod said in her clear voice, never loud, but distinct and ringing like the tap of a sterling teaspoon on a crystal goblet, "I did tell you, Ewen, did I not, that you should have got a girl in to help her with the housework? She would have rested more."

"I couldn't afford to get anyone in," my father said. "If you thought she should've rested more, why didn't you ever—oh God, I'm out of my mind tonight—just go back to bed, Mother, please. I must get back to Beth."

When my father went down to the front door to let Dr. Cates in, my need overcame my fear and I slipped into my parents' room. My mother's black hair, so neatly pinned up during the day, was startlingly spread across the white pillowcase. I stared at her, not speaking, and then she smiled and I rushed from the doorway and buried my head upon her.

"It's all right, honey," she said. "Listen, Vanessa, the baby's just going to come a little early, that's all. You'll be all right. Grandmother MacLeod will be here."

"How can she get the meals?" I wailed, fixing on the first thing that came to mind. "She never cooks. She doesn't know how."

"Yes, she does," my mother said. "She can cook as well as anyone when she has to. She's just never had to very much, that's all. Don't worry—she'll keep everything in order, and then some."

My father and Dr. Cates came in, and I had to go, without ever saying anything I had wanted to say. I went back to my own room and lay with the shadows all around me. I listened to the night murmurings that always went on in that house, sounds which never had a source, rafters and beams contracting in the dry air, perhaps, or mice in the walls, or a sparrow that had flown into the attic through the broken skylight there. After a while, although I would not have believed it possible, I slept.

The next morning I questioned my father. I believed him to be not only the best doctor in Manawaka, but also the best doctor in the whole of Manitoba, if not in the entire world, and the fact that he was not the one who was looking after my mother seemed to have something sinister about it.

"But it's always done that way, Vanessa," he explained. "Doctors never attend members of their own family. It's because they care so much about them, you see, and—"

"And what?" I insisted, alarmed at the way he had broken off. But my father did not reply. He stood there, and then he put on that difficult smile with which adults seek to conceal pain from children. I felt terrified, and ran to him, and he held me tightly.

"She's going to be fine," he said. "Honestly she is. Nessa, don't cry—"

Grandmother MacLeod appeared beside us, steel-spined despite her apparent fragility. She was wearing a purple silk dress and her ivory pendant. She looked as though she were all ready to go out for afternoon tea.

"Ewen, you're only encouraging the child to give way," she said. "Vanessa, big girls of ten don't make such a fuss about things. Come and get your breakfast. Now, Ewen, you're not to worry. I'll see to everything."

Summer holidays were not quite over, but I did not feel like going out to play with any of the kids. I was very superstitious, and I had the feeling that if I left the house, even for a few hours, some disaster would overtake my mother. I did not, of course, mention this feeling to Grandmother MacLeod, for she did not believe in the existence of fear, or if she did, she never let on. I spent the morning morbidly, in seeking hidden places in the house. There were many of these—odd-shaped nooks under the stairs, small and loosely nailed-up doors at the back of clothes closets, leading to dusty tunnels and forgotten recesses in the heart of the house where the only things actually to be seen were drab oil paintings stacked upon the rafters, and trunks full of outmoded clothing and old photograph albums. But the unseen presences in these secret places I knew to be those of every person, young or old, who had ever belonged to the house and had died, including Uncle Roderick who got killed on the Somme, and the baby who would have been my sister if only she had managed to come to life. Grandfather MacLeod, who had died a year after I was born, was present in the house in more tangible form. At the top of the main stairs hung the mammoth picture of a darkly uniformed man riding upon a horse whose prancing stance and dilated nostrils suggested that the battle was not yet over, that it might indeed continue until Judgment Day. The stern man was actually the Duke of Wellington, but at the time I believed him to be my Grandfather MacLeod, still keeping an eye on things.

We had moved in with Grandmother MacLeod when the Depression got bad and she could no longer afford a housekeeper, but the MacLeod house never seemed like home to me. Its dark red brick was grown over at the front with Virginia creeper that turned crimson in the fall, until you could hardly tell brick from leaves. It boasted a small tower in which Grandmother MacLeod kept a weedy collection of anaemic ferns. The verandah was embellished with a profusion of wrought-iron scrolls, and the circular rose-window upstairs contained glass of many colours which permitted an outlooking eye to see the world as a place of absolute sapphire or emerald, or if one wished to look with a jaundiced eye, a hateful yellow. In Grandmother MacLeod's opinion, these features gave the house style.

Inside, a multitude of doors led to rooms where my presence, if not actually forbidden, was not encouraged. One was Grandmother MacLeod's bedroom, with its stale and old-smelling air, the dim reek of medicines and lavender sachets. Here resided her monogrammed dresser silver, brush and mirror, nail-buffer and button hook and scissors, none of which must even be fingered by me now, for she meant to leave them to me in her will and intended to hand them over in the same flawless and unused condition in which they had always been kept. Here, too, were the silver-framed photographs of Uncle Roderick—as a child, as a boy, as a man in his Army uniform. The massive walnut spool bed had obviously been designed for queens or giants, and my tiny grandmother used to lie within it all day when she had migraine, contriving somehow to look like a giant queen.

The living room was another alien territory where I had to tread warily, for many valuable objects sat just-so on tables and mantelpiece, and dirt must not be tracked in upon the blue Chinese carpet with its birds in eternal motionless flight and its water-lily buds caught forever just before the point of opening. My mother was always nervous when I was in this room.

"Vanessa, honey," she would say, half apologetically, "why don't you go and play in the den, or upstairs?"

"Can't you leave her, Beth?" my father would say. "She's not doing any harm."

"I'm only thinking of the rug," my mother would say, glancing at Grandmother MacLeod, "and yesterday she nearly knocked the Dresden shepherdess off the mantel. I mean, she can't help it, Ewen, she has to run around—"

"Goddamn it, I know she can't help it," my father would growl, glaring at the smirking face of the Dresden shepherdess.

"I see no need to blaspheme, Ewen," Grandmother MacLeod would say quietly, and then my father would say he was sorry, and I would leave.

The day my mother went to the hospital, Grandmother MacLeod called me at lunch-time, and when I appeared, smudged with dust from the attic, she looked at me distastefully as though I had been a cockroach that had just crawled impertinently out of the woodwork.

"For mercy's sake, Vanessa, what have you been doing with yourself? Run and get washed this minute. Here, not that way—you use the back stairs, young lady. Get along now. Oh—your father phoned."

I swung around. "What did he say? How is she? Is the baby born?"

"Curiosity killed a cat," Grandmother MacLeod said, frowning. "I cannot understand Beth and Ewen telling you all these things, at your age. What sort of vulgar person you'll grow up to be, I dare not think. No, it's not born yet. Your mother's just the same. No change."

I looked at my grandmother, not wanting to appeal to her, but unable to stop myself. "Will she—will she be all right?"

Grandmother MacLeod straightened her already-straight back. "If I said definitely yes, Vanessa, that would be a lie, and the MacLeods do not tell lies, as I have tried to impress upon you before. What happens is God's will. The Lord giveth, and the Lord taketh away."

Appalled, I turned away so she would not see my face and my eyes. Surprisingly I heard her sigh and felt her papery white and perfectly manicured hand upon my shoulder.

"When your Uncle Roderick got killed," she said, "I thought I would die. But I didn't die, Vanessa."

At lunch, she chatted animatedly, and I realized she was trying to cheer me in the only way she knew.

"When I married your Grandfather MacLeod," she related, "he said to me, 'Eleanor, don't think because we're going to the prairies that I expect you to live roughly. You're used to a proper house, and you shall have one.' He was as good as his word. Before we'd been in Manawaka three years, he'd had this place built. He earned a good deal of money in his time, your grandfather. He soon had more patients than either of the other doctors. We ordered our dinner service and all our silver from Birks' in Toronto. We had resident help in those days, of course, and never had less than twelve guests for dinner parties. When I had a tea, it would always be twenty or thirty. Never any less than half a dozen different kinds of cake were ever served in this house. Well, no one seems to bother much these days. Too lazy, I suppose."

"Too broke," I suggested. "That's what Dad says."

"I can't bear slang," Grandmother MacLeod said. "If you mean hard up, why don't you say so? It's mainly a question of management, anyway. My accounts were always in good order, and so was my house. No unexpected expenses that couldn't be met, no fruit cellar running out of preserves before the winter was over. Do you know what my father used to say to me when I was a girl?"

"No," I said. "What?"

"God loves Order," Grandmother MacLeod replied with emphasis. "You remember that, Vanessa. God loves Order—he wants each one of us to set our house in order. I've never forgotten those words of my father's. I was a MacInnes before I got married. The MacInnes is a very ancient clan, the lairds of Morven and the constables of the Castle of Kinlochaline. Did you finish that book I gave you?"

"Yes," I said. Then, feeling some additional comment to be called for, "It was a swell book, Grandmother."

This was somewhat short of the truth. I had been hoping for her cairngorm brooch on my tenth birthday, and had received instead the plaid-bound volume entitled *The Clans and Tartans of Scotland*. Most of it was too boring to read, but I had looked up the motto of my own family and those of some of my friends' families. *Be then a wall of brass. Learn to suffer. Consider the end. Go carefully*. I had not found any of these slogans reassuring. What with Mavis Duncan learning to suffer, and Laura Kennedy considering the end, and Patsy Drummond going carefully, and I spending my time in being a wall of brass, it did not seem to me that any of us were going to lead very interesting lives. I did not say this to Grandmother MacLeod.

"The MacInnes motto is *Pleasure Arises from Work,*" I said.

"Yes," she agreed proudly. "And an excellent motto it is, too. One to bear in mind."

She rose from the table, rearranging on her bosom the looped ivory beads that held the pendant on which a fullblown ivory rose was stiffly carved.

"I hope Ewen will be pleased," she said.

"What at?"

"Didn't I tell you?" Grandmother MacLeod said. "I hired a girl this morning, for the housework. She's to start tomorrow."

When my father got home that evening, Grandmother MacLeod told him her good news. He ran one hand distractedly across his forehead.

"I'm sorry, Mother, but you'll just have to unhire her. I can't possibly pay anyone."

"It seems distinctly odd," Grandmother MacLeod snapped, "that you can afford to eat chicken four times a week."

"Those chickens," my father said in an exasperated voice, "are how people are paying their bills. The same with the eggs and the milk. That scrawny turkey that arrived yesterday was for Logan MacCardney's appendix, if you must know. We probably eat better than any family in Manawaka, except Niall Cameron's. People can't entirely dispense with doctors or undertakers. That doesn't mean to say I've got any cash. Look, Mother, I don't know what's happening with Beth. Paul thinks he may have to do a Caesarean. Can't we leave all this? Just leave the house alone. Don't touch it. What does it matter?"

"I have never lived in a messy house, Ewen," Grandmother MacLeod said, "and I don't intend to begin now."

"Oh Lord," my father said. "Well, I'll phone Edna, I guess, and see if she can give us a hand, although God knows she's got enough, with the Connor house and her parents to look after."

"I don't fancy having Edna Connor in to help," Grandmother MacLeod objected.

"Why not?" my father shouted. "She's Beth's sister, isn't she?"

"She speaks in such a slangy way," Grandmother MacLeod said. "I have never believed she was a good influence on Vanessa. And there is no need for you to raise your voice to me, Ewen, if you please."

I could barely control my rage, I thought my father would surely rise to Aunt Edna's defence. But he did not.

"It'll be all right," he soothed her. "She'd only be here for part of the day, Mother. You could stay in your room."

Aunt Edna strode in the next morning. The sight of her bobbed black hair and her grin made me feel better at once. She hauled out the carpet sweeper and the weighted polisher and got to work. I dusted while she polished and swept, and we got through the living room and front hall in next to no time.

"Where's her royal highness, kiddo?" she enquired.

"In her room," I said. "She's reading the catalogue from Robinson & Cleaver."

"Good Glory, not again?" Aunt Edna cried. "The last time she ordered three linen tea-cloths and two dozen serviettes. It came to fourteen dollars. Your mother was absolutely frantic. I guess I shouldn't be saying this."

"I knew anyway," I assured her. "She was at the lace handkerchiefs section when I took up her coffee."

"Let's hope she stays there. Heaven forbid she should get onto the banqueting cloths. Well, at least she believes the Irish are good for two things—manual labour and linen-making. She's never forgotten Father used to be a blacksmith, before he got the hardware store. Can you beat it? I wish it didn't bother Beth."

"Does it?" I asked, and immediately realized this was a wrong move, for Aunt Edna was suddenly scrutinizing me.

"We're making you grow up before your time," she said. "Don't pay any attention to me, Nessa. I must've got up on the wrong side of the bed this morning."

But I was unwilling to leave the subject.

"All the same," I said thoughtfully, "Grandmother MacLeod's family were the lairds of Morven and the constables of the Castle of Kinlochaline. I bet you didn't know that."

Aunt Edna snorted. "Castle, my foot. She was born in Ontario, just like your Grandfather Connor, and her father was a horse doctor. Come on, kiddo, we'd better shut up and get down to business here."

We worked in silence for a while.

"Aunt Edna—" I said at last, "what about Mother? Why won't they let me go and see her?"

"Kids aren't allowed to visit maternity patients. It's tough for you, I know that. Look, Nessa, don't worry. If it doesn't start tonight, they're going to do the operation. She's getting the best of care."

I stood there, holding the feather duster like a dead bird in my hands. I was not aware that I was going to speak until the words came out.

"I'm scared," I said.

Aunt Edna put her arms around me, and her face looked all at once stricken and empty of defences.

"Oh, honey, I'm scared, too," she said.

It was this way that Grandmother MacLeod found us when she came stepping lightly down into the front hall with the order in her hand for two dozen lace-bordered handkerchiefs of pure Irish linen.

I could not sleep that night, and when I went downstairs, I found my father in the den. I sat down on the hassock beside his chair, and he told me about the operation my mother was to have the next morning. He kept on saying it was not serious nowadays.

"But you're worried," I put in, as though seeking to explain why I was.

"I should at least have been able to keep from burdening you with it," he said in a distant voice, as though to himself. "If only the baby hadn't got itself twisted around—"

"Will it be born dead, like the little girl?"

"I don't know," my father said. "I hope not."

"She'd be disappointed, wouldn't she, if it was?" I said bleakly, wondering why I was not enough for her.

"Yes, she would," my father replied. "She won't be able to have any more, after this. It's partly on your account that she wants this one, Nessa. She doesn't want you to grow up without a brother or sister."

"As far as I'm concerned, she didn't need to bother," I retorted angrily.

My father laughed. "Well, let's talk about something else, and then maybe you'll be able to sleep. How did you and Grandmother make out today?"

"Oh, fine, I guess. What was Grandfather MacLeod like, Dad?"

"What did she tell you about him?"

"She said he made a lot of money in his time."

"Well, he wasn't any millionaire," my father said, "but I suppose he did quite well. That's not what I associate with him, though."

He reached across to the bookshelf, took out a small leather-bound volume and opened it. On the pages were mysterious marks, like doodling, only much neater and more patterned.

"What is it?" I asked.

"Greek," my father explained. "This is a play called *Antigone*. See, here's the title in English. There's a whole stack of them on the shelves there. *Oedipus Rex. Electra. Medea*. They belonged to your Grandfather MacLeod. He used to read them often."

"Why?" I enquired, unable to understand why anyone would pore over those undecipherable signs.

"He was interested in them," my father said. "He must have been a lonely man, although it never struck me that way at the time. Sometimes a thing only hits you a long time afterwards."

"Why would he be lonely?" I wanted to know.

"He was the only person in Manawaka who could read these plays in the original Greek," my father said. "I don't suppose many people, if anyone, had even read them in English translations. Maybe he would have liked to be a classical scholar—I don't know. But his father was a doctor, so that's what he was. Maybe he would have liked to talk to somebody about these plays. They must have meant a lot to him."

It seemed to me that my father was talking oddly. There was a sadness in his voice that I had never heard before, and I longed to say something that would make him feel better, but I could not, because I did not know what was the matter.

"Can you read this kind of writing?" I asked hesitantly.

My father shook his head. "Nope. I was never very intellectual, I guess. Rod was always brighter than I, in school, but even he wasn't interested in learning Greek. Perhaps he would've been later, if he'd lived. As a kid, all I ever wanted to do was go into the merchant marine."

"Why didn't you, then?"

"Oh, well," my father said offhandedly, "a kid who'd never seen the sea wouldn't have made much of a sailor. I might have turned out to be the seasick type."

I had lost interest now that he was speaking once more like himself.

"Grandmother MacLeod was pretty cross today about the girl," I remarked.

"I know," my father nodded. "Well, we must be as nice as we can to her, Nessa, and after a while she'll be all right."

Suddenly I did not care what I said.

"Why can't she be nice to us for a change?" I burst out. "We're always the ones who have to be nice to her."

My father put his hand down and slowly tilted my head until I was forced to look at him.

"Vanessa," he said, "she's had troubles in her life which you really don't know much about. That's why she gets a migraine sometimes and has to go to bed. It's not easy for her these days, either—the house is still the same, so she thinks other things should be, too. It hurts her when she finds they aren't."

"I don't see—" I began.

"Listen," my father said, "you know we were talking about what people are interested in, like Grandfather MacLeod being interested in Greek plays? Well, your grandmother was interested in being a lady, Nessa, and for a long time it seemed to her that she was one."

I thought of the Castle of Kinlochaline, and of horse doctors in Ontario.

"I didn't know—" I stammered.

"That's usually the trouble with most of us," my father said. "You go on up to bed now. I'll phone tomorrow from the hospital as soon as the operation's over."

I did sleep at last, and in my dreams I could hear the caught sparrow fluttering in the attic, and the sound of my mother crying, and the voices of the dead children.

My father did not phone until afternoon. Grandmother MacLeod said I was being silly, for you could hear the phone ringing all over the house, but nevertheless I refused to move out of the den. I had never before examined my father's books, but now, at a loss for something to do, I took them out one by one and read snatches here and there. After I had been doing this for several hours, it dawned on me that most of the books were of the same kind. I looked again at the titles.

Seven-League Boots. Arabia Deserta. The Seven Pillars of Wisdom. Travels in Tibet. Count Lucknor the Sea Devil. And a hundred more. On a shelf by themselves were copies of the *National Geographic* magazine, which I looked at often enough, but never before with the puzzling compulsion which I felt now, as though I were on the verge of some discovery, something which I had to find out and yet did not want to know. I riffled through the picture-filled pages. Hibiscus and wild orchids grew in a soft-petalled confusion. The Himalayas stood lofty as gods, with the morning sun on their peaks of snow. Leopards snarled from the vined depths of a thousand jungles. Schooners buffeted their white sails like the wings of giant angels against the great sea winds.

"What on earth are you doing?" Grandmother MacLeod enquired waspishly, from the doorway. "You've got everything scattered all over the place. Pick it all up this minute, Vanessa, do you hear?"

So I picked up the books and magazines, and put them all neatly away, as I had been told to do.

When the telephone finally rang, I was afraid to answer it. At last I picked it up. My father sounded faraway, and the relief in his voice made it unsteady.

"It's okay, honey. Everything's fine. The boy was born alive and kicking after all. Your mother's pretty weak, but she's going to be all right."

I could hardly believe it. I did not want to talk to anyone. I wanted to be by myself, to assimilate the presence of my brother, towards whom, without ever having seen him yet, I felt such tenderness and such resentment.

That evening, Grandmother MacLeod approached my father, who, still dazed with the unexpected gift of neither life now being threatened, at first did not take her seriously when she asked what they planned to call the child.

"Oh, I don't know. Hank, maybe, or Joe. Fauntleroy, perhaps."

She ignored this levity.

"Ewen," she said, "I wish you would call him Roderick."

My father's face changed. "I'd rather not."

"I think you should," Grandmother MacLeod insisted, very quietly, but in a voice as pointed and precise as her silver nail-scissors.

"Don't you think Beth ought to decide?" my father asked.

"Beth will agree if you do."

My father did not bother to deny something that even I knew to be true. He did not say anything. Then Grandmother MacLeod's voice, astonishingly, faltered a little.

"It would mean a great deal to me," she said.

I remembered what she had told me—*When your Uncle Roderick got killed, I thought I would die. But I didn't die.* All at once, her feeling for that unknown dead man became a reality for me. And yet I held it against her, as well, for I could see that it had enabled her to win now.

"All right," my father said tiredly. "We'll call him Roderick."

Then, alarmingly, he threw back his head and laughed.

"Roderick Dhu!" he cried. "That's what you'll call him, isn't it? Black Roderick. Like before. Don't you remember? As though he were a character out of Sir Walter Scott, instead of an ordinary kid who—"

He broke off, and looked at her with a kind of desolation in his face.

"God, I'm sorry, Mother," he said. "I had no right to say that."

Grandmother MacLeod did not flinch, or tremble, or indicate that she felt anything at all.

"I accept your apology, Ewen," she said.

My mother had to stay in bed for several weeks after she arrived home. The baby's cot was kept in my parents' room, and I could go in and look at the small creature who lay there with his tightly closed fists and his feathery black hair. Aunt Edna came in to help each morning, and when she had finished the housework, she would have coffee with my mother. They kept the door closed, but this did not prevent me from eavesdropping, for there was an air register in the floor of the spare room, which was linked somehow with the register in my parents' room. If you put your ear to the iron grille, it was almost like a radio.

"Did you mind very much, Beth?" Aunt Edna was saying.

"Oh, it's not the name I mind," my mother replied. "It's just the fact that Ewen felt he had to. You know that Rod had only had the sight of one eye, didn't you?"

"Sure, I knew. So what?"

"There was only a year and a half between Ewen and Rod," my mother said, "so they often went around together when they were youngsters. It was Ewen's air-rifle that did it."

"Oh Lord," Aunt Edna said heavily. "I suppose she always blamed him?"

"No, I don't think it was so much that, really. It was how he felt himself. I think he even used to wonder sometimes if—but people shouldn't let themselves think like that, or they'd go crazy. Accidents do happen, after all. When the war came, Ewen joined up first. Rod should never have been in the Army at all, but he couldn't wait to get in. He must have lied about his eyesight. It wasn't so very noticeable unless you looked at him closely, and I don't suppose the medicals were very thorough in those days. He got in as a gunner, and Ewen applied to have him in the same company. He thought he might be able to watch out for him, I guess, Rod being—at a disadvantage. They were both only kids. Ewen was nineteen and Rod was eighteen when they went to France. And then the Somme. I don't know, Edna, I think Ewen felt that if Rod had had proper sight, or if he hadn't been in the same outfit and had been sent somewhere else—you know how people always think these things afterwards, not that it's ever a bit of use. Ewen wasn't there when Rod got hit. They'd lost each other somehow, and Ewen was looking for him, not bothering about anything else, you know, just frantically looking. Then he stumbled across him quite by chance. Rod was still alive, but—"

"Stop it, Beth," Aunt Edna said. "You're only upsetting yourself."

"Ewen never spoke of it to me," my mother went on, "until once his mother showed me the letter he'd written to her at the time. It was a peculiar letter, almost formal, saying how gallantly Rod had died, and all that. I guess I shouldn't have, but I told him she'd shown it to me. He was very angry that she had. And then, as though for some reason he were terribly ashamed, he said—*I had to write something to her, but men don't really die like that, Beth. It wasn't that way at all.* It was only after the war that he decided to come back and study medicine and go into practice with his father."

"Had Rod meant to?" Aunt Edna asked.

"I don't know," my mother said slowly. "I never felt I should ask Ewen that."

Aunt Edna was gathering up the coffee things, for I could hear the clash of cups and saucers being stacked on the tray.

"You know what I heard her say to Vanessa once, Beth? *The MacLeods never tell lies*. Those were her exact words. Even then, I didn't know whether to laugh or cry."

"Please, Edna—" my mother sounded worn out now. "Don't."

"Oh Glory," Aunt Edna said remorsefully, "I've got all the delicacy of a two-ton truck. I didn't mean Ewen, for heaven's sake. That wasn't what I meant at all. Here, let me plump up your pillows for you."

Then the baby began to cry, so I could not hear anything more of interest. I took my bike and went out beyond Manawaka, riding aimlessly along the gravel highway. It was late summer, and the wheat had changed colour, but instead of being high and bronzed in the fields, it was stunted and desiccated, for there had been no rain again this year. But in the bluff where I stopped and crawled under the barbed wire fence and lay stretched out on the grass, the plentiful poplar leaves were turning to a luminous yellow and shone like church windows in the sun. I put my head down very close to the earth and looked at what was going on there. Grasshoppers with enormous eyes ticked and twitched around me, as though the dry air were perfect for their purposes. A ladybird laboured mightily to climb a blade of grass, fell off, and started all over again, seeming to be unaware that she possessed wings and could have flown up.

I thought of the accidents that might easily happen to a person—or, of course, might not happen, might happen to somebody else. I thought of the dead baby, my sister who might as easily have been I. Would she, then, have been lying here in my place, the sharp grass making its small toothmarks on her brown arms, the sun warming her to the heart? I thought of the leather-bound volumes of Greek, and the six different kinds of iced cakes that used to be offered always in the MacLeod house, and the pictures of leopards and green seas. I thought of my brother, who had been born alive after all, and now had been given his life's name.

I could not really comprehend these things, but I sensed their strangeness, their disarray. I felt that whatever God might love in this world, it was certainly not order.

The Move

Gabrielle Roy

I have perhaps never envied anyone as much as a girl I knew when I was about eleven years old and of whom today I remember not much more than the name, Florence. Her father was a mover. I don't think this was his trade. He was a handyman, I imagine, engaging in various odd jobs; at the time of the seasonal movings—and it seems to me that people changed their lodgings often in those days—he moved the household effects of people of small means who lived near us and even quite far away, in the suburbs and distant quarters of Winnipeg. No doubt, his huge cart and his horses, which he had not wanted to dispose of when he came from the country to the city, had made him a mover.

On Saturdays Florence accompanied her father on his journeys, which, because of the slow pace of the horses, often took the entire day. I envied her to the point of having no more than one fixed idea: Why was my father not also a mover? What finer trade could one practise?

I don't know what moving signified to me in those days. Certainly I could not have had any idea what it was like. I had been born and had grown up in the fine, comfortable house in which we were still living and which, in all probability, we would never leave. Such fixity seemed frightfully monotonous to me that summer. Actually we were never really away from that large house. If we were going to the country for a while, even if we were only to be absent for a day, the problem immediately arose: Yes, but who will look after the house?

To take one's furniture and belongings, to abandon a place, close a door behind one forever, say good-bye to a neighborhood, this was an adventure of which I knew nothing; and it was probably the sheer force of my efforts to picture it myself that made it seem so daring, heroic, and exalted in my eyes.

"Aren't we ever going to move?" I used to ask Maman.

"I certainly hope not," she would say. "By the grace of God and the long patience of your father, we are solidly established at last. I only hope it is forever."

She told me that to her no sight in the world could be more heartbreaking, more poignant even, than a house moving.

"For a while," she said, "it's as if you were related to the nomads, those poor souls who slip along the surface of existence, putting their roots down nowhere. You no longer have a roof over your head. Yes indeed, for a few hours at least, it's as if you were drifting on the stream of life."

Poor Mother! Her objections and comparisons only strengthened my strange hankering. To drift on the stream of life! To be like the nomads! To wander through the world! There was nothing in any of this that did not seem to me complete felicity.

Since I myself could not move, I wished to be present at someone else's moving and see what it was all about. Summer came. My unreasonable desire grew. Even now I cannot speak of it lightly, much less so with derision. Certain of our desires, as if they knew about us before we do ourselves, do not deserve to be mocked.

Each Saturday morning I used to go and wander around Florence's house. Her father—a big dirty-blond man in blue work clothes, always grumbling a little or even, perhaps, swearing— would be busy getting the impressive cart out of the barn. When the horses were harnessed and provided with nose bags of oats, the father and his little daughter would climb onto the high seat; the father would take the reins in his hands; they would both, it seemed to me, look at me then with slight pity, a vague commiseration. I would feel forsaken, of an inferior species of humans unworthy of high adventure.

The father would shout something to the horses. The cart would shake. I would watch them set out in that cool little morning haze that seems to promise such delightful emotions to come. I would wave my hand at them, even though they never looked back at me. "Have a good trip," I would call. I would feel so unhappy at being left behind that I would nurse my regret all day and with it an aching curiosity. What would they see today? Where were they at this moment? What was offering itself to their travelers' eyes? It was no use my knowing that they could go only a limited distance in any event. I would imagine the two of them seeing things that no one else in the world could see. From the top of the cart, I thought, how transformed the world must appear.

At last my desire to go with them was so strong and so constant that I decided to ask my mother for permission—although I was almost certain I would never obtain it. She held my new friends in rather poor esteem and, though she tolerated my hanging continually about them, smelling their odor of horses, adventure, and dust, I knew in my heart of hearts that the mere idea that I might wish to accompany them would fill her with indignation.

At my first words, indeed, she silenced me.

"Are you mad? To wander about the city in a moving wagon! Just picture yourself," she said, "in the midst of furniture and boxes and piled-up mattresses all day, and with who knows what people! What can you imagine would be pleasant about that?"

How strange it was. Even the idea, for instance, of being surrounded by heaped-up chairs, chests with empty drawers, unhooked pictures— the very novelty of all this stimulated my desire.

"Never speak of that whim to me again," said my mother. "The answer is no and no it will remain."

Next day I went over to see Florence, to feed my nostalgic envy of their existence on the few words she might say to me.

"Where did you go yesterday? Who did you move?"

"Oh I'm not sure," Florence said, chewing gum—she was always either chewing gum or sucking a candy. "We went over to Fort Rouge, I think, to get some folks and move them way to hell and gone over by East Kildonan."

These were the names of quite ordinary suburbs. Why was it that at moments such as these they seemed to hold the slightly poignant attraction of those parts of the world that are remote, mysterious, and difficult to reach?

"What did you see?" I asked.

Florence shifted her gum from one cheek to the other, looking at me with slightly foolish eyes. She was not an imaginative child. No doubt, to her and her father the latter's work seemed banal, dirty, and tiring, and nothing more similar to one household move than another household move. Later I discovered that if Florence accompanied her father every Saturday, it was only because her mother went out cleaning that day and there was no one to look after the little girl at home. So her father took her along.

Both father and daughter began to consider me a trifle mad to endow their life with so much glamor.

I had asked the big pale-blond man countless times if he wouldn't take me too. He always looked at me for a moment as at some sort of curiosity—a child who perhaps wasn't completely normal—and said, "If your mother gives you permission..." and spat on the ground, hitched up his huge trousers with a movement of his hips, then went off to feed his horses or grease the wheels of his cart.

The end of the moving season was approaching. In the blazing heat of summer no one moved except people who were being evicted or who had to move closer to a new job, rare cases. If I don't soon manage to see what moving is like, I thought, I'll have to wait till next summer. And who knows? Next summer I may no longer have such a taste for it.

The notion that my desire might not always mean so much to me, instead of cheering me, filled me with anxiety. I began to realize that even our desires are not eternally faithful to us, that they wear out, perhaps die, or are replaced by others, and this precariousness of their lives made them seem more touching to me, more friendly. I thought that if we do not satisfy them they must go away somewhere and perish of boredom and lassitude.

Observing that I was still taken up with my "whim," Maman perhaps thought she might distract me from it by telling me once more the charming stories of her own childhood. She chose, oddly enough, to tell me again about the long journey of her family across the prairie by covered wagon. The truth must have been that she herself relived this thrilling voyage into the unknown again and again and that, by recounting it to me, she perhaps drained away some of that heartbreaking nostalgia that our life deposits in us, whatever it may be.

So here she was telling me again how, crowded together in the wagon—for Grandmother had brought some of her furniture, her spinning wheel certainly, and innumerable bundles—pressed closely in together, they had journeyed across the immense country.

"The prairie at that time," she said, "seemed even more immense than it does today, for there were no villages to speak of along the trail and only a few houses. To see even one, away far off in the distance, was an adventure in itself."

"And what did you feel?" I asked her.

"I was attracted," Maman admitted, bowing her head slightly, as if there were something a bit wrong, or at least strange, about this. "Attracted by the space, the great bare sky, the way the tiniest tree was visible in the solitude for miles. I was very much attracted."

"So you were happy?"

"Happy? Yes, I think so. Happy without knowing why. Happy as you are, when you are young—or even not so young—simply because you are in motion, because life is changing and will continue to change and everything is being renewed. It's curious," she told me. "Such things must run in families, for I wonder whether there have ever been such born travelers as all of us."

And she promised me that later on I too would know what it is to set forth, to be always seeking from life a possible beginning over—and that perhaps I might even become weary of it.

That night the intensity of my desire wakened me from sleep. I imagined myself in my mother's place, a child lying, as she had described it, on the floor of the wagon, watching the prairie stars—the most luminous stars in either hemisphere, it is said—as they journeyed over her head.

That, I thought, I shall never know; it is a life that is gone beyond recall and lost—and the mere fact that there were ways of life that were over, extinct in the past, and that we could not recover them in our day, filled me with the same nostalgic longing for the lost years as I had felt for my own perishable desires. But, for lack of anything better, there was the possible journey with our neighbors.

I knew—I guessed, rather—that, though we owe obedience to our parents, we owe it also to certain of our desires, those that are strangest, piercing, and too vast.

I remained awake. Tomorrow—this very day, rather—was a Saturday, moving day. I had resolved to go with the Pichettes.

Dawn appeared. Had I ever really seen it until now? I noticed that before the sky becomes clean and shining, it takes on an indecisive color, like badly washed laundry.

Now, the desire that was pushing me so violently, to the point of revolt, had no longer anything happy or even tempting about it. It was more like an order. Anguish weighed upon my heart. I wasn't even free now to say to myself, "Sleep. Forget all that." I had to go.

Is it the same anguish that has wakened me so many times in my life, wakens me still at dawn with the awareness of an imminent departure, sad sometimes, sometimes joyful, but almost always toward an unknown destination? Is it always the same departure that is involved?

When I judged the morning to be sufficiently advanced, I got up and combed my hair. Curiously enough, for this trip in a cart, I chose to put on my prettiest dress. "Might as well be hung for a sheep as a lamb," I said to myself, and left the house without a sound.

I arrived soon at the mover's. He was yawning on the threshold of the barn, stretching his arms in the early sun. He considered me suspiciously.

"Have you got permission?"

I swallowed my saliva rapidly. I nodded.

A little later Florence appeared, looking bad-tempered and sleepy.

She hitched herself up onto the seat beside us.

"Giddup!" cried the man.

And we set out in that cool morning hour that had promised me the transformation of the world and everything in it—and undoubtedly of myself.

2

And at first the journey kept its promise. We were passing through a city of sonorous and empty streets, over which we rolled with a great noise. All the houses seemed to be still asleep, bathed in a curious and peaceful atmosphere of withdrawal. I had never seen our little town wearing this absent, gentle air of remoteness.

The great rising sun bleached and purified it, I felt. I seemed to be traveling through an absolutely unknown city, remote and still to be explored. And yet I was astonished to recognize, as if vaguely, buildings, church spires, and street crossings that I must have seen somewhere before. But how could this be, since I had this morning left the world I had known and was entering into a new one?

Soon streetcars and a few automobiles began to move about. The sight of them looming upon the horizon and coming toward us gave me a vivid sense of the shifting of epochs.

What had these streetcars and automobiles come to do in our time, which was that of the cart? I asked myself with pleasure. When we reached Winnipeg and became involved in already heavy traffic, my sense of strangeness was so great that I believed I must be dreaming and clapped my hands.

Even at that time a horse-drawn cart must have been rare in the center of the city. So, at our side, everything was moving quickly and easily. We, with our cumbrous and reflective gait, passed like a slow, majestic film. I am the past, I am times gone by, I said to myself with fervor.

People stopped to watch us pass. I looked at them in turn, as if from far away. What did we have in common with this modern, noisy, agitated city? Increasingly, high in the cart, I became a survivor from times past. I had to restrain myself from beginning to salute the crowds, the streets, and the city, as if they were lucky to see us sweeping by.

For I had a tendency to divide into two people, actor and witness. From time to time I was the crowd that watched the passage of this astonishing cart from the past. Then I was the personage who considered from on high these modern times at her feet.

Meanwhile the difficulty of driving his somewhat nervous horses through all this noise and traffic was making the mover, whom I would have expected to be calmer and more composed, increasingly edgy. He complained and even swore noisily at almost everything we encountered. This began to embarrass me. I felt that his bad temper was spoiling all the pleasure and the sense of gentle incongruity that the poor people of the present era might have obtained from our appearance in their midst. I should have very much liked to disassociate myself from him. But how could I, jammed in beside him as I was?

Finally, we took to small, quieter streets. I saw then that we were going toward Fort Garry.

"Is that the way we're going?"

"Yes," replied Monsieur Pichette ungraciously. "That's the way."

The heat was becoming overpowering. Without any shelter, wedged between the big bulky man and Florence, who made no effort to leave me a comfortable place, I was beginning to suffer greatly. At last, after several hours, we were almost in the country.

The houses were still ranked along narrow streets, but now these were short and beyond them the prairie could be seen like a great recumbent land—a land so widespread that doubtless one would never be able to see either its end or its beginning. My heart began once more to beat hard.

There begins the land of the prairies, I said to myself. There begins the infinite prairie of Canada.

"Are we going to go onto the real prairie?" I asked. "Or are we still really inside the city limits?"

"You are certainly the most inquisitive little girl I've ever seen in my life," grumbled Monsieur Pichette, and he told me nothing at all.

Now the roads were only of dirt, which the wind lifted in dusty whirlwinds. The houses spaced themselves out, became smaller and smaller. Finally they were no more than badly constructed shacks, put together out of various odds and ends—a bit of tin, a few planks, some painted, some raw—and they all seemed to have been raised during the night only to be demolished the next day. Yet, unfinished as they were, the little houses still seemed old. Before one of them we stopped.

The people had begun to pile up their belongings, in the house or outside it, in cardboard cartons or merely thrown pell-mell into bedcovers with the corners knotted to form rough bundles. But they were not very far along, according to Monsieur Pichette, who flew into a rage the moment we arrived.

"I only charge five dollars to move people," he said, "and they aren't even ready when I get here."

We all began to transport the household effects from the shack to the cart. I joined in, carrying numerous small objects that fell to my hand—saucepans with unmatching covers, a pot, a chipped water jug. I was trying, I think, to distract myself, to keep, if at all possible, the little happiness I had left. For I was beginning to realize that the adventure was taking a sordid turn. In this poor, exhausted-looking woman with her hair plastered to her face, and in her husband—a man as lacking in amiability as Monsieur Pichette—I was discovering people who were doomed to a life of which I knew nothing, terribly gray and, it seemed to me, without exit. So I tried to help them as much as I could and took it upon myself to carry some rather large objects on my own. At last I was told to sit still because I was getting in everyone's way.

I went to rejoin Florence, who was sitting a short distance away on a little wooden fence.

"Is it always like this?" I asked.

"Yes, like this—or worse."

"It's possible to be worse?"

"Much worse. These people," she said, "have beds, and dressers...."

She refused to enlighten me further.

"I'm hungry," she decided and she ran to unpack a little lunch box, took out some bread and butter and an apple and proceeded to eat under my nose.

"Didn't you bring anything to eat?" she asked.

"No."

"You should have," she said, and continued to bite hungrily into her bread, without offering me a scrap.

I watched the men bring out some soiled mattresses, which they carried at arm's length. New mattresses are not too distressing a sight; but once they have become the slightest bit worn or dirty I doubt that any household object is more repugnant. Then the men carried out an old torn sofa on their shoulders, some bedposts and springs. I tried to whip up my enthusiasm, to revive a few flames of it, at least. And it was then, I think, that I had a consoling idea: we had come to remove these people from this wretched life; we were going to take them now to something better; we were going to find them a fine, clean house.

A little dog circled around us, whimpering, starving, perhaps anxious. For his sake more than my own maybe, I would have liked to obtain a few bits of Florence's lunch.

"Won't you give him a little bit?" I asked.

Florence hastily devoured a large mouthful.

"Let him try and get it," she said.

The cart was full now and, on the ground beside it, almost as many old things still waited to be stowed away.

I began to suffer for the horses, which would have all this to pull.

The house was completely emptied, except for bits of broken dishes and some absolutely worthless rags. The woman was the last to come out. This was the moment I had imagined as dramatic, almost historic, undoubtedly marked by some memorable gesture or word. But this poor creature, so weary and dust-covered, had apparently no regret at crossing her threshold, at leaving behind her two, three, or perhaps four years of her life.

"Come, we'll have to hurry," she said simply, "if we want to be in our new place before night."

She climbed onto the seat of the cart with one of the younger children, whom she took on her knees. The others went off with their father, to go a little way on foot, then by streetcar, to be ahead of us, they said, at the place where we were going.

Florence and I had to stand among the furniture piled up behind.

The enormous cart now looked like some sort of monster, with tubs and pails bouncing about on both sides, upturned chairs, huge clumsy packages bulging in all directions.

The horses pulled vigorously. We set out. Then the little dog began to run along behind us, whimpering so loudly in fear and despair that I cried, imagining that no one had thought of him, "We've forgotten the little dog. Stop. Wait for the little dog."

In the face of everyone's indifference, I asked the woman, whose name was Mrs. Smith, "Isn't he yours?"

"Yes, he's ours, I suppose," she replied.

"He's coming. Wait for him," I begged.

"Don't you think we're loaded up enough already?" the mover snapped dryly, and he whipped his horses.

For a long moment more the little dog ran along behind us.

He wasn't made for running, this little dog. His legs were too short and bowed. But he did his best. Ah yes! He did his best.

Is he going to try to follow us across the whole city? I thought with distress. Awkward, distracted, and upset as he was, he would surely be crushed by an automobile or a streetcar. I don't know which I dreaded most: to see him turn back alone toward the deserted house or try to cross the city, come what might. We were already turning onto a street that was furrowed with tracks. A streetcar was approaching in the distance; several cars passed us, honking.

Mrs. Smith leaned down from the seat of the cart and shouted at the little dog, "Go on home."

Then she repeated, more loudly, "Go on home, stupid."

So he had a sort of name, even though cruel, yet he was being abandoned.

Overcome with astonishment, the little dog stopped, hesitated a moment, then lay down on the ground, his eyes turned toward us, watching us disappear and whimpering with fright on the edge of the big city.

And a little later I was pleased, as you will understand, that I did not need to look at him any longer.

3

I have always thought that the human heart is a little like the ocean, subject to tides, that joy rises in it in a steady flow, singing of waves, good fortune, and bliss; but afterward, when the high sea withdraws, it leaves an utter desolation in our sight. So it was with me that day.

We had gone back across almost the whole enormous city—less enormous perhaps than scattered, strangely, widely spread out. The eagerness of the day diminished. I even think the sun was about to disappear. Our monster cart plunged, like some worn-out beast, toward the inconvenient, rambling neighborhoods that lay at the exact opposite end of the city to the one from which we had come.

Florence was whiling away the time by opening the drawers of an old chest and thrusting her hand into the muddle inside—the exact embodiment, it seemed to me, of this day—bits of faded ribbon; old postcards on whose backs someone had one day written: Splendid weather, Best love and kisses; a quill from a hat; electricity bills; gas reminders; a small child's shoe. The disagreeable little girl gathered up handfuls of these things, examined them, read, laughed. At one point, sensing my disapproval, she looked up, saw me watching her rummage, and thumbed her nose in spite.

The day declined further. Once more we were in sad little streets, without trees, so much like the one from which we had taken the Smiths that it seemed to me we had made all this journey for nothing and were going to end up finally at the same shack from which I had hoped to remove them.

At the end of each of these little streets the infinite prairie once more appeared but now almost dark, barely tinted, on the rim of the horizon, with angry red—the pensive, melancholy prairie of my childhood.

At last we had arrived.

Against that red horizon a small lonely house stood out black, quite far from its neighbors—a small house without foundations, set upon the ground. It did not seem old but it was already full of the odor and, no doubt, the rags and tatters of the people who had left it a short time ago. However, they had not left a single light bulb in place.

In the semidarkness Mrs. Smith began to search through her bundles, lamenting that she was sure she had tucked two or three carefully away but no longer remembered where. Her husband, who had arrived a short time before us, distressed by the dimness and the clumsiness of his wife, began to accuse her of carelessness. The children were hungry; they started to cry with fretful frightened voices, in an importunate tone that reminded me of the whimpering of the little dog. The parents distributed a few slaps, a little haphazardly, it seemed to me. Finally Mrs. Smith found a light bulb. A small glow shone forth timidly, as if ashamed at having to illuminate such a sad beginning.

One of the children, tortured by some strange preference, began to implore, "Let's go home. This isn't our home. Oh let's go back home!"

Mrs. Smith had come across a sack of flour, a frying pan and some eggs while she was searching for light bulbs and now she courageously set to work preparing a meal for her family. It was this, I think, that saddened me most: this poor woman, in the midst of complete disorder and almost in the dark, beginning to make pancakes. She offered some to me. I ate a little, for I was very hungry. At that moment I believe she was sorry she had abandoned the little dog. This was the one small break in the terrible ending of this day.

Meanwhile Monsieur Pichette, in a grumbling anxiety to be finished, had completely emptied the cart. As soon as everything was dumped on the ground in front of the door, he came and said to Mr. Smith, "That's five dollars."

"But you have to help me carry it all in," said Mr. Smith.

"Not on your life. I've done all I have to."

Poor Mr. Smith fumbled in his pocket and took out five dollars in bills and small change, which he handed to the mover.

The latter counted the money in the weak glimmer that came from the house and said, "That's it. We're quits."

In this glimmer from the house I noticed that our poor horses were also very tired. They blinked their eyes with a lost expression, the result of too many house movings, no doubt. Perhaps horses would prefer to make the same trip over and over again—in this way they would not feel too estranged from their customary ways. But, always setting out on new routes, toward an unknown destination, they must feel disconcerted and dejected. I had time, by hurrying, to fetch them each a handful of tender grass at the end of the street where the prairie began.

What would we have had to say to each other on our way back? Nothing, certainly, and so we said nothing. Night had fallen, black, sad, and impenetrable, when we finally reached the old stable, which had once seemed to me to contain more magic and charm than even the cave of Aladdin.

The mover nevertheless reached out his hand to help me down from the cart. He was one of those people—at least I thought so then—who, after being surly and detestable all day, try at the last moment to make amends with a pleasant word for the bad impression they have created. But it was too late, much too late.

"You're not too tired?" he asked, I believe.

I shook my head and after a quick good night, an unwilling thank you, I fled. I ran toward my home, the sidewalk resounding in the silence under my steps.

I don't believe I thought of rejoicing at what I was returning to—a life that, modest as it was, was still a thousand miles away from that of the Pichettes and the Smiths. And I had not yet realized that this whole shabby, dull, and pitiless side of life that the move had revealed to me today would further increase my frenzy to escape.

I was thinking only of my mother's anxiety, of my longing to find her again and be pardoned by her—and perhaps pardon her in turn for some great mysterious wrong whose point I did not understand.

She was in such a state of nervous tension, as a matter of fact—although neighbors had told her I had gone off early with the Pichettes— that when she saw me it was her exasperation that got the upper hand. She even raised her hand to strike me. I did not think of avoiding punishment. I may even have wanted it. But at that moment a surge of disillusionment came over me—that terrible distress of the heart after it has been inflated like a balloon.

I looked at my mother and cried, "Oh why have you said a hundred times that from the seat of the covered wagon on the prairie in the old days the world seemed renewed, different, and so beautiful?"

She looked at me in astonishment.

"Ah, so that's it!" she said.

And at once, to my profound surprise, she drew me toward her and cradled me in her arms.

"You too then!" she said. "You too will have the family disease, departure sickness. What a calamity!"

Then, hiding my face against her breast, she began to croon me a sort of song, without melody and almost without words.

"Poor you," she intoned. "Ah, poor you! What is to become of you!"

The Bottle Queen

W.P. Kinsella

When I was just a kid, my father, Paul Ermineskin, took off for the city, and I only seen him a few times in the last ten years. He hang around the bars and missions in the city and last time I seen him he was in bad shape and I didn't figure he had long left to live. So it sure is a surprise when he come walking into the Hobbema Pool Hall one afternoon.

"Hey, Silas," he say to me, and give my hand a shake. There is something sneaky about Pa, maybe it is the way he walks kind of sideways, with his eyes always darting all over the place. The weather is cold and it due to snow any minute but Pa is wearing only a red-silk western shirt, have black fringes all down the sleeves, and pants look like they come from a businessman's suit.

He buys a round of pop and Frito chips for me and my friends, tells us stories that make us laugh and shows us a new way to play 8-Ball that we never seen before. Pa smells of whisky, but he ain't drunk; in fact he looks healthier than I ever remember seeing him.

"You know I sure would like to see the other kids, Silas," he say to me. "I wonder if you might sort of ask your Ma if it would be okay?"

Pa smile at me when he say that and I can see that him and me look quite a lot alike. I frown some. Me and Ma and all the kids but Delores got more than our share of bad memories about Pa. Delores, she wasn't even born yet, though Ma's belly was big with her, when Pa left for good.

"Hey, Silas, look at me," says Pa. "You ever seen me lookin' so good? I straightened myself out some. Been off the booze and eatin' good meals. Even got a job lined up." He smile again and slap me on the arm.

"A guy who's able to charm the warts off a toad," is how Mad Etta, our medicine lady, describe Paul Ermineskin.

"Hmmfff," Ma say when I tell her Pa is back on the reserve. "He better not come around when he's drunk, if he know what's good for him." Then when I mention he want to see the kids, "They're all big enough to make their own minds up," she says. "Just let me know so's I can be away if he comes around."

Of the kids, only Delores is interested. Thomas, and Hiram, and Minnie, young as they were, all have enough bad thoughts about Pa not to want to see him.

Pa stay with an old friend of his, Isaac Hide. He keep asking me for my sister Illianna's address in Calgary but I keep pretending I forgot to look it up. Illianna is married to a white man, live in a big, new house. Pa wouldn't be comfortable there.

Delores has never had a father, and I guess has always wished for one. She keep a picture of Jay Silverheels the movie actor, and Allen Sapp the artist, pinned to the wall, and I heard her tell a girlfriend once that the picture of Allen Sapp was really one of her father.

Pa and me was still a hundred yards from the cabin when Delores explode out the door and hang herself on his neck. If you want to see somebody get hugged, you look at Paul Ermineskin that afternoon. Delores glue herself to his hand and lead him around the reserve like he never been here before. She tell him all about how she is the best bottle collector there is, and show him the forty or so dozen beer bottles stacked by the side of the cabin.

Ordinarily, bottles left around like that would disappear real quick, but me and my friends Frank Fence-post and Rufus Firstrider let it be known anybody stealing from Delores have to deal with us. The younger kids is enough afraid, especially of Frank who like to act tough, that they leave things be.

People who know her, call Delores *The Bottle Queen*. That is because she is able to collect more beer bottles and pop bottles than anybody around the reserve.

"If you throw a bottle out the door of your cabin, Delores Ermineskin will catch it before it hits the ground," Mad Etta say of her, and she say it with a prideful smile.

Delores take dancing lessons from Molly Thunder and Carson Longhorn. They is about the best chicken dancers around. Twice a week, Delores pack up her costume what Ma made out of an old dress, stuff it in a shopping bag comes from the Shoppers Drug Mart in Wetaskiwin, and head down to Blue Quills Hall for her lesson.

Carson Longhorn tell me she is really good. She win the prize for Girls Under 12 at our own pow-wow, and she win again, a five dollar prize, at the Rocky Mountain House rodeo. "If she had the money to travel to more pow-wows, she'd win almost every time," Carson tell me.

Delores is sometimes shy and sometimes bold. She can be as determined as a bird pulling a worm out of the ground. Her eyes is black and move fast as a crow's. She can spot a bottle in a ditch from a hundred yards. Sometimes when we drive back from Wetaskiwin or Ponoka, even at night, she spot a glint in the ditch, no more of a shine than a firefly, and she make me stop the truck. I watch her disappear into the ditch, walking real determined, hiking up her jeans, her pigtails what by that time of day coming undone, bouncing on her shoulders in the glow from the truck lights. In a minute she come back, usually with a bottle in each hand, grinning like somebody just give her a dollar. In winter, she can tell whether a hole in a snow drift been made by wind, an animal, or a bottle. She wade right in, have almost to swim against the drifts sometimes, but she come out grip a bottle in her mitten, have snow on her clothes right up to the armpit.

Delores have a reason for collecting all the bottles she does. Molly Thunder, her dance teacher, also make costumes. Boy, at the pow-wows you see some dancers decked up in costumes make them look like a rainbow when they twirl around as they dance. Molly make those kind, fancy ones with real coloured feathers in the bustle and headdress, and the jackets and moccasins she makes be solid beadwork done on real buckskin. Molly sell them costumes for sometimes a thousand dollars and Indian dancers from all over Canada order their dancing dress from her.

Molly promise to sell Delores a costume at cost for only $300. "A champion dancer should have fancy duds," is what Molly says, and Delores she look at them costumes, finger the beadwork and feathers every time she at Molly's cabin.

"How can somebody who's only ten years old earn three hundred dollars?" Delores ask me. I suggest she collect bottles, but I thought she'd get tired of it in a few days, like kids do, not that she'd take her collecting serious as a religion. Every day after school she go off with her gunnysack dragging behind her and walk the ditches of Highway 2A either south or north from Hobbema. She also stay up late on weekend nights when people are partying and circulate from cabin to cabin. "Soon as an empty or nearly empty bottle been set down on a table it disappear under Delores' coat," people say. But they don't say it mean. Everybody is kind of proud to see a young girl work as hard as she does.

Sometimes Delores is like a growed up woman, especially when she is working, or counting her money which she collect in one dollar bills, "'Cause I look like I'm more rich that way." Other times when she smile up at me showing how one of her big front teeth is only half-way grown in, she is like a little girl.

She is like a little girl with Pa. If being loved could make you a better person then Pa would be about equal to an angel. And Pa, I guess is affected some by the way she treat him. One day after him and Isaac Hide been to town drinking he give to Delores a barrette for her hair. It not an ordinary one, but is made from leather with pretty beads all over it. "This here belong to your Grandma Ermineskin," I hear him tell Delores. "She used to dance in all the pow-wows and was as good as anybody. Guess you take after her."

Well, Delores couldn't of liked the barrette better if it was made of solid diamonds. She don't wear it in her hair but carry it on a thick string around her neck and show it to anybody she meet, whether they interested or not.

It make me mad to see Pa do that to her. It is the first I ever heard of my grandma being a dancer, though she did die before I was born and I don't know too much about her. But the idea of Pa carrying anything around with him for more than a month or so is not very likely. Pa, he don't own nothing but the clothes on his back, and when he's drunk I think he even sometimes lose some of them.

Him and Isaac Hide drink a lot at the Alice Hotel beer parlour the last couple of weeks and Pa look like he going back to his habit of not eating very often.

One afternoon when we hanging around the Hobbema Pool Hall, Bert Cardinal get off the southbound bus. Bert he been in jail for a few months for driving off with a car don't belong to him. "Hey, Paul, what you up to since you got out?" is the first thing he say to my papa.

Pa try to pretend like he don't hear the question, but Bert carry right on in a loud voice. "They had to throw Paul here out; he liked Fort Saskatchewan Jail so much he wanted to stay there permanent," and he slap Pa on the back.

So now I know why he ain't been drinking for a year and been eating good. "Hey, Silas," Bert says, "you should of seen your old man the day he got busted. Was walking out of Woodward's with a chainsaw in each hand. They give him eighteen months but they throw him out in twelve."

I look at Pa. "I never lied to you," he says, "you just never asked." But he got a foxy look about him anyway.

Quite a few times I take Delores out in Louis Coyote's pickup truck, look for bottles. I stop on the shoulder of the road let Delores out, and she head off down the ditch in kind of a zig-zag run. I drive ahead exactly a mile, stop and walk the ditch ahead, putting bottles in the gunnysack I'm dragging along. I'd only get a half-mile or so down the road when the truck catch up with me. I can see Delores kneeling on the front seat, grinning and steering as the truck bump down the shoulder.

When she want to stop, she disappear from sight and I know she pressing with all her might on both the clutch and the brake.

One time I even complained to her about all the bottles she was collecting. "You know me and Frank used to gather up bottles to buy gas for the truck," I said. "Now there ain't a bottle in all of Hobbema for us to find." I was sorry right away that I said it, but me and Frank wanted to take our girls for a ride, and we was broke.

"You and Frank don't collect bottles, you steal them," said Delores.

"Sometime Frank he borrow a case or two from somebody's yard...."

"Frank steals," said Delores, sounding like a nun or a school teacher.

After supper that night Delores come into our cabin with four cases of beer bottles stacked in her arms like cord-wood. I couldn't even see her face behind them.

"I'm sorry, Silas," she said. "These will give you enough gas money to get to town and back," and she set the bottles on the table and lean in and kiss my cheek. Of course I didn't take them, even though I really would of liked to.

One afternoon in the pool hall Pa he is bragging about how him and Isaac Hide going into business together, when I hit him up about giving that barrette to Delores. I checked with Ma and Mad Etta and they say Grandma Ermineskin, though she could build a teepee and run a cross-cut saw like a man, was never one to dance. "Why'd you tell Delores that?" I ask. "You know she gonna find you out for a liar." I notice Pa is still wearing that red shirt with the fringes; the silky material got a fine glaze of dirt over it now. "Hey, who's gonna tell her?" say Pa, "you?"

"It don't be long until Delores recognize that barrette as something come from a craft-store in Wetaskiwin," I say.

"She's just a little girl," says Pa. "Leave her be." And he look mean at me out of his bloodshot eyes.

Next afternoon Delores talk me into driving her and her bottles into Wetaskiwin to the bottle depot. An old man in a dirty parka and a long-billed red cap tote up her take, which come to $49 and she take it all in ones as usual.

"Only thirty more dollars and I got enough for my costume," she announce as we driving back. I try to talk her into spend a dollar or two for some burgers and Cokes but she won't do it.

We return Louis Coyote's truck to him and walk back to our cabin. Soon as we walk into the cabin I know something is wrong. There is a rustling noise from Delores' and Minnie's room, which is marked off by a sheet been throwed over some clothes-line cord.

When I move aside the sheet there is Paul Ermineskin, on his hands and knees, busy stuffing money into his pockets. Delores she keep her costume money stashed safe in a Kellogg's Corn Flake box, under some clothes on the floor of her room.

"What are you doing?" I yell, though there is no need to ask.

Pa look up and make kind of a sick smile. "Hey, I was just counting the money for the kid, ya know."

If I looked at him any meaner he'd be deep-fried.

"I thought you was low-down the last time I seen you," I say.

"Hey, I was gonna pay her back...."

Delores has followed me across the cabin and now she hangs on to my arm, real tight, and sniffles some. She looks at Pa, her eyes wide, not understanding. "All you had to do was ask," she say in a small, tear-choked voice.

"I was doing it for you," Pa says to Delores. "This other guy and me we going to go out and cut Christmas trees. We got a chance to make a lot of money..." and his voice kind of trail off. The money is laying there all mixed in with Delores' clothes. Pa takes some dollars from his shirt pocket and throws them down.

"Well, I better get going," Pa says, standing up, "got to head for Edmonton, find my partner and get to work." He push past me and head for the door.

"No," says Delores, "don't go yet." She let go of my arm, run over scoop up some money and hold it out to Pa, who has stopped and turned around.

Pa flash a smile at her, like a weasel just been invited into a hen house.

"You don't want to give him nothing, Delores," I say.

"Yes, I do," she say, real final like.

"You know I'm gonna pay you back," says Pa, smiling again.

I got my fists clenched, and even though I hardly ever raise up my hand against anybody, right now I'd like to punch that smile right through to the back of his neck.

"Just go," says Delores, pushing more money at Pa who is stuffing it in all his pockets, even pushing some down the neck of his shirt what don't have no buttons on the front. When Pa got the money all stashed he wheel around and skulk out the door, giving us a little wave over his shoulder.

When we can't hear his boots on the snow no more, Delores rush over and throw her arms around me and hug real hard. She sob loud into my chest.

Maybe she have just the slightest suspicion he was telling the truth. After a while her crying slow down some. I tip her head up so I can see her face, and kiss her forehead. She looks so much like Pa. Maybe that was it, maybe she can feel his blood travelling around in her.

She is wearing that beaded barrette Pa gave her, not in her hair, but hanging from around her neck, it rest in a spot where she gonna grow breasts in a couple of years.

Still sniffling, she undo the barrette and hold it in the palm of her hand.

"Did this really belong to my Grandma Ermineskin, Silas?" she say to me, looking me right in the face with her wet, black eyes.

This is sure my chance to tan Paul Ermineskin's hide. And I'm mad enough to do it. But when I look at Delores it seem to me she lost enough already today. I can't believe she doesn't know the truth. I think the woman in her does, but it is the little girl who is asking the question. And if she has to ask I know what answer she want to hear.

Of White Hairs and Cricket

Rohinton Mistry

The white hair was trapped in the tweezers. I pulled it taut to see if it was gripped tightly, then plucked it.

"Aaah!" grimaced Daddy. "Careful, only one at a time." He continued to read the *Times of India*, spreading it on the table.

"It *is* only one," I said, holding out the tweezers, but my annoyance did not register. Engrossed in the classifieds, he barely looked my way. The naked bulb overhead glanced off the stainless steel tweezers, making a splotch of light dart across the Murphy Radio calendar. It danced over the cherubic features of the Murphy Baby, in step with the tweezers' progress on Daddy's scalp. He sighed, turned a page, and went on scrutinizing the columns.

Each Sunday, the elimination of white hairs took longer than the last time. I'm sure Daddy noticed it too, but joked bravely that laziness was slowing me down. Percy was always excused from this task. And if I pointed it out, the answer was: your brother's college studies are more important.

Daddy relied on my nimble fourteen-year-old fingers to uproot the signposts of mortality sprouting week after week. It was unappetizing work, combing through his hair greasy with day-old pomade, isolating the white ones, or the ones just beginning to turn—half black and half white, and somehow more repulsive. It was always difficult to decide whether to remove those or let them go till next Sunday, when the whiteness would have spread upward to their tips.

The Sunday edition of the *Times of India* came with a tabloid of comics: Mandrake the Magician, The Phantom, and Maggie and Jiggs in "Bringing Up Father." The drab yellow tablecloth looked festive with the vivid colours of the comics, as though specially decorated for Sunday. The plastic cloth smelled stale and musty. It was impossible to clean perfectly because of the floral design embossed upon its surface. The swirly grooves were ideal for trapping all kinds of dirt.

Daddy reached up to scratch a spot on his scalp. His "aaah" surprised me. He had taught me to be tough, always. One morning when we had come home after cricket, he told Mummy and *Mamaiji*, "Today my son did a brave thing, as I would have done. A powerful shot was going to the boundary, like a cannonball, and he blocked it with his bare shin." Those were his exact words. The ball's shiny red fury, and the audible crack—at least, I think it was audible—had sent pain racing through me that nearly made my eyes overflow. Daddy had clapped and said, "Well-fielded, sir, well-fielded." So I waited to rub the agonized bone until attention was no longer upon me. I wish Percy had not lost interest in cricket, and had been there. My best friend, Viraf from A Block, was immensely impressed. But that was all a long time ago, many months ago, now Daddy did not take us for cricket on Sunday mornings.

I paused in my search. Daddy had found something in the classifieds and did not notice. By angling the tweezers I could aim the bulb's light upon various spots on the Murphy Radio calendar: the edges of the picture, worn and turned inward; the threadbare loop of braid sharing the colour of rust with the rusty nail it hung by; a corroded staple clutching twelve thin strips—the perforated residue of months ripped summarily over a decade ago when their days and weeks were played out. The baby's smile, posed with finger to chin, was all that had fully endured the years. Mummy and Daddy called it so innocent and joyous. That baby would now be the same age as me. The ragged perimeter of the patch of crumbled wall it tried to hide strayed outward from behind, forming a kind of dark and jagged halo around the baby. The picture grew less adequate, daily, as the wall kept losing plaster and the edges continued to curl and tatter.

Other calendars in the room performed similar enshroudings: the Cement Corporation skyscraper; the Lifebuoy Soap towel-wrapped woman with long black hair; the Parsi calendar, pictureless but showing the English and Parsi names for the months, and the *roje* in Gujarati beside each date, which Mummy and *Mamaiji* consulted when reciting their prayers. All these hung well past their designated time span in the world of months and years, covering up the broken promises of the Firozsha Baag building management.

"Yes, this is it," said Daddy, tapping the paper, "get me the scissors."

Mamaiji came out and settled in her chair on the veranda. Seated, there was no trace of the infirmity that caused her to walk doubled over. Doctors said it was due to a weak spine that could not erect against the now inordinate weight of her stomach. From photographs of Mummy's childhood, I knew *Mamaiji* had been a big handsome woman, with a majestic countenance. She opened her bag of spinning things, although she had been told to rest her eyes after the recent cataract operation. Then she spied me with the tweezers.

"Sunday dawns and he makes the child do that *duleendar* thing again. It will only bring bad luck." She spoke under her breath, arranging her spindle and wool; she was not looking for a direct confrontation. "Plucking out hair as if it was a slaughtered chicken. An ill-omened thing, I'm warning you, Sunday after Sunday. But no one listens. Is this anything to make a child do, he should be out playing, or learning how to do *bajaar*, how to bargain with butcher and *bunya*." She mumbled softly, to allow Daddy to pretend he hadn't heard a thing.

I resented her speaking against Daddy and calling me a child. She twirled the spindle, drawing fibres into thread from the scrap of wool in her left hand as the spindle descended. I watched, expecting—even wishing—the thread to break. Sometimes it did, and then it seemed to me that *Mamaiji* was overcome with disbelief, shocked and pained that it could have happened, and I would feel sorry and rush to pick it up for her. The spindle spun to the floor this time without mishap, hanging by a fine, brand new thread. She hauled it up, winding the thread around the extended thumb and little finger of her left hand by waggling the wrist in little clockwise and counter-clockwise half-turns, while the index and middle fingers clamped tight the source: the shred of wool resembling a lock of her own hair, snow white and slightly tangled.

Mamaiji spun enough thread to keep us all in *kustis*. Since Grandpa's death, she spent more and more time spinning, so that now we each had a spare *kusti* as well. The *kustis* were woven by a professional, who always praised the fine quality of the thread; and even at the fire-temple, where we untied and tied them during prayers, they earned the covetous glances of other Parsis.

I beheld the spindle and *Mamaiji*'s co-ordinated feats of dexterity with admiration. All spinning things entranced me. The descending spindle was like the bucket spinning down into the sacred Bhikha Behram Well to draw water for the ones like us who went there to pray on certain holy days after visiting the fire-temple. I imagined myself clinging to the base of the spindle, sinking into the dark well, confident that *Mamaiji* would pull me up with her waggling hand before I drowned, and praying that the thread would not break. I also liked to stare at records spinning on the old 78-rpm gramophone. There was one I was particularly fond of: its round label was the most ethereal blue I ever saw. The lettering was gold. I played this record over and over, just to watch its wonderfully soothing blue and gold rotation, and the concentric rings of the shiny black shellac, whose grooves created a spiral effect if the light was right. The gramophone cabinet's warm smell of wood and leather seemed to fly right out of this shellacked spiral, while I sat close, my cheek against it, to feel the hum and vibration of the turntable. It was so cosy and comforting. Like missing school because of a slight cold, staying in bed all day with a book, fussed over by Mummy, eating white rice and soup made specially for me.

Daddy finished cutting and re-reading the classified advertisement. "Yes, this is a good one. Sounds very promising." He picked up the newspaper again, then remembered what *Mamaiji* had muttered, and said softly to me, "If it is so *duleendar* and will bring bad luck, how is it I found this? These old people—" and gave a sigh of mild exasperation. Then briskly: "Don't stop now, this week is very important." He continued, slapping the table merrily at each word: "Every-single-white-hair-out."

There was no real enmity between Daddy and *Mamaiji;* I think they even liked each other. He was just disinclined towards living with his mother-in-law. They often had disagreements over me, and it was always *Mamaiji* versus Mummy and Daddy. *Mamaiji* firmly believed that I was underfed. Housebound as she was, the only food accessible to her was the stuff sold by door-to-door vendors, which I adored but was strictly forbidden: *samosa, bhajia, sevganthia*; or the dinners she cooked for herself, separately, because she said that Mummy's cooking was insipidity itself: "Tasteless as spit, refuses to go down my throat."

So I, her favourite, enjoyed from time to time, on the sly, hot searing curries and things she purchased at the door when Daddy was at work and Mummy in the kitchen. Percy shared, too, if he was around; actually, his iron-clad stomach was much better suited to those flaming snacks. But the clandestine repasts were invariably uncovered, and the price was paid in harsh and unpleasant words. *Mamaiji* was accused of trying to burn to a crisp my stomach and intestines with her fiery, ungodly curries, or of exposing me to dysentery and diphtheria: the cheap door-to-door foodstuff was allegedly cooked in filthy, rancid oil—even machine oil, unfit for human consumption, as was revealed recently by a government investigation. *Mamaiji* retorted that if they did their duty as parents she would not have to resort to secrecy and *chori-chhoopi*; as it was, she had no choice, she could not stand by and see the child starve.

All this bothered me much more than I let anyone know. When the arguments started I would say that all the shouting was giving me a headache, and stalk out to the steps of the compound. My guilty conscience, squirming uncontrollably, could not witness the quarrels. For though I was an eager partner in the conspiracy with *Mamaiji*, and acquiesced to the necessity for secrecy, very often I spilled the beans—quite literally—with diarrhoea and vomiting, which *Mamaiji* upheld as undeniable proof that lack of proper regular nourishment had enfeebled my bowels. In the throes of these bouts of effluence, I promised Mummy and Daddy never again to eat what *Mamaiji* offered, and confessed all my past sins. In *Mamaiji*'s eyes I was a traitor; but sometimes it was also fun to listen to her scatological reproaches: "*Muà ugheeparoo*! Eating my food, then shitting and tattling all over the place. Next time I'll cork you up with a big *bootch* before feeding you."

Mummy came in from the kitchen with a plateful of toast fresh off the Criterion: unevenly browned, and charred in spots by the vagaries of its kerosene wick. She cleared the comics to one side and set the plate down.

"Listen to this," Daddy said to her, "just found it in the paper: 'A Growing Concern Seeks Dynamic Young Account Executive, Self-Motivated. Four-Figure Salary and Provident Fund.' I think it's perfect." He waited for Mummy's reaction. Then: "If I can get it, all our troubles will be over."

Mummy listened to such advertisements week after week: harbingers of hope that ended in disappointment and frustration. But she always allowed the initial wave of optimism to lift her, riding it with Daddy and me, higher and higher, making plans and dreaming, until it crashed and left us stranded, awaiting the next advertisement and the next wave. So her silence was surprising.

Daddy reached for a toast and dipped it in the tea, wrinkling his nose. "Smells of kerosene again. When I get this job, first thing will be a proper toaster. No more making burnt toast on top of the Criterion."

"I cannot smell kerosene," said Mummy.

"Smell this then," he said, thrusting the tea-soaked piece at her nose, "smell it and tell me," irritated by her ready contradiction. "It's these useless wicks. The original Criterion ones from England used to be so good. One trim and you had a fine flame for months." He bit queasily into the toast. "Well, when I get the job, a Bombay Gas Company stove and cylinder can replace it." He laughed. "Why not? The British left seventeen years ago, time for their stove to go as well."

He finished chewing and turned to me. "And one day, you must go, too, to America. No future here." His eyes fixed mine, urgently. "Somehow we'll get the money to send you. I'll find a way."

His face filled with love. I felt suddenly like hugging him, but we never did except on birthdays, and to get rid of the feeling I looked away and pretended to myself that he was saying it just to humour me, because he wanted me to finish pulling his white hairs. Fortunately, his jovial optimism returned.

"Maybe even a fridge is possible, then we will never have to go upstairs to that woman. No more obligations, no more favours. You won't have to kill any more rats for her." Daddy waited for us to join in. For his sake I hoped that Mummy would. I did not feel like mustering any enthusiasm.

But she said sharply, "All your *shaik-chullee* thoughts are flying again. Nothing happens when you plan too much. Leave it in the hands of God."

Daddy was taken aback. He said, summoning bitterness to retaliate, "You are thinking I will never get a better job? I'll show all of you." He threw his piece of toast onto the plate and sat back. But he recovered as quickly, and made it into a joke. He picked up the newspaper. "Well, I'll just have to surprise you one day when I throw out the kerosene stoves."

I liked the kerosene stoves and the formidable fifteen-gallon storage drum that replenished them. The Criterion had a little round glass window in one corner of its black base, and I would peer into the murky depths, watching the level rise as kerosene poured through the funnel; it was very dark and cool and mysterious in there, then the kerosene floated up and its surface shone under the light bulb. Looking inside was like lying on Chaupatty beach at night and gazing at the stars, in the hot season, while we stayed out after dinner till the breeze could rise and cool off the walls baking all day in the sun. When the stove was lit and the kitchen dark, the soft orange glow through its little mica door reminded me of the glow in the fire-temple *afargaan*, when there wasn't a blazing fire because hardly any sandalwood offerings had been left in the silver *thaali*; most people came only on the holy days. The Primus stove was fun, too, pumped up hot and roaring, the kerosene emerging under pressure and igniting into sharp blue flames. Daddy was the only one who lit it; every year, many women died in their kitchens because of explosions, and Daddy said that though many of them were not accidents, especially the dowry cases, it was still a dangerous stove if handled improperly.

Mummy went back to the kitchen. I did not mind the kerosene smell, and ate some toast, trying to imagine the kitchen without the stoves, with squat red gas cylinders sitting under the table instead. I had seen them in shop windows, and I thought they were ugly. We would get used to them, though, like everything else. At night, I stood on the veranda sometimes to look at the stars. But it was not the same as going to Chaupatty and lying on the sand, quietly, with only the sound of the waves in the dark. On Saturday nights, I would make sure that the stoves were filled, because Mummy made a very early breakfast for Daddy and me next morning. The milk and bread would be arriving in the pre-dawn darkness while the kettle was boiling and we got ready for cricket with the boys of Firozsha Baag.

We always left by seven o'clock. The rest of the building was just starting to wake up: Nariman Hansotia would be aligning, on the parapet of his ground floor veranda, his razor and shaving brush and mirror beside two steaming cups, one of boiling water and the other of tea, and we often wondered if he ever dipped the brush in the wrong cup; and the old spinster Tehmina, still waiting for her cataracts to ripen, would be saying her prayers facing the rising sun, with her duster-coat hoisted up and slung over the left shoulder, her yellowing petticoat revealed, to untie and tie her thick rope-like *kusti* around the waist; and the *kuchrawalli* would be sweeping the compound, making her rounds from door to door with broom and basket, collecting yesterday's garbage. If she happened to cross Tehmina's line of vision, all the boys were sure to have a fine time, because Tehmina, though blurry with cataracts, would recognize the *kuchrawalli* and let loose at her with a stream of curses fouler than any filth in the garbage basket, for committing the unspeakable crime of passing in front of her, thereby polluting her prayers and vitiating their efficacy.

Even Daddy laughed, but he hurried us along as we lingered there to follow the ensuing dialogue. We picked our way through sleeping streets. The pavement dwellers would stretch, and look for a place to relieve themselves. Then they would fold up their cardboard pieces and roll away their plastics before the street sweepers arrived and the traffic got heavy. Sometimes, they would start a small fire if they had something to cook for breakfast, or else try to beg from people who came to the Irani restaurant for their morning *chai* and bun. Occasionally, Mummy would wrap up leftovers from the night before for Daddy and me to distribute to them along the way.

It had been such a long time since we last played cricket. Flying kites had also become a thing of the past. One by one, the things I held dear were leaving my life, I thought gloomily. And Francis. What about poor Francis? Where was he now, I wondered. I wished he was still working in the Baag. That awful thrashing he got in Tar Gully was the fault of Najamai and Tehmina, those stupid old women. And Najamai saying he stole eighty rupees was nonsense, in my opinion; the absent-minded cow must have forgotten where she left the money.

I put down the tweezers and reached for the comics. Daddy looked up. "Don't stop now, it should be perfect this week. There will be an interview or something."

Avoiding his eye, I said stolidly, "I'm going to read the comics," and walked out to the compound steps. When I turned at the doorway Daddy was still looking at me. His face was like *Mamaiji*'s when the thread broke and slipped through his fingers and the spindle fell to the floor. But I kept walking, it was a matter of pride. You always did what you said you were going to do.

The comics did not take long. It used to be more fun when Daddy and I had a race to the door to grab the *Times*, and pretended to fight over who would read the comics first. I thought of the lines on Daddy's forehead, visible so clearly from my coign of vantage with the tweezers. His thinning hair barely gave off a dull lustre with its day-old pomade, and the Sunday morning stubble on his chin was flecked with grey and white.

Something—remorse, maybe just pity—stirred inside, but I quashed it without finding out. All my friends had fathers whose hair was greying. Surely they did not spend Sunday mornings doing what I did, or they would have said something. They were not like me, there was nothing that was too private and personal for them. They would talk about anything. Especially Pesi. He used to describe for us how his father passed gas, enhancing the narrative with authentic sound effects. Now he was in boarding school. His father was dead.

From our C Block stone steps I could observe the entire length of the compound, up to A Block at the far end. Dr. Sidhwa's black Fiat turned in at the gate and trundled laboriously over the roughhewn flagstones of Firozsha Baag. He waved as he went past. He looked so much like Pesi's father. He had the same crow's-feet at the corners of his eyes that Dr. Mody used to have, and even their old cars seemed identical, except that Dr. Mody healed animals and Dr. Sidhwa, humans. Most of us had been treated by him at one time or another. His house and dispensary were within walking distance of Firozsha Baag, even a sick person's walking distance; he was a steadfast Parsi, seen often at fire-temples; and he always drove over for his house-calls. What more could we want in a doctor?

The car stopped at the far end of the compound. Dr. Sidhwa heaved out, he was a portly man, and reached in for his bag. It must be an emergency in A Block, I decided, for someone to call him on Sunday. He slammed the door, then opened and slammed it again, harder now. The impact rocked the old car a little, but the door shut properly this time. Viraf emerged from the steps of A Block. I waved to him to let him know I was waiting.

Viraf was my best friend. Together we learned bicycling, on a rented contraption of bent spokes and patchwork tyres from Cecil Cycles of Tar Gully: Fifty Paise Per Hour. Daddy used to take us to practise at Chaupatty on the wide pavements by the beach. They were deserted in the early morning—pavement dwellers preferred the narrow side streets—except for pigeons gathering in anticipation of the pigeon-man, who arrived when the streets stirred to life. We took turns, and Daddy ran behind, holding the seat to keep us steady. Daddy also taught the two of us to play cricket. Mummy had been angry when he brought home the bat and ball, asking where the money had come from. His specialty on his own school team had been bowling, and he taught us the leg break and off break, and told us about the legendary Jasu Patel, born with a defective wrist which turned out to be perfect for spin bowling, and how Jasu had mastered the dreaded curl spin which was eventually feared by all the great international batsmen.

Cricket on Sunday mornings became a regular event for the boys in Firozsha Baag. Between us we almost had a complete kit; all that was missing was a pair of bails, and wicket-keeping gloves. Daddy took anyone who wanted to play to the Marine Drive *maidaan*, and organized us into teams, captaining one team himself. We went early, before the sun got too hot and the *maidaan* overcrowded. But then one Sunday, halfway through the game, Daddy said he was going to rest for a while. Sitting on the grass a little distance away, he seemed so much older than he did when he was batting, or bowling leg breaks. He watched us with a faraway expression on his face. Sadly, as if he had just realized something and wished he hadn't.

There was no cricket at the *maidaan* after that day. Since we were not allowed to go alone, our games were now confined to the Firozsha Baag compound. Its flagstoned surface would not accept the points of stumps, and we chalked three white lines on the compound's black stone wall. But the compound was too cramped for cricket. Besides, the uneven ground made the ball bounce and rear erratically. After a few shattered panes of glass and several complaints from neighbours, the games ceased.

I waved again to Viraf and gave our private signal, "OO ooo OO ooo," which was like a yodel. He waved back, then took the doctor's bag and accompanied him into A Block. His polite demeanour made me smile. That Viraf. Shrewd fellow, he knew the things to do to make grownups approve of him, and was always welcome at all the homes in Firozsha Baag. He would be back soon.

I waited for at least half an hour. I cracked all my fingers and knuckles, even the thumbs. Then I went to the other end of the compound. After sitting on the steps there for a few minutes, I got impatient and climbed upstairs to find out why Viraf was buttering up the doctor.

But Dr. Sidhwa was on his way down, carrying his black bag. I said, "*Sahibji*, doctor," and he smiled at me as I raced up to the third floor. Viraf was standing at the balcony outside his flat. "What's all the *muskaa-paalis* for the doctor?"

He turned away without answering. He looked upset but I did not ask what the matter was. Words to show concern were always beyond me. I spoke again, in that easygoing debonair style which all of us tried to perfect, right arm akimbo and head tilted ever so slightly, "Come on *yaar*, what are your plans for today?"

He shrugged his shoulders, and I persisted, "Half the morning's over, man, don't be such a crybaby."

"Fish off," he said, but his voice shook. His eyes were red, and he rubbed one as if there was something in it. I stood quietly for a while, looking out over the balcony. His third-floor balcony was my favourite spot, you could see the road beyond Firozsha Baag, and sometimes, on a sunny day, even a corner of Chaupatty beach with the sun gleaming on the waves. From my ground floor veranda the compound's black stone wall was all that was visible.

Hushed voices came from the flat, the door was open. I looked into the dining-room where some A Block neighbours had gathered around Viraf's mother. "How about Ludo or Snakes-and-Ladders?" I tried. If he shrugged again I planned to leave. What else could I do?

"Okay," he said, "but stay quiet. If *Mumma* sees us she'll send us out."

No one saw as we tiptoed inside, they were absorbed in whatever the discussion was about. "*Puppa* is very sick," whispered Viraf, as we passed the sickroom. I stopped and looked inside. It was dark. The smell of sickness and medicines made it stink like the waiting room of Dr. Sidhwa's dispensary. Viraf's father was in bed, lying on his back, with a tube through his nose. There was a long needle stuck into his right arm, and it glinted cruelly in a thin shaft of sunlight that had suddenly slunk inside the darkened room. I shivered. The needle was connected by a tube to a large bottle which hung upside down from a dark metal stand towering over the bed.

Viraf's mother was talking softly to the neighbours in the dining-room. "...in his chest got worse when he came home last night. So many times I've told him, three floors to climb is not easy at your age with your big body, climb one, take rest for a few minutes, then climb again. But he won't listen, does not want people to think it is too much for him. Now this is the result, and what I will do I don't know. Poor little Viraf, being so brave when the doctor..."

Supine, his rotundity had spread into a flatness denying the huge bulk. I remembered calling Viraf a crybaby, and my face flushed with shame. I swore I would apologize. Daddy was slim and wiry, although there were the beginnings of a small pot, as Mummy called it. He used to run and field with us at cricket. Viraf's father had sat on the grass the one time he took us. The breath came loud and rasping. His mouth was a bit open. It resembled a person snoring, but was uneven, and the sound suggested pain. I noticed the lines on his brow, like Daddy's, only Daddy's were less deep.

Over the rasp of his breath came the voice of Viraf's mother. "...to exchange with someone on the ground floor, but that also is no. Says I won't give up my third-floor paradise for all the smell and noise of a ground-floor flat. Which is true, up here even B.E.S.T. bus rattle and rumble does not come. But what use of paradise if you are not alive in good health to enjoy it? Now doctor says intensive care but Parsi General Hospital has no place. Better to stay here than other hospitals, only..."

My eyes fixed on the stone-grey face of Viraf's father, I backed out of the sickroom, unseen. The hallway was empty. Viraf was waiting for me in the back room with the boards for Ludo and Snakes-and-Ladders. But I sneaked through the veranda and down the stairs without a word.

The compound was flooded in sunshine as I returned to the other end. On the way I passed the three white stumps we had once chalked on the compound wall's black stone. The lines were very faint, and could barely be seen, lost amongst more recent scribbles and abandoned games of noughts and crosses.

Mummy was in the kitchen, I could hear the roaring of the Primus stove. *Mamaiji*, sinister in her dark glasses, sat by the veranda window, sunlight reflecting off the thick, black lenses with leather blinders at the sides; after her cataract operation the doctor had told her to wear these for a few months.

Daddy was still reading the *Times* at the dining-table. Through the gloom of the light bulb I saw the Murphy Baby's innocent and joyous smile. I wondered what he looked like now. When I was two years old, there was a Murphy Baby Contest, and according to Mummy and Daddy my photograph, which had been entered, should have won. They said that in those days my smile had been just as, if not more, innocent and joyous.

The tweezers were lying on the table. I picked them up. They glinted pitilessly, like that long needle in Viraf's father. I dropped them with a shudder, and they clattered against the table.

Daddy looked up questioningly. His hair was dishevelled as I had left it, and I waited, hoping he would ask me to continue. To offer to do it was beyond me, but I wanted desperately that he should ask me now. I glanced at his face discreetly, from the corner of my eye. The lines on his forehead stood out all too clearly, and the stubble flecked with white, which by this hour should have disappeared down the drain with the shaving water. I swore to myself that never again would I begrudge him my help; I would get all the white hairs, one by one, if he would only ask me; I would concentrate on the tweezers as never before, I would do it as if all our lives were riding on the efficacy of the tweezers, yes, I would continue to do it Sunday after Sunday, no matter how long it took.

Daddy put down the newspaper and removed his glasses. He rubbed his eyes, then went to the bathroom. How tired he looked, and how his shoulders dropped; his gait lacked confidence, and I'd never noticed that before. He did not speak to me even though I was praying hard that he would. Something inside me grew very heavy, and I tried to swallow, to dissolve that heaviness in saliva, but swallowing wasn't easy either, the heaviness was blocking my throat.

I heard the sound of running water. Daddy was preparing to shave. I wanted to go and watch him, talk to him, laugh with him at the funny faces he made to get at all the tricky places with the razor, especially the cleft in his chin.

Instead, I threw myself on the bed. I felt like crying, and buried my face in the pillow. I wanted to cry for the way I had treated Viraf, and for his sick father with the long, cold needle in his arm and his rasping breath; for *Mamaiji* and her tired, darkened eyes spinning thread for our *kustis*, and for Mummy growing old in the dingy kitchen smelling of kerosene, where the Primus roared and her dreams were extinguished; I wanted to weep for myself, for not being able to hug Daddy when I wanted to, and for not ever saying thank you for cricket in the morning, and pigeons and bicycles and dreams; and for all the white hairs that I was powerless to stop.

Willie

Jim Burke

I often thought I should write it down, leave some record of the way that summer changed my life. But maybe that sounds a little dramatic because I guess it really didn't—change my life, I mean. I don't guess things would have turned out much different for me if I'd never met Willie. It wasn't all that long ago so maybe I shouldn't expect all memories to have faded away, much as I'd have liked it. Images still keep clutching at me like a dog ragging a bone and sometimes I can almost feel myself there with that burning sun shrivelling everything—even people's spirits—and making folks edgy and mean.

I might never have met Willie—him and his lopsided smile and clumsy innocence—if I hadn't come home from school that summer. I'd just finished my first year of university and couldn't get any kind of half-way decent work in the city so I figured I'd go back home to Rossville and help out my dad in his store. Dad's was one of only two general stores in town and the only one that sold gas and even though there were only about seven or eight hundred people in the area, the trade was enough to keep them both pretty busy. Country people don't shop like city folks. In the city, they usually do a week's shopping at one crack but back home they do it a little bit at a time. A farmer might come in for some tobacco in the morning and then get his cigarette papers that afternoon. Each visit's as much a social as business call and it wasn't uncommon to see three or four pick-ups and tractors in the dirt yard fronting the gas pumps.

I wasn't that keen on coming home for the summer. I'd met this girl at school and figured if I could get work and hang around the city, she and I might get to know each other pretty well—if you know what I mean. But no job and no girl, just pumping gas into beat-up pick-ups and stacking shelves in a country store. I've got to admit it was nice to be with my folks again—at first, anyway. That cafeteria food sure couldn't hold a candle to mom's roasts and homemade bread. There wasn't a heck of a lot to do in Rossville—for kicks, I mean—but I'd started to get interested in literature— Hemingway, Faulkner, and that crowd—and I figured I might try my hand at that racket—writing, that is. I'd always been one for making up stories—usually to get out of some jam—and I thought I might as well put some of them down on paper and see if someone would spot me as Rossville's answer to Sinclair Lewis. One of the Lit profs at school had said that my writing "showed promise." I wasn't quite sure what that meant but at least he didn't say my stuff was rotten. I was really impressed by profs in those days. I figured if you could get a pile of money just for talking to people like me, you had to have something going for you. It took me a while to find out that their talk was usually filled with someone else's ideas. But that came later.

For the first couple of days after I came home, I just lazied around except for when I was telling the folks all about my adventures in the big city. I've got to admit I cleaned them up a little—not that I had to all that much since that first year I was kind of new and just feeling my way around—no pun intended. Well, on about my third day back, I was kind of putting it on, telling my dad how we had these discussions in Philosophy class and some of us decided that God really didn't exist because of the shape the world was in and Him supposed to be perfect and all. Dad just "hmmmmed" and hinted that it was time that I got down to something a little more beneficial to mankind like maybe sweeping out the store.

And that was pretty well the way summer passed, with me working in the store just about every day with maybe a little time off for fishing or trying to find out if Mattie Simmons was as wild as the farm boys leeringly implied. I never did find out—if she was wild, I mean. At least not that summer.

I did find out something else though. I found out that the world would have to get along without the deathless prose of Clifton W. Freitel—I always thought my name would look right at home on a dust jacket; kind of dignified but gutsy. Anyway, I gave that clackety typewriter of ours a pretty good workout and all I had to show for it was an Everest of scrap paper. I started to think that maybe it was just the town and tried to picture Hemingway closeted in the back room of a country store, sitting down to write *The Sun Also Rises*. "If he'd been stuck in a place like this," I comforted myself by thinking, "he probably wouldn't have got enough inspiration to write his own name. Who couldn't write novels in Paris or London? But try it in some little jerkwater town where everybody thinks creativity means reproducing more hicks!" It's not every day you find out you're not going to be another Hemingway so maybe I can be excused for the disappointment that made me a little bitter toward the townspeople and caused me to think of them as turned-in, strait-jacketed drudges. If they ever thought about anything but crops or herds, they kept it pretty well hidden. Plodding here and herding themselves there, they seemed to have all the characteristics of the animals they raised. It was like they had laid out a blueprint for themselves a long way back and stuck to it day by day, every once in a while checking to see if they'd stepped off the line. Anyway, they seldom did—step off, I mean—and if they did, their neighbors were quick to call it to their attention.

Most of the farmers in the area and quite a few of the townspeople were of German descent; hard-working upright citizens who approached their two main interests—work and worship—with the same single-minded purpose and unquestioning faith.

Well, my dad had to make quite a few business trips to the city and mom spent most of her day puttering in the garden or gossiping with the neighbour women so sometimes I was in complete charge of the store and I admit it made me feel kind of important to stand behind the counter and have people ask me for this and that. I'd made a point of finding out just where everything was and I'd try to be crisp and professional. Somebody'd ask for an item and I'd go right to it and whip it on the counter with a smooth "There you are, sir." I thought that would really impress them. Well, that's what I thought, anyway.

It was on one of those days when I was alone, standing behind the showcase and drumming my fingers on the counter-top, that I heard the screen door bang shut and looked up to see this big farm boy who didn't look at all familiar. He was a good six feet and didn't look like the kind of guy you'd want to tangle with. Everything about that broad, raw-boned frame spelled strength from those tree-trunk legs to that bull-neck set between a pair of the most massive shoulders I'd ever seen. Aside from his build, he looked about the same as most of the young men in those parts: blonde, blue-eyed, and dressed in scuffed overalls and a heavy plaid workshirt. He looked about eighteen or nineteen and, though it was only the end of May, he already had the makings of a typical farmer's tan. His face and neck as far as the vee of his shirt collar were a deep rust as were his arms, at least to the bases of his rolled-up sleeves. It was always that way with the farmers around here. They worked outside all day long and figured it was bad enough that the sun got at their faces and arms without them giving it a chance at the rest of them.

Well anyway, this fellow stood there in the middle of the store and looked around him at all the shelves, those blue eyes wide and shining and his smile all big but kind of hanging to one side and his mouth a little open. I couldn't help but stare at him. It wasn't often that you saw a smile like that in these parts. The farmers were mostly a pretty sour lot as if they had some inside knowledge that smiling was sinful and might jeopardize their chances of getting into that big wheat-field in the sky. The smile seemed even stranger stuck in the middle of a face that was completely strange to me. Like my mom and dad, I knew about everyone around here, particularly boys around my own age, but I sure couldn't place this one. Another thing that caught my eye was his boots, black and shiny even with a thin layer of dust filming them. Around here, the only time you'd see boots that shiny was on Sunday and here it was just Friday. He was a strange one alright.

But if I was surprised when I first spotted him—and I admit I was—it was nothing to what I felt when he started speaking—if you could call it that. He just kind of grunted out the words, twisting his face all up so that his tongue lolled to one side and you could see his jaw muscles standing out as though the words were jammed in there and he was doing his damnedest to squeeze them out. Well, he finally squeezed them out alright but that didn't end it because it took me just about as long to make out his meaning. That slow, painful way he had of talking caused me to concentrate on each word as it was shaped and sounded and I'd even find myself shaping the words along with him. Picking it up this way, it seemed as though each word seemed to stand by itself rather than as part of a meaningful sentence and it was a while before I could string them together.

Finally, I decided he said something like: "You got can-dy got quar-ter pay you." He said it a couple of times and by now I got the idea all right, him scuffing the floor with the toe of one of those shiny boots and squeezing that coin until the tips of his fingers were white. That old joke flashed into my head. You know the one: "Our town was so small, everyone took turns being the village idiot." Here's someone, I thought, who could take on the job full time and immediately I was ashamed at having such an idea. This wasn't the first time that I'd seen someone who was retarded or subnormal or whatever they call them now so I really had no excuse. I'd always felt really sorry for them even though they usually looked happier than most of the so-called normal people that gaped at them.

Still trying to figure out who he could be, I went about serving him. This wasn't the easiest thing in the world either. I showed him the candy counter and found that I was starting to fall into baby-talk myself, saying something like: "Can-dy o-ver here. See can-dy?" and "What kind you want?" He'd just look, his eyes so big I think he saw every candy on every shelf at the same time. I started pointing to different boxes but he'd just shake his head—and I mean shake. His head went in an arc that covered about two feet. He didn't do anything by halves, that was plain. Anyway, I finally stuck my finger into a box of chocolate creams and saw that blonde bullethead nod its approval. That head went a good eight or nine nods, with that chin smacking right down into that barrel chest every time. By the time the nodding stopped, I already had those creams in a bag. It was a big bag—holding about half a pound—and it didn't take him long to dig in. When he pushed open the door to leave, he turned and fastened that lopsided smile on me again and I could see that his lips were pretty well smeared with melted chocolate.

He gave a little wave as he stepped out and the door slapped shut before I could get one off in return. Just looking at him with his chocolate-coated smile gave me a good feeling—seeing him so happy over something so small. It really picked me up and I was even whistling when my dad got back from the city. This in itself was enough to make him suspicious since I'd never given him reason to think that tending the store was my favorite pastime.

I told him about my candy-fancying visitor, hoping to get some clues about who he was but dad was just as much in the dark as me. "Maybe he was just passing through," I thought. But no, come next Friday, there was that powerful body shuffling up to the candy counter again. Every Friday—regular as clock-work—he showed up at the store and gradually I got to know him a little better. Not that we ever had any real conversations—just smiled at each other a lot—but at least I found out that his name was Willie.

I found out quite a bit more about him though, picking up bits and pieces of conversations here and there and I got a pretty good picture of his situation. His full name was Willie Rentel, and as soon as I heard that last name it rang a bell, but I couldn't connect it up right away. Then I remembered that there was an old man by that name farming west of town and the pieces started to fall into place. Old man Rentel came into the store once in a while but he never said much and he never looked as though he wanted anyone else to say anything either. So I never did, except "Can I help you, sir," that is. My dad had known him or at least dealt with him for almost twenty years but it seemed that they never exchanged more than a dozen words, usually about the weather or what a rotten job the government was doing selling grain. Like many of the older people in the area, his English was overlaid with a heavy German accent. It always sounded like he was trying to talk and clear his throat at the same time.

He was small and wiry and it made you wonder how he could have fathered a Goliath of a son like Willie. Dad said there'd been four other Rentel boys helping the old man at one time or another but they'd all moved on; some to the city and others to farms in the area. Old man Rentel wasn't renowned for a sweet disposition and there was talk that the boys all got fed up with his slavedriving, miserly ways.

One day, a couple of guys that I went to high school with came in and I got the full story. It seems that Willie'd been in one of those homes in the city. You know the kind: for kids who are kind of slow or slightly disturbed; not dangerous but just a little off. Well, he just turned eighteen and the rules of the place said he'd have to leave. They just kept them up to juvenile age and now he'd had to go somewhere else. He really didn't have any other place to go so it wasn't very surprising that he ended up with his old man. It was plain that Mr. Rentel was making pretty good use of him and— knowing him—not going overboard on wages. For some time, he'd been living in that grey, weather-beaten shack of his by himself, taking on hired hands for work he couldn't handle alone. Now he had Willie, and the way they both worked, that was probably enough. The old man must have been pushing sixty but he was a match for anyone half his age. And Willie, well he was something that entirely defied classification. Just watching him pitch hay or feed livestock was enough to make you tired. The first time I saw him pick up a bale and throw it like a softball, my mouth dropped full open. He was just about the strongest person I'd ever seen and he wasn't even full-grown yet. He did everything effortlessly, smiling all the while or whistling through his teeth.

So that was the way it went for a couple of months, with Willie and his dad coming in about once a week—but never together. The old man was only seen with his son when they were working and even then, it didn't look as though they talked at all. Just a couple of work machines—one a blonde, smiling giant and the other a wizened, glowering dwarf.

Once I got used to the way Willie talked, we kind of hit it off. I like kids anyway and he was just a bigger model—lots bigger. Once, I asked him what he liked doing and he said in that slow, wheezing way of his: "I like to look at things...pret-ty things...like touch...smell them." He really went for flowers and such. Through the window, I'd often seen him crouching at the side of the road, snuffling away at some daisies or buttercups and even smiling at the damn things. Sometimes when he came in, he'd have pollen dust all over his nose, he'd push in so close. He never picked any though. "I don't want break them...make them die," he'd say. That's the kind of guy he was. Powerful enough to crush you but too gentle to even knock a petal off a withered wildflower. He reminded me of that kid's story I read years back about a bull who didn't want to fight but just lay around smelling flowers—that was Willie alright.

And there were times when Willie would have been well within his rights to use those muscles to straighten somebody out. Some of the farm boys took a cruel delight in giving him a rough time. They'd trip him, grab his bag of candies, and call him names like "dum-dum" or "goof," and he'd just smile and kind of cock his head to one side and look at his tormentors the way a St. Bernard might view a couple of little kids tugging at his ears. After a while, they stopped baiting him but that didn't mean they were his friends. Most people sort of felt uncomfortable around him.

That huge powerful body just didn't fit with that little-kid way he talked and acted. Mentally, he was probably about eight or nine and he just didn't fit in with the rest of us. It was plain to see that he was lonely. Sometimes he'd just hang around the store until that candy was pretty well gone; not saying much, just looking at everything and hoping that you'd nod or smile at him so he could nod and smile back. He really hated to leave but he knew his old man would be steaming if he stayed too long and he usually hustled on his way home. He never once showed up on a truck or tractor; always on foot. I guess his dad didn't trust him with a machine—with good reason, probably. Mr. Rentel wouldn't drive him down either though, so Willie had to make a three-mile hike each way—just for that bag of candy. When he left, it was at a steady lope and I would have bet that he didn't slow down along the way.

Well, he kept coming in but after a while, he wasn't alone anymore. He'd usually have a couple of town kids in tow—they couldn't have been more than nine or ten years old. It was funnier than hell seeing that crew lined up in front of the candy counter, him towering over them but with the same little-kid face pressing against the glass. They really made a production out of buying candy and I'd usually go along with it as though it was the biggest deal I'd swung all day. After a while, the novelty wore off for the little kids and Willie was pretty well alone—except for Lisa Parton. Lisa was about the prettiest eight-year-old girl I'd ever seen, and her mother always made sure that she was decked out better than any girl in town. Her chestnut curls always had bright ribbons in them and her clothes—even her jeans—were spotless.

The way she talked to Willie really knocked me out. She'd say: "Those mints look nice, Willie. Maybe we should get some of those." Her voice would be all prim and grown-up and it was really comical to see that doll-like creature counselling her hulking companion. Willie always nodded sagely at her advice as though really thinking about it but I knew he was set on the chocolate creams and I already had a bag ready. He'd listen to Lisa, incline his head to one side and put one finger up beside his cheek but when I pointed at those creams, that big boulder head of his would sweep into those looping nods.

Now that he had a friend, he wouldn't hang around inside the store so much. They'd be outside doing all those kid things, skipping rope and such. You haven't seen anything until you've seen a six foot, two-hundred-pounder skip rope. It was like watching an elephant take tapdancing lessons. They'd often go walking along the edge of the road—Lisa leading him by the hand—stopping occasionally to look into gopher holes or sniff the flowers. I guessed he must have been happier now, having a friend and all, although his smile seemed just about the same. His eyes seemed different though—softer and less shiny than before—and darker, as though there was something in there looking out. Before his eyes seemed like mirrors, just reflecting the outside world but now it looked like there was something in him that was really in touch with something he saw out there—something that had meaning for him.

And that was how the summer passed. July had snuck up on me and I was starting to think about getting ready to go back to university. Not that I had a lot of getting ready to do; it was just that I wasn't really excited about staying in the country since I'd discovered the girls out here weren't all that fired up about sex even though they'd seen bulls do their stuff and knew what the score was. Another myth shot down. It's funny; all the guys in Rossville figured the city girls must be hot stuff and the guys at college thought that the next best thing to a nymphomaniac was a farm girl.

After a while, Willie started coming to town more often—two, sometimes three times a week and he'd always be with Lisa. They were inseparable. Her folks weren't too keen on this set-up though. One day, I was in the stock room in back and I heard Mr. Parton's voice, loud and angry.

"I told Lisa not to have anything to do with that ape," he snapped. "He's been away in that nut house for years for good reason and he might do anything. You read about those sex maniacs all the time. I don't know why the hell he's running around loose with all these kids around."

Then my dad tried to cool him down in that low soothing voice of his: "Willie's harmless. He's just an overgrown kid. I've never seen anyone more gentle in my life. He worships Lisa and wouldn't think of doing her any harm."

"Wouldn't think? That's the whole trouble; he probably *can't* think. And that's why we've got to protect our kids from him. I'm gonna talk to Rentel and tell him he's got to keep that freak away from our kids."

I guess he must have followed up on it because I didn't see Willie for about three weeks. When he finally showed up, he didn't seem like his old self. The mouth was kind of hanging open as usual but it wasn't smiling. His eyes seemed dull and disinterested and no longer swept over the shelves. The only place he looked was over his shoulder and he did it like he was expecting somebody that he wasn't too crazy about seeing. He just rattled a quarter onto the counter-top and stuck a stubby forefinger against the glass in front of the chocolate creams—so hard the whole case shook a little. I could see he was in no mood to talk, so I just handed him the bag without saying anything. He grabbed it and started for the door then turned and waved, with just a quiver of a smile. Then he was through the door and gone.

I went to the window and watched him start off down the road. He was just getting into that gallop of his when a girl's high-pitched squeal piped out: "Willie, wait up!" It was Lisa and she was running just about as fast as those little legs could go, breathlessly shouting for Willie to stop. He pulled up and turned around and she came up to him. I could see them talking, then she reached up and grabbed his hand, leading him to a wild rose bush at the side of the road and they both started smelling the blossoms and lightly touching them.

Then Lisa plucked one of the rich red blossoms and, cupping it in her hand, held it up to him. Willie looked at it for a long while, then took it and twined it among her shining curls. It was a sight I'll never forget and I admit I had a catch in my throat and my eyes weren't as dry as they could've been. I guess we were all pretty caught up in it: Lisa, Willie, and I, because none of us heard Mr. Rentel's rusty pick-up until it jarred to a dusty stop in front of them. Rentel was out of the truck before the dust had settled and I could hear his voice, shrill and angry.

As he headed toward the pair, I could see him undoing his belt and by the time he came abreast of them, it was already in his hand. Still yelling, he started cleaving the air with that belt, buckle-end out. Again and again it slashed against Willie's arms as he tried to shield himself. The old man was no slouch though and some of those swipes managed to get through his defence, opening angry red welts on his cheek and forehead. Her piercing screams shattering the country silence, Lisa fled, running blindly, falling, and scrambling to her feet, heedless of the thorns that stung her legs.

Willie just stood there and took it. With his size and strength, he could have tossed his father aside like a rag doll but he just stood there until the old man wore himself out. For a time I felt paralyzed and sick to my stomach. I wanted desperately to do something—to end the horror, but I couldn't move. By the time I pushed open the door and went outside, Mr. Rentel was slipping his belt on, his chest heaving and his breath coming hard. He pointed to the back of the pick-up and Willie clambered in, still holding his hands over his face.

Then the truck rattled off with me watching until all I could see was a settling cloud of dust. Well, the story of what happened got around pretty quick and I must admit I had something to do with it. I told mom and dad and I guess they told a few others. It seemed I *had* to talk about it—to try and make some sense of it all. I felt rotten about it and wondered if maybe I shouldn't have done something—but what? For a while, I just moped around thinking a lot but not really getting anywhere.

But after a while, I forgot about it; not completely, it's true, but at least the nightmarish image of that belt whipping down dimmed a little and I no longer felt sick when I thought about it—just sad. We were into August now and I should have been looking forward to going back to school, but I wasn't. School and the city seemed like a completely different world and about a million miles away. Here I was in a tiny world that I'd grown up in and it seemed that I couldn't get to first base figuring it out.

It seemed like I had a lot of nerve sitting in some university in the city and thinking I had all the answers because I'd read a few books. What I'd been hiding deep inside jumped out at me and I knew that I didn't want to go back to school—at least not until I found out a few answers—and I didn't want to stay in Rossville among people that seemed to sleepwalk through life, going through the motions but not connecting them up with anything meaningful. Probably what I wanted to get away from most was myself, but I didn't know that then.

So there I was, watching my mother get my stuff ready and listening to my dad tell his friends that I was going to make those profs sit up and take notice, and not wanting any part of it. It was one of those late summer days with a dry wind sweeping in and I was thinking about what I should do, when I heard the high-pitched wail of a siren and—looking out the front window—saw a bigger rush of traffic than that old road had probably ever carried. Through the billowing dust, I could make out an R.C.M.P. squad car in the lead, followed closely by an ambulance with a blinking red light and a siren going full out. The other cars seemed to be filled with people tagging along out of curiosity.

By the time they all zoomed by, I counted eight cars in all. I think I would have joined in myself if I hadn't been tending the store. But I couldn't, so it was a couple of hours before I heard what the fuss was about.

They'd been heading west toward the Rentel place and I figured maybe the old man had a heart attack or something but they didn't stop there, continuing further along until they reached the place where the railroad track crosses the road. When I heard what had happened, I was glad that I wasn't able to get down there. When that gang of cars got there, a long freight train was straddling the road, all silent and shut-down. The engineer and some other trainmen were perched on the steps of the diesel, not talking at all, and they got up slowly when the mounties pulled up.

The brakeman told the story. He'd been looking down the track as they lugged their chain of cattle cars south and he'd noticed something on the tracks way ahead. He couldn't make out what it was right away but he gave a couple of blasts on the horn just to be on the safe side. He kept his eye on the track and saw that whatever it was moved. He called the engineer over and it didn't take them long to figure out that it was a man's body draped across the rails. They were about a hundred yards away and going at a pretty fair clip when the brake was jammed on, and all the while the horn was blasting, but it was no use. Half the train had passed over the prostrate form before it ground to a shuddering halt.

There wasn't much left of him but from the description of the brakeman and engineer and from the clothes, it was pretty certain that it was Willie Rentel scattered there beneath those cars. Later on, they found a pair of still-shiny boots and that cinched it. They said that he just laid himself on the track and waited for that train to crush the life out of him and couldn't understand how somebody could do something so horrible. "He must have been crazy," they said.

A lot of people around here thought that. A lot of them said: "But he was always smiling and seemed so happy. Why would he do it?" Others guessed that "he's probably better off like this. What kind of life could a loony like that have, anyway?" That "better off" business kind of threw me at first. I couldn't figure how anyone could be better off with pieces of him strewn along half a mile of track. But that was just another question I couldn't answer.

Well, I didn't go back to school that fall and I didn't stay home either. Mom and dad took it pretty hard but I just took off and I've been on the road for about a year now, hitting different places. I don't have all the answers yet, that's for sure, but I think I'm getting somewhere and maybe someday I'll stand behind that candy counter again, think about Willie and get that good feeling I had when I first saw his crooked smile. I hope so, because sometimes it gets kind of lonely and the world doesn't seem to have the time to smile at flowers.

The Ride

Anne Marriott

The day of the ride was a fine day. No dust blew. That alone set it apart from the rest of the summer.

Other days, by dinner time (which was noon) the wind had risen. After dinner, when I went down the yard to the outhouse, there was at least a faint brown film in the air, making me blink and sniffle. If the wind were rising, the film would thicken, until the atmosphere was full of grit, collecting in the corners of the eyes and grinding between the teeth.

On the worst days, a choking cloud of soil moved across the country, a dark blizzard piling up dry drifts against the paintless farmhouses, sagging barns and sheds. It seemed to pile above me, filling the sky; I could feel the weight of it, pressing down, smothering. Days like that, I tried not to go outside at all. Before my rest I would use the chamber pot upstairs.

The afternoon rest was the tag-end of my convalescence. I had been ill, close to death, for a long time the previous winter and spring, and my visit to the prairies—a high, dry climate—to my father's sister-in-law was to finish the cure. (My parents, obviously, had not believed the reports of the drought which appeared in the eastern papers.)

I would lie on the bed and listen to the wind outside the house slapping a loose piece of siding against the wall near my head. The wind had a curious whine, lonely, foreboding; the sound increased the state of fear I was in constantly that year—most of all the fear of death. I had escaped death so narrowly, and some day—any day!—I would not escape it at all.

I went on the ride with my cousin Harry—not that he wanted me to go.

He came into the kitchen where I was finishing a late breakfast and said to my aunt, "It's such a good day I think I'll go down into the hills and look for those two damn colts."

He gave me a wink, something that happened often and which I had decided was his special signal for me. Something just between the two of us, recognition of a bond holding us together—and holding us apart.

A first cousin was the next thing to a brother—my parents had stressed this when seeing me off on the train west. So I was at ease with Harry, not stupid with shyness as with all other boys—who were automatically potential boy-friends. He had bright red hair and blue eyes, and the reddish, perpetually chapped-looking skin that sometimes goes with that colouring. I thought him the most handsome boy I had ever seen, and fallen in love with him my second day on the farm, a love sharpened by the knowledge that it could never reach its climax—a white wedding.

When he told my aunt he was going to ride after the colts, "Can I come?" I cried. "Can I go with you, Harry? Please, Harry? Please?"

"It's too hot for you," said my aunt.

"It's too far for you," said Harry. "I might go all of twenty miles before I'm through, and you were never on a horse in your life until last week."

"It's not too far," I said. "And heat's good for me—the doctor said so. Please, Harry, please—"

I kept on until he got angry and shouted at me, "Okay, then come on, but don't blame me if you don't have a good time."

By noon, we had ridden nearly ten miles, over summer fallow that rose like dry cocoa around the horses' hooves; over crackling stubble and stunted crop, and into the shallow, dead-grass-covered hills which lay to the south of the farm.

I was dizzy with heat. Once in a while Harry, riding ahead, looked over his shoulder at me with a sarcastic grin.

Coming up through a narrow, stifling draw, we arrived suddenly at a small level area. There were a few rusting pieces of farm machinery on it, half buried in dust, Russian thistle and pigweed, in the middle of the flat ground, and on the far side, looking at first glance like an outcrop of the hill beyond, was a house.

"I'll be damned," Harry said, "I'll bet you this is the James place."

"Who're they?" My mouth was so dry I could hardly shape the words.

"The James—who else?" He smiled more kindly, then. "I don't know that much about them—nobody does. Some say they came from England years back. Others say they're from the States. There's tales Bert James was only a jump ahead of the law and that's why they hid out down here in the hills—but then people'll make up tales like that. Anything to give spice to life these days."

A screen door in the front of the house was flung open. A broad woman in a brownish dress came out and stared.

"Company!" It was a shout. "Lord love us, we got company!" She turned, called into the dark hole of doorway behind her. "Rosella! D'you hear? We got company! And one of 'em's a *girl*!"

We rode around a half-buried stoneboat (poking fun at my ignorance, Harry had identified such common objects for me my first few days at the farm). We rode up to the house.

"Why, it's Harry, isn't it?" the woman said. "Harry Burton. I seen you last year at the Stampede."

"That's right," Harry said. "Never come across your place before, though. —This is my cousin, Irene Gray, from down east."

"Pleased to meet you," Mrs. James said. "Well—don't just sit there, get down, come on in. —Rosella!" she called into the doorway again, "Girl looks about your age, too!"

A tremendous greasy smell of onions suddenly gusted out of the door. I could almost see it, thick on the air.

"You're just in time for dinner," Mrs. James said.

"Harry," I said urgently, "We—we can't stop, can we? We've got *that*," I pointed to the lardpail tied to Harry's saddle. On the other side hung a quart sealer of hard well-water flavoured with Watkins' lemon crystals. I had been dreaming of our picnic for hours, Harry sprawled on the dry grass beside me—

"It's not much of a meal," Mrs. James said. Her hearty voice dropped a little. "But you'd be more than welcome—"

"Of course we'll stay—be glad to," Harry said. "A hot dinner's better than a bunch of sandwiches any time." He gave me a sharp look as he got off his horse.

"Put the horses in the barn, Harry, there's shade for 'em there if nothing else," Mrs. James said. "Rosella! What's wrong with that girl?—Stiff, eh?" she turned her attention to me, as I forced a leg around over the horse's rump and then dismounting caught at the stirrup to save myself falling full length on the ground. Harry watched me.

"Come in, then!" Mrs. James held the ragged screen door open. As I passed her, I stumbled, bumped against her huge buttocks, feeling them wobble inside her worn, patched dress.

After the harsh brilliant light outside, the inside of the house seemed pitch dark, but after some moments I made out a girl—Rosella, I supposed—standing motionless beside a long table. As her mother had said, Rosella like me was in her late teens. Unlike me, she was extremely pretty.

"Hello," I said nervously. Rosella continued to stare at me in silence. I looked away, around the room. It was large; as my eyes adjusted further, I saw the wallpaper was cracked and faded; here and there a strip hung down. The window sills were crammed with sickly plants in tomato cans—Rosella moved and I looked back at her. She wore a shapeless, greyish dress with a random pattern in places, a design of lighter dots and lines.

She moved again. The design was not a design. It was Rosella's pale skin, showing through holes and tears.

A wave of onion odour came from the wide cook-stove at the end of the room. The familiar panic swelled in my chest. I was going to vomit—to faint—to have a heart attack. I was going to die—*here*!

"Give her a chair, Rose!" Mrs. James spoke urgently. "She's come over swimmy."

Rosella pushed a wooden kitchen-chair, wired together at the back, toward me and I lurched onto it.

"Too much sun," Mrs. James said, nodding her large head. She had a mass of sandy-grey, wiry curls. "Need your dinner, too." She slammed pots and pans about on the stove.

"We can't stay—really, we can't," I said desperately, trying to get to my feet. "It's very kind of you to ask us but Harry has to find—"

"Won't get him going again till he's had his meal," she said, but she looked disturbed. "It's not much, as I said, but lucky we got a crop of spuds if nothing else. And them Swedes over west give Bert a bag of onions." She poured water from a black kettle into the frying-pan, and steam rushed up, an oily geyser. "Rosella! Don't stand there mooning! Get the table set before Dad and the boys come in!—always wishing and wishing there was a girl to talk to," she said to me, "And now there is one, cat's got her tongue!—Not that *I* ever thought girls was that good company!"

Harry was in the doorway. The screen slapped shut behind him. He came into the room, laughing. He gave Mrs. James a wink.

"Harry!" I said, "I—I don't feel well."

For a moment he looked anxious. But then Mrs. James said, "She was saying you had to leave, but I think she'll feel better if she has her dinner."

Harry's expression changed. "You will feel better when you've eaten, Irene," he said with meaning.

My eyes filled with tears. Blinking, I turned toward Rosella. Mechanically she was putting bent and blackened cutlery between the chipped enamel plates already spaced down each side of the table. Every time she leaned forward her breasts pushed against her dress and I expected it to rip further.

She caught my look, interpreted it wrongly and spoke at last. "Them's awful plates, all right." Her voice had a mechanical sound; she spoke slowly. But having once spoken she went on, sounding more natural. "If the gove'ment sends us that relief money, then we get new dishes. I got 'em all picked out. In the catalogue. Roses on 'em—that's my flower." She got to the end of the table nearer to me and said in an undertone, with a glance at Harry, "I'll show you—after dinner. I'm getting something else, too. Something special. I might show you that too. I might."

"Here's the men!" Mrs. James pounded a lopsided wooden masher into a pot. "Put the bread on, Rose, while I make the tea! Then we'll dish up."

"This is Bert James, Irene—my cousin from down east." I realized the door had opened and closed.

"Pleased to meet you." He wore a sticky-looking cap; he pushed it back as he spoke but left it on his head. He was smaller than his wife, dark, weasel-looking. His eyes looked hot. In spite of the lines on his sweaty face I thought he was younger than Mrs. James—certainly younger than my own father, who was fifty.

He glanced at Rosella and she at him. Her face was blank. He went to the water-bucket, drank, dipping water with an old tobacco can which floated on the water. He poured the surplus back into the bucket. Nausea rose faintly in my gullet.

In turn, five young boys who had slipped into the room behind him, so quickly and quietly I had scarcely noticed their arrival, drank from the tobacco can. They looked at me sideways from shy-animal faces. Their hair-cuts and shirt-collars were ragged, though their clothes were neatly patched and darned. One by one, in a little darkish-looking water, they washed their faces and hands. Bert James did not wash.

"Sit down!" Mrs. James set an enamel washbasin full of potatoes on the table. "Sorry we've no meat, but the bread's fresh." She carried the chair, from which I had just risen, to the head of the table. Mr. James sat down in it. He jerked his head at Rosella and she moved in behind the table, along the wooden bench which ran the table's length against the wall. "Sit by me!" she murmured, and I got in beside her. Harry sat next.

"Move down there!" Mrs. James said to the five boys, who were on another long bench, on the other side of the table. They made little noises of protest.

"Lots of space over here," Harry said, "or would be if Irene didn't take up so much room." He gave me a shove and Mrs. James plumped down at the end.

It was the first time I had been so close to Harry. His arm, hip-bone and thigh were pressed against mine; I was surprised at the hardness of them. He seemed quite unaware of any contact with me, turning away and laughing at something Mrs. James had said in an undertone to him.

Rosella held the basin for me to take the potatoes. They were streaked with dark lines and my nausea came back, stronger. I couldn't swallow them. Nor the greasy-looking gravy—

Harry dug his elbow into me, making me flinch. I picked up the bent fork and began to eat. To my surprise the potatoes and the onion gravy tasted good. I realized I was hungry after all. The fresh bread was delicious, even though there was no butter. I had second helpings.

While I ate, I managed to edge even closer to Harry. He pulled away. But with Mrs. James' bulk beyond him he could not get far. I realized I was quite happy.

I felt Rosella catch her breath, just as I became aware of a sound outside—a truck approaching, grinding over the hills. Mrs. James stopped talking. The truck came closer, into the yard. There was silence around the table except for a faint snickering from one of the boys.

I was surprised that no one moved. My aunt would have been up and at the window at the first noise of an engine, eager to see who was coming, out to welcome them—as Mrs. James had welcomed Harry and me.

The truck door slammed. Mr. James scraped his chair a few inches over the cracked linoleum, closer to Rosella. Everyone looked over at the door.

A figure appeared in the doorway, black against the dry brilliance of the yard outside.

"Come on in, Bob, you're just in time," Mrs. James said. Her voice was hospitable enough. I saw Mr. James glare at her. "Rose, get another plate—"

"No, no thanks, I've eaten. I'll just get a drink of water." He was a middle-sized man, about midway between Mr. James and Harry in age.

He was rather fat. "Howdy, all." I saw he was carrying a large parcel, in brown paper. It looked like a dress box. "I brought you something, Rose."

She did not look up at him. "It's a dress," he said, "Pink, your colour. You've been needing a dress." His eyes (I thought) ran over her torn one. "You ought to like a pink dress," he said.

She stared into her cup, at the blob of tea-leaves congested in the bottom. He set the parcel against the wall.

Mr. James was looking at her with his beady, hot brown eyes. Suddenly he hit the table with his fist. The knives and forks jumped and thudded; the enamel plates clanked. I jumped, too, harder into Harry. He pushed me away with his forearm.

"God damn it to hell!" Mr. James shouted, apparently at Mrs. James. "Why d'you let her go around like—like—"

Her red face became purplish. She leaned forward, around Harry, her breasts bulging out the front of her dress against the plate in front of her.

"As if you don't know I can't do nothing with her, not any more!" she shouted back at him. "Not since—" His eyes wavered away.

"Give us more tea," he muttered. The boys passed the big, broken-spouted brown pot to him. Everyone ate dessert—stewed Saskatoon berries, dry and seedy. Bob leaned against the wall, picking his teeth with a match which he carefully whittled to a point before he began.

"This here's Bob Lewis," Mrs. James suddenly realized no one had been introduced. "Pleased to meet you," he said.

Harry had been looking at him carefully. "I saw you at the Stampede last year," he said.

"That's right," Bob nodded, the match-stick jiggling.

The Stampede—where Harry had also met Mrs. James. No doubt Rosella had been there too. My mind put the romance together in a flash. She was so pretty—if only I had fair hair and blue eyes—Bob had fallen in love—

"How are the crops where you are?" Harry was asking, "Anything over there in the valley?"

"Not as much as it used to be," Bob said. "But compared to most folks I guess we've got a lot to be thankful for." He was solemn. "We need to count our blessings."

"That's right," Harry's voice was as solemn as Bob's, but it also had a certain sound I had learned to beware of. But if he were making fun of Bob, he let it rest there.

"Got some pliers and some spare wire in the truck," Bob said to Bert James. "Noticed last time I was around you've got some fence down along the pasture. I'll give you a hand with it."

"We can look after ourselves," Bert said, but scarcely loud enough to carry to where Bob stood. Mrs. James spoke loudly. "I don't know what's the use of mending fences when there's nothing to keep inside 'em—and not likely to be whether it ever rains or it doesn't!"

No, it didn't, I thought vaguely, look as if anything would grow in the hills. But my attention was on Harry. Before I could think of anything to say to hold him, he got up, as Bert rose to his feet at the head of the table. Mrs. James got up to let Harry out. Gulping down the last of the strong bitter tea, the boys got up too.

One after another, the men and boys went out. Mrs. James grabbed up the last boy in line, the one who did not look to me more than five. "Here, ducks, you're too little to go off with them men, listen to their kind of talk. You stay with Mum this afternoon, that's my baby!"

"I ain't no baby!" He struggled free and ran after the others.

Mrs. James shook her head. "He ain't, that's the truth. And he's the last, seems like, more's the pity." She sighed, went to the door and stared out, bulging against the dazzle, then closed the door and came back. She started to clear the table.

She told me, over the clatter, "That last one, there, Bert and Rosella, they helped me when the time come. Something didn't go right, that last one—none of their fault, it wasn't, but I was laid up a long time. Since then something seemed to drop, like—I can feel it—" she pointed with one of the forks at her sprawling abdomen. "Bearing down. Since, seems I can't carry no more children. Hurts, too when Bert—"

She stood still, staring at the fork, then her red face went back to its former cheerfulness. "Well, if we get them relief payments maybe I'll get someone to drive me to town, see the doctor, get fixed up as good as new." She laughed, went to the bucket and began to dip water out sparingly with the tobacco can into a bent dishpan which she placed on the stove.

All this time Rosella had been sitting, motionless, at the table. She was staring at the opposite wall. Mrs. James looked anxious.

"Rosella! You're mooning again! Why don't you show Irene—" she jerked her head toward the door at the opposite end of the long room.

Rosella made no response.

"*Rose*!"

Rosella stared at her mother. Abruptly she sprang up. "Come on, then," she took hold of my hand as if we were little girls. As I took mine away I was startled by the roughness of her palm.

"She's the artistic one," Mrs. James said behind us.

Art was my best subject at school so perhaps we had something in common after all. But I followed her without much interest.

She opened the door and we went into a very small bedroom almost entirely filled with a very large bed—the largest bed I had ever seen. It was, I realized, more like a platform, of boards on boxes, covered with old mattresses and faded patchwork quilts. I stared at it. However many of them slept in here, all in one bed? And—who slept next to who? I sat down on the edge.

Rosella was dragging something from underneath the platform. It was a large, dilapidated cardboard box, the name of a farm machinery company on the side. She hesitated, then, over opening it, squatting beside it with her hand on one of the flaps but not lifting it any further.

I still did not feel much interest. I looked away, staring around the room with its rows of winter coats and caps hung on nails. There was an old mirror which gave a distorted image of the opposite wall. There were some faded pictures of girls holding flowers, and kittens, cut from magazines and put up with straight pins—

"See?" Rosella laid something on my lap.

I looked down. I cried out. Not, I realize later, as loudly as I thought—at least Rosella did not start or show surprise.

I began to tremble. My fears—my greatest fear—liquefied my bones. It was an omen—it must be.

She had laid a tombstone on my lap.

It was not, I saw after a few seconds, as large as a normal tombstone, but in shape and general effect it could have been one of the stones I had seen on an unwilling visit to my uncle's grave last Sunday. (My uncle who at thirty had been kicked in the stomach by the unpredictable horse which had bucked him off in the snow, then—still unpredictable—had stood by him all night.)

"Everything all right?" Mrs. James looked in the door. (She must have heard me, at any rate.)

"Yes, thank you," I managed.

"It's my flower, see?" Rosella said. She was pointing to the centre of the slab. "I always do this design." It was a wreath of roses, painted in palest pink.

"What—what is it for?" I asked.

"I dunno." She looked vague. "I just like doing them. I couldn't buy no more paper, and then the little one, he found this clay down in the draw. Mixed with water it sets real hard."

"She puts it in my old meat tin, and it makes a real good block for painting on," Mrs. James said, still in the dooway. Rosella frowned.

"I got more," Rosella said to me in a whisper. She began tossing sheets of old newspapers and catalogues out of the box, on to the floor, and carefully, edge symmetrical with edge, laying out more and more of the slabs on the bed. Each one had exactly the same rose wreath, exactly in the centre. Some were pale pink, some pale blue, some pale yellow. The last were grey.

"I run out of everything but black, and then clean out." She bent over, searching among the papers in the bottom of the box.

"How did you—where did you get the design?" I asked.

"A transfer—one of them things for embroidering, you know? It come in an old country magazine, in a box with some of them relief clothes one time. Being it was my flower, I took it." She straightened up, something in her hand. As she did so I heard her dress rip again.

She opened the thing in her hand, held it out to me. "Run right out," she said.

It was a paintbox, the smallest, cheapest type. It had originally, I judged, held the primary colours and black. But it was scrubbed clean, no trace of tints remaining. There was a small brush, thread-bare. I looked at the immaculate paintbox, at Rosella's torn and—certainly—dirty dress. I was suddenly aware that the tombstone still rested on my knee; I snatched it up and held it out to Rosella. She had turned back to her box. I tossed the slab past her, onto the bed, then for a moment was terrified I might have cracked it. I had not. Staring at the paintbox, Rosella had not noticed what I had done.

Her face became lively for the first time. "Now I'll show you what's special, what I told you about!" Carefully she laid down the paintbox, bent and pulled the mail order catalogue from under the bed. She flipped over the crumpled pages, found one quickly. She read out "Dee-lux paintbox. Twenty different shades.—Twenty, could you imagine it? Think of all the roses I'll be able to paint, pink and mauve and—"

"Think you'll find any horses this way?" Harry was pushing past me, looking into the box of plaques, his reddish eyebrows raised. Rosella glared at him; she held out her arms as if to shield her creations. His blue eyes moved over them but he showed no interest. "Let's hit the trail," he said to me.

Rosella whispered to me, "I got dozens more—waiting for the paints. Stacked out back of the barn—"

It was on the tip of my tongue to tell her that I would send her a paintbox—with forty colours, if there were such a thing. But I hesitated.

If only Harry wasn't listening—he might think I sounded like a rich city girl, showing off. He'd teased me about that more than once.

"Come on, Irene," Harry said, straightening up and turning back toward the kitchen.

When Harry had brought the horses over to the door, and we were all standing outside, Mrs. James exclaimed, "Well, it done my heart good, seeing new faces! Come again—any time. And stay longer! If that relief comes through we'll give you something better than spuds and gravy."

"It was a damn good dinner," Harry said.

"I'll make a wreath just for you if you'll come and get it," Rosella murmured to me.

"We'll have roast beef and Yorkshire," Mrs. James promised recklessly. She grabbed me, her thick arms pressing me against her. Her breasts were against mine, I could feel them moving and squashing. She gave me a smacking kiss. "Goodbye, lovie! Hope you feel all right now. Have a nice ride back!"

She turned to Harry, held out her hand. "Aren't you going to give me a kiss?" he asked, his eyes sparkling.

"You bet your life I am!" She seized him, her face crimson. The loud kiss landed on Harry's mouth; he was kissing her back. "How's that?" she asked him.

"You could still teach the young ones a thing or two," Harry said to her.

"I thought you were in a hurry to get started!" I said furiously to him.

I turned toward my horse and tried to leap into the saddle. I was still so stiff that my muscles did not respond. I was stuck, one foot in the stirrup, the other poking at the air instead of swinging over the horse's rump.

"Give her a push!" Mrs. James cried, laughing. They all laughed. Rosella caught my helpless ankle, pushed my leg over. Mrs. James pushed on my rear. I was, finally, astride.

Harry mounted lightly on the other horse. "Thanks again," he said. "Yes, thank you very much." I made a great effort to sound grateful and pleased.

We began to jog slowly away. After a dozen yards or so we looked back, waved. "Goodbye!"

"Goodbye!" Mrs. James waved. Rosella waved. Her dress split open—"Get *up*!" I kicked my horse, yelling, "Get up! Get up!" The horse as always paid no attention and ambled on at the same gait.

Harry said nothing until we were in the draw. Mrs. James, Rosella, the house were out of sight behind us. Then, "You don't think I've never seen one of those things before, do you?" He added, in a regretful voice, "I guess it's just all the way you've been brought up, Irene. So sheltered."

A movement above us caught my eye. On the rim of the yellow-grey knoll, Bob was working with pliers on the broken, sagging wire fence. Why, if no one wanted him to? Against the blue sky his fat stomach was noticeable, yet he looked hardier, stronger, than I had thought indoors. He saw us and saluted with a gloved hand.

We went around the next bend in the gully and Bob was hidden.

"He wants to marry her, you know," Harry said. "You'd think she'd jump at anyone, to get away from that place. And her old man—"

I took hold of the saddle horn. I was dizzy again—but it was not really a physical dizziness. I did not know what it was.

One thing I did know, though, abruptly and very clearly. Life was not what I had thought it to be, not like that at all. What it was—For a few seconds I was more afraid of living even than I had been of dying. I *wanted* to die. If I had died, last winter—I saw my grave, also perfectly clearly, a peaceful mound, with one of Rosella's tombstones placed dead centre.

"Giddap!" Harry yelled.

He whacked my horse across its rear. We bounded up, out of the draw, onto a level plateau, the tombstone falling and shattering behind me. It was glorious, exhilarating; the sky, so close to us, still perfectly clear, the sun brilliant, and Harry and I alone together, for the whole yellow afternoon.

But in a few seconds the rubbing of the hard saddle against my chafed thighs made me cry out, "Slow down, Harry! Please! Slow down!"

I tried to pull the horse in and at the same time hold onto the saddle horn and stand in the stirrups, so that my legs would be away from the hot leather. "Harry! It hurts!"

But all Harry did was gallop on, laughing.

Biographies

Aske

Roger Aske was born in 1928 in Nottingham, England, where he lived until he went to sea at age 14. Much of his life has revolved around, or on, the oceans. He has been sailor, master mariner, and, after coming to Canada, a marine insurance broker. He is married with four children, and makes his home in Saint John, New Brunswick, where he is a part-time writer.

Several of his short stories have been published by Holt Rinehart and Winston in their school anthologies, and others have won recognition by the New Brunswick Writers' Association and the Canadian Authors' Association. His story "Birds," included in this volume, has not been published before. In his own words, he "writes for pleasure, for the love of words and the sense of literary fulfilment."

Atwood

Margaret Atwood was born in Ottawa in 1939, and moved to Toronto six years later. She graduated from Victoria College, University of Toronto, in 1961, and received an A.M. from Harvard in 1962. She has taught English at a number of Canadian universities, was writer in residence at the University of Toronto for two years, and was president of the Writers' Union of Canada in 1982-83. She now lives near Alliston, Ontario.

Since the publication of her first volume of poems, *Double Persephone*, in 1961, Atwood has published steadily. Her works include nine poetry collections, seven novels, two collections of short stories and one of "short fiction and prose poems," an anthology, two children's books and two works of criticism. Among these are: *The Journals of Susanna Moody* (1970); *Survival: A Thematic Guide to Canadian Literature* (1972); *Surfacing* (1972); *The New Oxford Book of Canadian Verse in English* (1982); *Murder in the Dark* (1983); and *Bluebeard's Egg* (1987). For her efforts, she has received the Governor General's Award, The Bess Hopkins Prize, the Molson Prize, a Guggenheim Fellowship Award and honorary degrees from five universities. In addition, two recent novels, *The Handmaid's Tale* (1986) and *Cat's Eye* (1989), were both nominated for England's Booker Prize.

Burke

Jim Burke was born in 1939 in Winnipeg. A graduate of the University of Winnipeg, he has worked as a community development worker with Native organizations, a political organizer with the Liberal Party, a reporter with CKY-TV in Winnipeg, and a freelance researcher for "W-5." He is currently living in Winnipeg, where he divides his time between freelance reporting and working on his upcoming novel.

Burke's first publication was a study of Native American housing in Manitoba, and he has since published two further studies: *Evaluation of Stedman Federal School* (1980); and *Native Clan Organization Review of Rehabilitative Services for Native Offenders* (1986). On the subject of Native life, he has published a collection of essays entitled *Native Studies: In Search of Canada* (1977). His short fiction collection is called *Willie: Winnipeg Short Stories* (1974). He has published two non-fiction trade books: *If It Weren't For Sex, I'd Have To Get A Job* (1984), and *Paper Tomahawks* (1976). His first novel, *Fatal Choices,* was published in 1990, and the sequel, *The Death Dealers,* came out in early 1991. For his efforts, Burke has been awarded two grants from the Manitoba Arts Council, and one from the Ontario Arts Council.

Burnard

Bonnie Burnard has devoted her attention as a writer to short fiction, and has been steadily published in Canadian literary magazines and journals. Her talent was first highlighted in *Coming Attractions* in 1983, and has been recognized in *Best Canadian Stories* (1984, 1988). She was also editor of a collection of short fiction, *The Old Dance* (1987). For her collection of stories, *Women of Influence* (1988), she received the Commonwealth Writer's Prize for Best First Book.

Gallant

Mavis Gallant was born in Montreal in 1922, and attended seventeen different schools there and in the eastern United States. After working for the National Film Board and as a writer for the *Montreal Standard,* she left Canada for Europe in 1950. She has lived in Paris periodically since 1950, working as a full-time writer and correspondent.

Gallant's literary success is due primarily to the dozens of short stories she has written since she began her career in 1944. She has maintained a long relationship with *The New Yorker,* which has published virtually all of her stories, and has also collected her stories in six volumes. Among these are *The Other Paris* (1959) and *Home Truths: Selected Canadian Stories* (1981), which won a Governor General's Award. Her stories are highly complex and often deal with the theme of the difficulty of entering an alien culture. Gallant has also published two novels, *Green Water, Green Sky* (1959), and *A Fairly Good Time* (1970), and was made an Officer of the Order of Canada in 1981. Her most recent publications are *In Transit* (1989), and *Overhead in a Balloon* (1989).

Garner

Hugh Garner was born in 1913 in Batley, Yorkshire, and died in Toronto in 1979. Having arrived in Toronto in 1919 with his family, Garner attended a technical high school for two years before leaving Toronto on his own at age 16. During the worst years of the Depression, Garner worked at various unskilled jobs, riding freight trains from job to job across North America. He enlisted in the Abraham Lincoln Brigade, which fought on the side of the Loyalists in the Spanish Civil War. During the Second World War, Garner served on a corvette with the Canadian Navy—an experience which became the basis for his first novel, *Storm Below*, published in 1949.

After his return from the war, Garner became a full-time writer, and over the next thirty years published more than fifty short stories. The most successful of these revolve around the lives of outsiders in Canadian society, and his collection, *Hugh Garner's Best Stories*, won the Governor General's Award in 1963. Among his many publications are the novels *The Silence on the Shore* (1962) and *The Intruders* (1973), and an autobiography, *One Damn Thing After Another* (1973). He also produced three police novels set in Toronto, *Sin Sniper* (1970), *Death in Don Mills* (1975), and *Murder Has Your Number* (1978).

Havemann

Ernst Havemann, the son of Afrikaner farmers, was born in 1918 in Zululand, South Africa. He attended the village school, and then went on to the University of Natal, where he received a degree in Social Science. Between 1940 and 1945, he served in the Union Defence Forces, attached to the British Army in the Middle East. After ten years working in state and national government, he began work for the Royal Dutch/Shell Oil Group, where he remained until his retirement in 1978. He emigrated to Canada with his wife Isabel in 1979, and now lives on Kootenay Lake, British Columbia. He continues to write, give readings, and conduct writing workshops.

After attending creative writing classes at the (now defunct) David Thompson University Centre in Nelson, B.C., Havemann turned his attention seriously to writing. His short stories have appeared in literary magazines and anthologies throughout Canada and the United States. His first collection of short stories, *Bloodsong* (1987), received a National Magazine Award for fiction, and has been translated into German and

French. Havemann has been twice awarded both second and first prize in the annual CBC Literary Competition.

Kinsella

W.P. Kinsella was born in 1935 in Edmonton, Alberta. He spent nearly two decades working as a civil servant, life insurance salesman, cab driver and manager of a pizza parlour before enrolling in the Creative Writing Department of the University of Victoria in 1972. He received a B.A. from the University in 1974, and then enrolled in the Writer's Workshop at the University of Iowa, where he earned his M.F.A. in 1978. He taught for several years at the University of Calgary, and now lives in White Rock, B.C.

Kinsella has written four books of Indian stories: *Dance Me Outside* (1977); *Stars* (1978); *Born Indian* (1981); and *The Moccasin Telegraph* (1983). All of these embody what Jeffrey Heath has termed a "euphoric anti-authoritarianism." He has also published a collection of baseball stories, *Shoeless Joe Jackson Comes to Iowa* (1980), which became the foundation for his 1982 novel *Shoeless Joe*. This novel is a mixture of fantasy and reality, and earned Kinsella both the "Books in Canada" First Novel Award and the Houghton Mifflin Literary Fellowship. In 1988, *Shoeless Joe* was made into a major American film, *Field of Dreams*.

Kleiman

Ed Kleiman was born in 1932 in Winnipeg, Manitoba. He did his undergraduate work at the University of Manitoba, and went on to receive his M.A. from the University of Toronto in 1959. After teaching in London for two years, he returned to the University of Manitoba, where he has been teaching and writing as a member of the English Department since 1961. He reads from his work regularly at bookstores and universities, and has taught Creative Writing at the Manitoba Arts Festival. He currently lives in Winnipeg with his wife and four children.

Kleiman's short stories have been published in most Canadian journals, and several of them have been broadcast by the CBC. He has also published two collections of stories: *The Immortals* (1980), and *A New-Found Ecstasy* (1989). Fascinated by the Pacific coast's attraction for prairie dwellers who are all too aware of the savagery of Canadian winters, Kleiman took a sabbatical in Victoria, B.C., in 1989 to study the West Coast's effects on the prairie consciousness. His observations form the foundation for his upcoming collection, *Grand Canyon Suite*.

Krueger

Lesley Krueger was born in 1954 in Vancouver, and studied political science at the University of British Columbia. Trained as a journalist, she worked for the *Toronto Star* and the *Vancouver Sun* before taking a year to travel throughout Europe and Asia. After returning to Toronto, she worked first as a producer, then as a freelancer, for CBC. She began writing full-time while her husband held a Nieman Fellowship at Harvard, and currently lives and writes in Rio de Janeiro.

Krueger's first published story appeared in the *Tamarack Review* and she has since published in a variety of literary journals. The abundance of details in her stories reflects her awareness that the more the world is studied, the more mysterious it becomes. Her observations of this mystery form the backbone of her writing. She was highlighted in Helwig and Martin's *Coming Attractions* in 1986, and published her first book, *Hard Travel*, in 1989.

Laurence

Margaret Laurence was born in 1926 in Neewapa, Manitoba, the model for her fictional town of "Manawaka." She graduated from United College in Winnipeg in 1947, and worked for several years as a reporter for the Winnipeg *Citizen*, during which time she met her husband, Jack Laurence. In 1949, the two moved to England, and then on to Somalia and Ghana, Africa, until 1957. After separating from her husband in 1962, she lived for ten years in England before moving to Lakefield, Ontario, where she lived until her death in 1989.

Laurence led a prolific literary life, publishing novels, children's books, magazine articles, and short stories. Her writings come directly out of her experiences, both in Africa—*This Side Jordan* (1960), *The Tomorrow Tamer* (1962), and *The Prophet's Camel Bell* (1963)—and in the small prairie towns of her childhood—*The Stone Angel* (1961), *A Jest of God* (1966), *The Fire Dwellers* (1966), *A Bird in the House* (1970) and *The Diviners* (1974). The latter four are all set in Manawaka, the fictional town which is, as suggested by Joan Woodward, "an amalgam of all prairie small towns infused with the spirit of their Scots-Presbyterian founders."

Laurence collected her magazine articles in *Heart of A Stranger* (1976), and many of her short stories and novels have been dramatized for radio and television. She served as Chancellor of Trent University for eight years, and received numerous literary awards, including two Governor General's Awards, the President's Medal of the University of Western Ontario, and a Molson Prize.

Marriott

Anne Marriott was born in Victoria, British Columbia in 1913. She has spent the majority of her life in British Columbia, and her experiences during the Depression serve as a foundation for many of her most successful documentary poems. She currently lives in North Vancouver, where she is an active member of the League of Canadian Poets and serves on the Editorial Board of *Event* magazine. Her recent energies have been concentrated on a new manuscript of poems, which was published in early 1991.

Since she received the Governor General's Award for *Calling Adventures* (1941), Marriott has been widely recognized for the sensitivity and power of her poetry. While her early poems are concerned with the lives of prairie farmers during the Depression years, her recent poems revolve around her experiences on the west coast. Her published collections of poems include *The Wind Our Enemy* (1939), *Sandstone and Other Poems* (1945), *Countries* (1971), the widely anthologized *The Circular Coast* (1981) and *Letters From Some Islands* (1985), for which she was short-listed for the British Columbia Book prize for poetry. Marriott also harbours a love of fiction, but has only published one collection of short stories, *A Long Way To Oregon* (1984), from which "The Ride" is taken.

Mistry

Rohinton Mistry was born in Bombay, India in 1952. After emigrating to Toronto in 1975, he began work at a bank while taking night classes at the University of Toronto in pursuit of a B.A. in English and philosophy. He began writing short stories in 1983, and focused his attention exclusively on writing in 1985. He currently lives in Brampton, Ontario, where he writes fulltime.

Mistry's stories are a rich evocation of life in the Parsee community of Bombay, and his firsthand knowledge of this community infuses his characters with fullness and vitality. He has collected many of his stories in *Swimming Lessons and Other Stories From Firozsha Baag* (1987), for which he was short-listed for the Governor General's Award. Mistry has received two awards from the Hart House literary contest, and has been awarded a *Canadian Fiction*'s Contributor's prize. He is currently working on his first novel, entitled *Such a Long Journey*.

O'Flaherty

Patrick O'Flaherty was born in Long Beach, Newfoundland in 1939. He received his formal education from St. Bonaventure's College and Memorial University of Newfoundland, and the University of London in 1962. Since then, he has worked as a university teacher and professor, and is currently a Professor of Writing at Memorial University in St. John's, Newfoundland.

O'Flaherty writes in various genres—literary criticism, fiction, journalism, history and biography. His writings up to 1985 are primarily non-fiction, while recent publications reflect a new interest in the world of fiction. Among his non-fiction works are *By Great Waters* (1974) and *Part of the Main* (1983). He has also published two short story collections, *Summer of the Greater Yellowlegs* (1987) and *A Small Place in the Sun* (1989) and a novel, *Priest of God* (1989).

Pittman

Al Pittman was born in St. Leonard's, Placentia Bay, Newfoundland in 1940. After attending Salem State Teachers College in Massachusetts, he went on to receive his M.A. from St. Thomas University of Fredericton, New Brunswick. He taught school in several different locations before moving to St. John's to teach at Memorial University of Newfoundland. The opening of Sir Wilfred Grenfell College in 1978 gave him the opportunity to return to Corner Brook—the city of his childhood—where he is currently a professor of English.

Pittman has been prolific in a variety of literary forms, having written poetry, plays, short stories, essays, children's books and scripts for CBC radio and television. Best known as a poet, his collections include *Seaweed and Rosaries* (1969), *Through One More Window* (1974), and *Once When I Was Drowning* (1978). He has also published two children's books, *Down By Jim Long's Stage* (1976) and *One Wonderful Fine Day For A Sculpin Named Sam* (1983), and one play, *A Rope Against the Sun* (1974). His most recent publication is a collection of short stories entitled *The Boughwolfen and Other Stories* (1984), which examines the guilt-ridden world of Catholic childhood and adolescence. His newest children's book, *On a Wing and a Wish: Rhymes for Salt Water Birds*, is to be released during 1991. His work has been honoured with such awards as the Lydia Campbell Award for Writing and the Stephen Leacock Centennial Award.

Riches

Brenda Riches was born in India in 1942 and moved to England at age four. She was educated in Taunton, Somerset, and at the University of Cambridge, and went on to teach English and Creative Writing in secondary schools in London and Liverpool. She emigrated to Saskatchewan in 1974 with her husband and three children, and became involved in the Saskatoon literary community. She has taught creative writing and served as editor of *Grain* literary magazine. She currently lives in Regina, where she teaches creative writing and literature at the University of Regina.

After seeing many of her short stories published in a variety of Canadian literary magazines and journals, Riches published her first book, *Dry Media,* in 1981. She has continued to write short stories which have appeared in numerous anthologies. Her second book, *Rites,* was published in 1988.

Roy

Born in Saint-Boniface, Manitoba in 1909, Gabrielle Roy was educated at the Winnipeg Normal School, and taught for several years in rural Manitoba. She travelled in France and England, and, during this period, began to develop her career as a writer. The war forced her to return to Canada, where she continued to write stories and articles in Montreal. Elected to the Royal Society of Canada in 1947, she was also made a Companion of the Order of Canada in 1967. She lived and wrote in Quebec City until her death in 1983.

While fluent in both French and English, Roy wrote almost exclusively in the language of her favourite city, Quebec. Her first novel, *Bonheur d'Occasion* (1945), gained her immediate recognition as a gifted craftsperson. She published two other novels, *Alexandre Chenevert* (1955) and *La Montagne Secrète* (1961), as well as seven collections of linked short stories, among them *La Poule de Ma Vie* (1950), *Rue Deschambault* (1955), and *Ces Enfants de Ma Vie* (1979). For her works, Roy received three Governor General's Awards, the Prix David and the Molson Prize.

Vanderhaeghe

Guy Vanderhaeghe was born in Esterhazy, Saskatchewan in 1951. He received his Bachelor and Master's degrees in History from the University of Saskatchewan, and went on to pursue further studies at the University of Regina, where he earned his B.Ed. in 1978. He has worked as a teacher, archivist and researcher, and is now working on a collection of short stories. He currently resides in Saskatoon.

Vanderhaeghe began experimenting with short stories in the late 1970s, and has been widely published in Canadian literary magazines. In 1980, his story "The Watcher" was the winner of *Canadian Fiction Magazine*'s annual contributor's prize for short fiction. He has published two collections of short stories, *Man Descending* (1982) and *The Trouble With Heroes* (1983), the former of which won him a Governor General's Award for fiction. Recurrent themes in his writing are loneliness and the struggle for authenticity and dignity—themes which he explores in his novels *My Present Age* (1984) and *Homesick* (1989).

Van Herk

Aritha Van Herk was born in Alberta in 1954, and grew up only a few miles from the Battle River. She worked as a secretary, bush cook, hired hand, teacher and editor before returning to school and receiving her M.A. in English from the University of Alberta in 1978. Since then, she has worked in several positions as an editor and has been both President and Vice-President of the Writers Guild of Alberta. She currently lives in Calgary, where she divides her time between her writing and an associate professorship at the University of Calgary.

Fascinated by human myth, Van Herk draws on the variety of her experience in all her works. She has seen many of her short stories published in literary magazines and anthologies. For her novel, *Judith* (1978), she received the Seal First Novel Award, and was named one of Canada's Ten Best Young Fiction Writers in 1986. Other publications include *The Tent Peg* (1981) and *No Fixed Address* (1986), for which she was nominated for the Governor General's Award for Fiction.

Acknowledgements

"Gall" was first published in *The Capilano Review* No. 14, then in *More Stories From Western Canada*. It is included in the book *Dry Media* by Brenda Riches, Turnstone Press, 1980. Reprinted by permission of the author.

"Striptease." From *The Boughwolfen and Other Stories*, 1984, by Al Pittman. Reprinted by permission of Breakwater.

"Crush." From *Double Bond*, C. Heath ed., 1984. Reprinted by permission of the author.

"Hurricane Hazel." From *Bluebeard's Egg and Other Stories*, 1984, by Margaret Atwood. Reprinted by permission of the Canadian Publishers, McClelland and Stewart, Toronto.

"Cages." From *Man Descending* by Guy Vanderhaeghe, © 1982. Reprinted by permission of Macmillan of Canada, a Division of Canada Publishing Corporation.

"A Manly Heart." From *Best Stories*, 1983, by Hugh Garner. Reprinted by permission of McGraw-Hill Ryerson, Ltd.

"Maiden Aunt." From *A Small Place in the Sun*, 1989, by Patrick O'Flaherty. Reprinted by permission of Breakwater.

"Never Sisters," originally published under the title "Transitions," in *Miss Chatelaine*, August 1978. Copyright © 1978 by Aritha van Herk. Reprinted by arrangement with Virginia Barber Literary Agency. All rights reserved.

"Growing Up Rosie." From *Tamarack Review*, Winter 1981. Reprinted by permission of the author.

"The Immortals" is reprinted from *The Immortals*, by Ed Kleiman (Edmonton: NeWest Press, 1980), by permission of the publishers.

"Death of a Nation." From *Bloodsong and Other Short Stories of South Africa*, 1989, by Ernst Havemann. © 1987 by Ernst Havemann. Reprinted by permission of Houghton Mifflin Company.

"In A War." Reprinted by permission of Georges Borchardt Inc., and the author. Copyright © 1989 by Mavis Gallant. First appeared in *The New Yorker*.

"To Set Our House In Order." From *A Bird In The House* by Margaret Laurence. Used by permission of the Canadian Publishers, McClelland & Stewart, Toronto, and the Lucinda Vardey Agency. © 1963 by Margaret Laurence.

"The Move." From *The Road Past Altamont* by Gabrielle Roy. Used by permission of the Canadian Publishers, McClelland & Stewart, Toronto. © Fonds Gabrielle Roy.

"The Bottle Queen." From *The Moccasin Telegraph*. Copyright © W.P. Kinsella, 1983. Reprinted by permission of Penguin Books Canada Ltd. and David R. Godine, Publisher, Inc.

"Of White Hairs and Cricket." From *Tales from Firozsha Baag* by Rohinton Mistry. Copyright © Rohinton Mistry, 1987. Reprinted by permission of Penguin Books Canada Ltd. and Houghton Mifflin Company.

"Willie." From *Winnipeg Stories*, Joan Paar, ed. Reprinted by permission of Queenston House Publishing Co. Ltd.

"The Ride." From *A Long Way to Oregon* by Anne Marriott, Mosiac Press, 1984. Reprinted by permission of the author.

Every effort has been made to protect copyright material used. The publisher would be pleased to be informed of any instance where further acknowledgement is required or permission for further use is to be sought.